# The Evolution of China's Banking System, 1993–2017

This book traces the development of China's banking system through the first 25 years of China's socialist market economy up to the present. It examines how China's leaders have chosen their own path for reforming and regulating the banking sector and shows how this approach has differed significantly from the neoliberal approach promoted by the West. The book demonstrates the effectiveness of the Chinese approach, contrasting China's relative success in weathering the Asian financial crisis with the huge disruption experienced by other East and Southeast Asian nations which had followed the neoliberal model much more closely. The book explains how China's officials were able to resist the persistent efforts of foreign financial institutions to gain control of China's financial sector, particularly around the time of China's entry to the World Trade Organization. It argues that China's increasing influence in international financial institutions after the global financial crisis can help mitigate the risk of future financial crises and promote global financial stability.

**Guy Williams** completed his doctorate at the University of Cambridge.

**Routledge Studies on the Chinese Economy**
Series Editor
Peter Nolan
*Director, Centre of Development Studies;*
Chong Hua
*Professor in Chinese Development; and Director of the Chinese Executive
Leadership Programme (CELP), University of Cambridge*

Founding Series Editors
Peter Nolan
*University of Cambridge*
and
Dong Fureng
*Beijing University*

The aim of this series is to publish original, high-quality, research-level work by
both new and established scholars in the West and the East, on all aspects of the
Chinese economy, including studies of business and economic history.

# The Evolution of China's Banking System, 1993–2017

Guy Williams

Routledge
Taylor & Francis Group

LONDON AND NEW YORK

First published 2019 by Routledge

2 Park Square, Milton Park, Abingdon, Oxfordshire OX14 4RN

52 Vanderbilt Avenue, New York, NY 10017

*Routledge is an imprint of the Taylor & Francis Group, an informa business*

First issued in paperback 2020

*British Library Cataloguing-in-Publication Data*
A catalogue record for this book is available from the British Library

*Library of Congress Cataloging-in-Publication Data*
Names: Williams, Guy, 1981– author.
Title: The evolution of China's banking system, 1993–2017 / Guy Williams.
Description: Abingdon, Oxon ; New York, NY : Routledge, 2019. |
Series: Routledge studies on the Chinese economy | Includes
bibliographical references and index.
Identifiers: LCCN 2018011139| ISBN 9781138496972 (hardback) |
ISBN 9781351020022 (ebook)
Subjects: LCSH: Banks and banking–China–History. | Financial
institutions–China–History.
Classification: LCC HG3334 .W55 2019 | DDC 332.10951–dc23
LC record available at https://lccn.loc.gov/2018011139

ISBN: 978-1-138-49697-2 (hbk)
ISBN: 978-0-367-58912-7 (pbk)

Typeset in Times New Roman
by Wearset Ltd, Boldon, Tyne and Wear

# Contents

# Illustrations

## Figures

## Tables

# Selected milestones in the reform of China's banking sector

1978: 'Reform and Opening' economic policy announced

1979: Agricultural Bank of China (ABC) and Bank of China (BoC) established

1983: China Construction Bank (CCB) established

1984: Industrial and Commercial Bank of China (ICBC) established, People's Bank of China (PBoC) becomes an independent central bank

1987–88: Establishment of six shareholding banks (Bank of Communications (BoCom), CITIC Industrial Bank, China Merchants Bank, Fujian Industrial Bank, Guangdong Development Bank and Shenzhen Development Bank)

1993: Three further shareholding banks established (China Everbright Bank, Hua Xia Bank and Shanghai Pudong Development Bank)

1993: Establishment of the socialist market economy

1993: Financial institutions begin pilot implementation of risk supervision according to the standards of the 1988 Basel Accord

1994: China's three policy banks established (Agricultural Development Bank of China, China Development Bank and Export-Import Bank of China)

1994–97: Regulators segregate commercial banks from security, trust and insurance sectors

1995: Guiding documents for regulatory development established, namely *The Law of the PRC on the PBoC* and *The PRC Commercial Bank Law*

1997: Asian financial crisis

1997: The First National Financial Work Meeting is held

1998: Officials announce the closure of the Guangdong International Trust and Investment Corporation (GITIC) and the restructuring of Guangdong Enterprises (GDE)

1998: The Central Financial Work Committee (CFWC) is established

1998: Recapitalisation of China's banks to the value of RMB 270 billion

1999: Asset Management Companies (AMCs) established for disposal of non-performing loans (NPLs)

1999–2002: Trust sector restructured

2001: China's entry into the World Trade Organisation (WTO)

2002: Programme of shareholding reform announced at the Second National Financial Work Meeting

2003: China Banking Regulatory Commission (CBRC) established

2004: Five-tier loan classification system adopted by all banking institutions

2004: Guidelines on corporate governance reforms issued for large state-owned banks

2004–06: Minority stakes taken in China's large state-owned banks by external investors

2005–10: Initial Public Offerings (IPOs) of China's 'Big Four' state-owned banks

2008: Global financial crisis

2009: China becomes a member of the Financial Stability Board (FSB) and the Basel Committee of Banking Supervision (BCBS)

2013: Loan rate floor abolished as part of gradual liberalisation of interest rates

2013: China's implementation of Basel III capital standards deemed 'compliant' by the BCBS

2015: Deposit rate ceiling abolished, interest rate liberalisation achieved

2016: Deposit insurance scheme introduced for all deposit-taking financial institutions

2018: Merger of the CBRC and the China Insurance Regulatory Commission (CIRC) into one regulatory body, the China Banking and Insurance Regulatory Committee (CBIRC). PBoC to assume responsibility of the legislative and rule-making functions of the CBRC and CIRC. Please note this merger is not covered in this book as it was announced just prior to publication

# Preface

This book is about the evolution of China's banking sector after the establishment of the socialist market economy in 1993. It covers a 25-year period. I have chosen this starting point because it was only after the establishment of the socialist market economy that China's leaders decided to focus on the development of a robust and comprehensive system of banking regulation in order to maintain economic and social stability. While 1978 marks the beginning of China's economic reforms, in the early reform period the state did not prioritise the development of market regulation and credit was still allocated predominantly through the planning system. The establishment of the socialist market economy was the beginning of a highly explorative process as officials sought to find the best way to regulate the banking sector. Officials established new central bank and commercial bank laws which became guiding documents for the reform process. China's large state-owned banks were unified and transformed from 'specialised banks' to 'state-owned commercial banks'. In 1993 it was announced that banks would abide by important elements of the first Basel Accord, a notable milestone in China's selective adoption of international standards of regulation.

The introduction lays out the theoretical framework of this book. It argues that the evolution of China's banking sector should not be viewed as conformance with a neoliberal model. It argues instead that change in China's banking sector should instead be viewed as an evolution of institutions which reflect historical patterns of political and economic organisation in China. Chapter 2 (800–1990) is a background chapter that examines the history of Chinese banking and identifies important features such as the pattern of strong bureaucratic control over market activity, along with the devastating effects of instability and the loss of economic sovereignty as officials sought to establish a modern banking system. It details the development of China's banking system under Reform and Opening policies prior to 1993 and shows the persistence of the aforementioned historical patterns in this process.

Chapter 3 (1990–96) examines how China's officials gradually and pragmatically constructed a system of banking regulation for the socialist market economy. It details a highly exploratory process of regulatory development that was designed to establish financial order and contain market risk. It shows how

Western concepts were adapted in an effort to develop systems for close regulation and supervision of the banks at a time when these principles were being forgotten by the West. Chapter 4 (1997–2002) details how the Asian financial crisis
(AFC) alerted Chinese officials to the dangers of integration into an under-
regulated and dangerous global financial system and the immediate systemic risk
posed by the high levels of bad loans to China's banking system. It shows how
the crisis drove measures to contain financial risk, including the centralisation of
party governance of the banking sector and the adoption of international standards of regulation. It shows how officials resisted intense pressure from foreign
financial institutions to allow foreign control of financial assets, despite the weak
state of the banking sector.

Chapter 5 (2003–07) demonstrates how fundamental reforms of bank governance and risk management, led by new banking regulator China Banking Regulatory Commission (CBRC), created a much stronger and more resilient banking
system. It explains how Western concepts of corporate governance were adapted
alongside a party system which remained deeply embedded within the corporate
governance structure of the banks, and details the important contribution of
minority investors to the development of the banking sector. Chapter 6
(2008–17) shows how China's leaders sought to mitigate new forms of risk in
the banking sector which emerged after the global financial crisis (GFC). In
response to the crisis, regulators sought to reform and further develop its systems
of supervision and regulation and use the party system to limit executive compensation and root out corruption. This approach was in contrast to the culture of
deregulation and unbridled financial innovation that was ultimately behind the
GFC. After the crisis, China's officials were able to use China increasing influence in international institutions to advance their ideas on how to establish a
more stable global financial system.

The conclusion identifies the major institutional features of the evolution of
China's banking system. It demonstrates the importance of China's bureaucratic
tradition, and the focus of officials on stability and pragmatic reform, to the
transformation and improvement of the banking system. It examines how
China's officials, wary of Western economic self-interest, adapted Western ideas
selectively to facilitate the development of a stable, well-regulated banking
system that promoted economic development by serving the real economy. It
identifies future reform priorities and China's potential role in the future governance of the global financial system.

This study of the institutional evolution China's banking sector has utilised
qualitative research methods to shed light on the thought processes of policymakers and the nature of banking reform. Two primary sources of data, qualitative interviews and documentary data, were gathered. The principal subjects
of the qualitative interviews were officials from the CBRC, the primary agency
charged with regulation and supervision of China's banking system from 2003
to 2017. Interviews were held with employees of CBRC's head office, which is
located in central Beijing. The interviews were conducted on two occasions, the
first in Beijing in October and November of 2014 and the second in Beijing and

Shanghai during February and March of 2015. A total of ten semi-structured interviews of CBRC head office personnel were conducted. Interviewees were asked their opinions on the overall process of reform of the banking sector since Reform and Opening began. Questions covered major reform events and the future direction of reform. Interviewees were also asked questions relating to their roles and responsibilities at the CBRC as well as their previous work history. One goal of the interviews was to understand the philosophy of the organisation and its staff towards regulation, and what has influenced this philosophy. Thirteen other interviews were conducted with a variety of persons with personal knowledge and experience of China's banking reform. The other principal source of information was documentary data. Documents referred to include CBRC annual reports, bank annual reports, official government reports and publications of international organisations.

Completing this book has been a difficult but extremely rewarding task. I could not have achieved this without the considerable support of a number of people along the way. First, I would like to thank my PhD supervisor, Professor Peter Nolan for his patience, encouragement and honest and constructive criticism. I also want to thank him for sharing his passion for Chinese civilisation and deep understanding of China's banking sector. I would also like to thank the administrative staff at the Centre of Development Studies, Cambridge University for their all their help and assistance, particularly Doreen and Nathalie. I would also like to thank Dr Kun-Chin Lin for his support of what is now known as the Cambridge Society for the Study of the Political Economy of China, a society that was established by myself and other graduate students, including Vasiliki Mavroeidi. I am also grateful for the friendship and support of my fellow students at the Centre of Development Studies. I wish to thank Joao and Fu Zhenyu in particular.

I would like to thank all the people who generously offered their time to me for interviews and advice during my research for this book. I offer special thanks to Zhu Yuanqian and the staff at CBRC headquarters. I am also especially indebted to Leon Walker at ANZ, Professor Wang Dashu at Peking University and David Chin of UBS for going out of their way to help me and taking a real interest in my work.

I also want to thank all of the people outside of my academic life that have supported me. To my friends in Cambridge and New Zealand, thank you for sticking by me throughout my research. I wish to thanks my parents Anne and Lyn for their constant support from so far away! Thanks also to Dongmei, Eric and Zha for hosting me in Beijing when I conducted my interviews. I am grateful also to Tom Chan and his family for so generously providing a 'home away from home' in the United Kingdom and treating me like family. Thank you also to the staff of Darwin College, Cambridge University for looking after me during my PhD.

# Abbreviations

| | |
|---|---|
| ABC | Agricultural Bank of China |
| AFC | Asian Financial Crisis |
| AMC | Asset Management Company |
| ANZ | Australia and New Zealand Banking Group |
| BCBS | Basel Committee for Banking Supervision |
| BoC | Bank of China |
| BoCom | Bank of Communications |
| CASS | Chinese Academy of Social Sciences |
| CBIRC | China Banking and Insurance Regulatory Commission |
| CBRC | China Banking Regulatory Commission |
| CCB | China Construction Bank |
| CCDI | Central Commission for Discipline Inspection |
| CCP | Chinese Communist Party |
| CFWC | Central Financial Work Committee |
| CIRC | China Insurance Regulatory Commission |
| CITIC | China International Trust Investment Corporation |
| COD | Central Organisational Department |
| CRS | Contract Responsibility System |
| CSRC | China Securities Regulatory Commission |
| FDI | Foreign Direct Investment |
| FSB | Financial Stability Board |
| GDE | Guangdong Enterprises |
| GDP | Gross Domestic Product |
| GFC | Global Financial Crisis |
| GITIC | Guangdong International Trust and Investment Corporation |
| HKSE | Hong Kong Stock Exchange |
| HR | Human Resources |
| ICBC | Industrial and Commercial Bank of China |
| IFC | International Finance Corporation |
| IMF | International Monetary Fund |
| IPO | Initial Public Offering |
| IT | Information Technology |
| ITIC | International Trust and Investment Corporation |

| | |
|---|---|
| JV | Joint Venture |
| LGFV | Local Government Financing Vehicle |
| M&A | Merger and Acquisition |
| MOF | Ministry of Finance |
| NAO | National Audit Office |
| NBFI | Non-Banking Financial Institution |
| NDRC | National Development and Reform Commission |
| NPC | National People's Congress |
| NPLs | Non-performing loans |
| P2P | Peer-to-Peer |
| PBoC | People's Bank of China |
| PCBC | People's Construction Bank of China |
| PWC | Price Waterhouse Coopers |
| RCC | Rural Credit Cooperative |
| SAFE | State Administration of Foreign Exchange |
| SASAC | State-owned Assets Supervision and Administration Commission |
| SOCB | State-owned Commercial Bank |
| SEZ | Special Economic Zone |
| SMEs | Small and Medium-Sized Enterprises |
| SOE | State-owned enterprise |
| TIC | Trust and Investment Corporation |
| UCC | Urban Credit Cooperative |
| WMPs | Wealth Management Products |
| WTO | World Trade Organisation |

# 1   Introduction

This book addresses what many in the West view as a contradiction: the successful transformation of China's banking sector and the refusal of China's officials to adopt a reform path recommended by international institutions such as the World Bank and International Monetary Fund (IMF) or international bankers with considerably more knowledge of modern banking methods. It will explain how China's banking sector has evolved since the establishment of the socialist market economy in 1993. It contends that it is the Chinese state that has driven the modernisation of China's banking sector, even as Western ideas and technology have been adapted for this purpose. The state has implemented a coherent reform strategy that has relied upon lessons learned from the China's past. The defining features of the state's role in the governance and regulation of China's banking sector can be linked to historical patterns of political and economic organisation. China's officials have incorporated Western ideas and technology to develop the banking sector within these historical patterns of political and economic organisation according to the principle 'Chinese learning for the fundamental principles, Western learning for practical application' (中體西用 *zhongti xiyong*) (see Levenson 1964). The banking sector reform path has also been influenced by China's economic conditions and important events which have affected the banking sector. Articulating the approach of officials to banking reform, the first Head of the CBRC, Liu Mingkang, stated that 'no reform can ignore the actual situation in our country. Only by paying attention to China's national conditions and drawing lessons from advanced countries' successful experiences can reform be successful' (Liu, Mingkang 刘明康 2009, 122). It is argued that the orthodox view of reform mischaracterises China's banking reform because it fails to identify the positive role played by the state and the influence of China's historical patterns of political and economic organisation. This book will demonstrate how these historical patterns have defined the evolution of China's banking sector.

Between 1993 and 2017, China's banking sector has undergone a remarkable transformation. With the introduction of the socialist market economy in 1993, China began to formally establish a system of market regulation and commercialise its large state-owned banks. These banks struggled to cope with the rapid pace of economic development. By the late 1990s China's banks were widely considered by external observers to be technically insolvent (Liu, Mingkang

刘明康 2009). Today China is home to four of the top five banks in the world (measured by Tier 1 capital), with twelve further banks placed within the top fifty in the world (see Table 1.1). As of 2015, the average rate of non-performing loans (NPLs) in the banking sector was only 1.9 per cent (CBRC 2016, 196). China has now developed a robust regulatory system and a sustainable banking system that is resilient to risk.

The evolution of China's banking system has been a vital component in the transformation of China's economy since the introduction of Deng Xiaoping's Reform and Opening policy. China's economy has grown at an unprecedented rate since the implementation of this policy in 1978. Between 1978 and 2016, China's economy grew at an average rate of approximately 10 per cent per year (World Bank 2016). During this time, China's economy has been transitioning from a planned economy to a market economy. The industrial plants of the planned economy have been transformed into modern commercial enterprises. The modernisation of the country has required an enormous investment in

*Table 1.1* China's banks in world top 200 by tier 1 capital 2017

| Country rank | World rank | Bank |
| --- | --- | --- |
| 1 | 1 | Industrial and Commercial Bank of China |
| 2 | 2 | China Construction Bank |
| 3 | 4 | Bank of China |
| 4 | 6 | Agricultural Bank of China |
| 5 | 11 | Bank of Communications |
| 6 | 23 | China Merchants Bank |
| 7 | 25 | China Citic Bank |
| 8 | 27 | Shanghai Pudong Development Bank |
| 9 | 28 | Industrial Bank |
| 10 | 29 | China Minsheng Bank |
| 11 | 31 | Postal Savings Bank of China |
| 12 | 49 | China Everbright Bank |
| 13 | 59 | Ping An Bank |
| 14 | 67 | Hua Xia Bank |
| 15 | 73 | Bank of Beijing |
| 16 | 85 | Bank of Shanghai |
| 17 | 93 | China Guangfa Bank |
| 18 | 117 | Bank of Jiangsu |
| 19 | 131 | China Zheshang Bank |
| 20 | 145 | Evergrowing Bank |
| 21 | 146 | Bank of Nanjing |
| 22 | 166 | Chongqing Rural Commercial Bank |
| 23 | 168 | Huishang Bank |
| 24 | 175 | Bank of Ningbo |
| 25 | 187 | Shanghai Rural Commercial Bank |
| 26 | 190 | Shengjing Bank |
| 27 | 199 | Bank of Tianjin |
| 28 | 200 | China Bohai Bank |

Source: data adapted from thebankerdatabase.com, 'Ranking – Top 1000 World Banks by Tier 1 and Assets – 2017'.

infrastructure. According to McKinsey, between 1992 and 2011 China's average investment in infrastructure was 8.5 per cent of Gross Domestic Product (GDP), the highest in the world over this period and well ahead of the United States and EU countries, which each averaged 2.6 per cent (Chen, Matzinger and Woetzel 2018). The provision of credit from China's banks has been vital to all these processes of transformation. Banks have remained dominant in China's financial sector over the course of reform despite the diversification that has occurred in the financial sector. As of 2016, banking institutions still held 68.4 per cent of assets in the financial system (IMF 2017, 60).

## Part I: the orthodox view of reform

The orthodox view of reform in the academic literature on this subject is derived from neoliberalism and evaluates China's banking sector according to the degree of implementation of free market policies. Neoliberalism is an economic philosophy that advocates for free markets and against state intervention which has been influential in global economic policy since the 1970s. The neoliberal philosophy originates from two main schools of economic thought, neoclassical economics, which provides the analytical tools, and the Austrian-Libertarian tradition, which is responsible for the moral and political philosophy. The fundamental tenet of neoliberalism is that economic activity should be left to the market with limited, if any, intervention by the state. Neoliberal theorists advocate prices determined by market forces for efficient allocation of resources, as well as the private ownership of firms and protection of property rights of shareholders to provide a profit motive and incentive for investment. According to this theory, there should be no restrictions on competition, which drives firms to be more efficient. State intervention is considered by neoliberal theorists to cause efficiency losses. For example, protectionism in the banking sector is characterised as 'regulatory capture' by the state. Neoliberal policies recommended by the International Monetary Fund (IMF), World Bank and United States Treasury Department (known as the Washington Consensus) include the abolition of policies which restrict market entry and competition; liberalisation of interest rates; privatisation; adoption of a competitive exchange rate; and the establishment of a system of property rights (Williamson 1989).

This book relies on the work of Geoffrey Hodgson to both critique the orthodox view of reform and offer an alternative explanation for the reform path of China's banking sector. According to Hodgson, the emergence of neoliberal theory is part of a trend in the social sciences towards the search for a general theory, 'a single theoretical framework', which would provide universal laws and principles which apply to all economic systems (Hodgson 2001, 3). The search for a 'general theory' can be contrasted with an empirical approach that relies on gaining knowledge through observed experience. Neoliberals view their economic system as 'natural' and other systems as 'unnatural', and consider the implementation of neoliberal policies as the means to achieve the 'one ideal, pure market system' (Hodgson 2001, 29, 31).

The use of a single theoretical framework or universal laws and principles is prevalent in the literature which analyses China's banking system. The principal work cited in this book that uses such a framework is *Red Capitalism*. Its authors, Walter and Howie, write that 'China's economy is no different from any other' and consider any China-specific explanations of banking reform as part of what they consider to be 'the Great China Development Myth' (Walter and Howie 2012, xvii, 3). In this way, Walter and Howie neglect historical patterns of political and economic organisation and focus instead on China's perceived conformance with neoliberal economic policies. For Walter and Howie, China's establishment of the socialist market economy marked the commencement of reforms that '... followed a path of deregulation blazed by the United States' (Walter and Howie 2012, 3).

The orthodox view of reform is supported by the academic literature, institutions of global financial governance and also by large international financial conglomerates and their governments. In academic literature related to the banking sector, the justification for neoliberal policies is supported by cross-sectional studies such as Barth, Caprio and Levine (2004), which finds that restriction of banks' activities and entry of foreign banks is associated with bank fragility, and that government ownership is linked with negative banking outcomes. Studies on China's banking sector typically recommend the adoption of neoliberal policies (see for example Mo 1999; Bonin and Huang 2001; Bekier, Huang and Wilson 2005; Dobson and Kashyap 2006; Feyzioglu, Porter and Takáts 2009; Huang, Wang and Lin 2010; Kwong 2011). Yiping Huang (2001) concludes that while China's economic performance over reform has been 'remarkable', the state's exit from the banking sector and the introduction of competition from private and foreign sectors is necessary for the 'completion of the transition to the market economy' (Huang 2001, 1, 156). The Western developed countries that designed and controlled institutions of global financial governance have sought to promote neoliberal policies. As recently as July 2015, the World Bank described China's financial sector in a chapter of its China Economic Update, later redacted, as 'unbalanced, repressed, costly to maintain and potentially unstable', attributes which in its view had led to 'the poor performance of the financial system' (Wildau 2015).

China's officials have perceived the orthodox view of reform to be an instrument of power for developed countries, whose financial conglomerates sought to gain control over China's best financial assets. In his speech at the Second National Financial Work Meeting, then General Secretary Jiang Zemin cited the view expressed in Huntington's book *Clash of Civilisations* that control and operation of the international financial system, hard currency and international capital markets were all strategic objectives for Western civilisation (Du, Hua 杜华 2007). The pressure from foreign financial institutions and their governments was particularly acute in the late 1990s after China announced its entry into the World Trade Organisation (WTO). Large financial conglomerates from developed countries, which had emerged in the 1990s following the deregulation of the global financial services industry, had aggressively pursued merger and acquistions (M&A) deals for financial firms in developing countries. China's financial sector was considered the next major objective and international financial conglomerates, with support from their governments, lobbied intensely for the deregulation of China's financial sector to allow acquisition of China's financial assets by foreign firms. Recalling this time, former Federal Reserve Chairman Alan Greenspan commented that 'with the geopolitical pressure of the cold war removed, the United States had the historic opportunity to knit the international economy more closely together' (Greenspan 2007, 149). There was deep fear and uncertainty among banking executives and regulators in China regarding the future of the banking sector. One official in the financial regulatory sector commented at the time that 'they [the international financial conglomerates] will walk all over us'.

## The orthodox view of reform and the role of the state

The orthodox view of reform rejects the idea of an active role for the state to promote economic development and transformation. State intervention in China's banking system is deemed to be the result of mere political self-interest rather than seen as a legitimate policy for economic development. Walter and Howie state that 'greed is the driving force behind the protectionist walls of the "state-owned" economy "inside the system" and money is the language' (Walter and Howie 2012, 23). State intervention exists, in their opinion, to serve the needs of the political elite with the 'true nature' of the state-owned economy considered to be 'a patronage system centred on the Party's *nomenklatura*' (Walter and Howie 2012, 24). In his 2008 book *Factions and Finance in China*, Victor Shih of North Western University writes that this political self-interest manifests itself through local and central party factions whose 'dominant presence' in the financial sector 'ultimately shape policy-making' (Shih 2008, 3). According to Shih, 'top leaders desire for power and the uncertain political environment in which they operate compel them to pursue factional politics, which creates ... the dearth of significant financial market reform' (Shih 2008, 47). According to Nicholas Lardy, his book *Markets over Mao* 'counters the argument ... that the real engine of Chinese economic progress has been the government's adoption of an economic model that eschews reliance on the market' (Lardy 2014, 2). According to Lardy, 'The key theme ... of this book is that virtually every dimension of China's economic success over the last three decades plus can be attributed to the rise of markets and private businesses' and that 'attempts to produce a model of state capitalism have actually failed' (*Nicholas Lardy on Markets over Mao: The Rise of Private Business in China* 2014). These works contend that state intervention is an obstacle for reform of China's banking sector and that a free market system with limited government intervention is preferable.

Many journal articles on China's banking system attempt to find evidence of efficiency losses associated with state intervention. These losses of efficiency are considered to be the impact of China's non-conformance with free market policies. Studies attempt to establish a causal relationship between state owner-ship and the relatively weak performance of China's centrally controlled banks relative to other banks in the sector (Shih, Zhang and Liu 2007; Berger, Hasan and Zhou 2009; Fu and Heffernan 2009; García-Herrero, Gavilá and Santa-bárbara 2009; Jia 2009; Lin and Zhang 2009). Other studies attempt to demon-strate the negative impact of financial repression or lack of competition on the performance of the banking system (Fu and Heffernan 2009; García-Herrero, Gavilá and Santabárbara 2009).

In general, the academic literature perceives state influence over the govern-ance of China's banks to be unfavourable because it has a negative impact on the efficient allocation of capital. State influence has been cited as the principal reason for problems of corporate governance within China's banks (Huang 2010; Huang, Wang and Lin 2010). Studies also claim that excessive state influence is the major contributing factor behind high rates of NPLs during the 1990s and the high proportion of loans allocated to local government financing platforms for low-return infrastructure and utility projects following the state's expansionary monetary policy in 2009 (Mo 1999; Bonin and Huang 2001; Cull and Xu 2003; Kwong 2011). According to the literature, the state's influence prevents capital flowing to the most desirable recipients of funds, private firms, which exhibit the highest rates of growth and investment (Huang, Wang and Lin 2010; Lardy 2014). Studies have criticised the banking sector's lending to state-owned enter-prises (SOEs), which it suggests is politically motivated and not responsive to commercial principles (Park and Sehrt 2001; Podpiera 2006; Firth *et al.* 2009; W. Zhou 2009). A recent IMF working paper assessing the default risks for Chinese firms found that the cost of debt for firms was detached from economic fundamentals and determined by implicit guarantees (Law and Roache 2015).

The orthodox view of reform disregards the positive role that the Communist Party has played in the governance of the banking sector. Party institutions have been central to the values and ideology of officials in the banking sector. They have been responsible for the appointment, monitoring and discipline of officials in the banking sector. Party institutions have also adapted to the evolution of the banking sector. These institutions have been utilised to implement policy initi-atives and mitigate risk in China's banking sector.

The orthodox view of reform neglects the role that the Chinese state has played in economic development and transformation. China's banks have made a significant contribution to the country's transition from a planned economy. To reform its SOEs, the state has pulled together plants from the planned economy era to create unified, centrally controlled enterprises which have been commer-cialised and have developed modern structures of corporate governance. To quote Australian and New Zealand Banking Group (ANZ) economist Zhou Hao, China's banks have been a 'mirror of the economy' as the liabilities of these enterprises have represented the bulk of banking assets (Interview with ANZ economist Zhou Hao, 24 April 2015). China's large state-owned banks have taken the leading role in providing capital to SOEs as the state has transitioned from grant-based funding to loan-based funding, supporting them as price controls and barriers to competition have been removed (Laurenceson and Chai 2001; Naughton 2007). State intervention has been fundamental to the development of the banking sector. In contrast with neoliberal policy, China has employed protectionist measures in the banking sector to enable the transformation of its SOEs such as the regulation of bank interest rates and control of the capital account. State intervention into the allocation of credit has been part of a strategy of economic transformation. For example, important state infrastructure and industrial projects have retained priority over credit, even when these loans are not profitable (Yeung 2009).

The Chinese state has played an important role in determining the pace and sequencing of reform. Current General Secretary Xi Jinping recently commented that 'the market and the government should complement and coordinate with each other to promote sustained and sound economic development' (Xi 2014, 128). Officials considered factors such as the suitability of reforms to China's national conditions, the level of difficulty and the potential impact on economic stability when determining the reform agenda. In Liu Mingkang's words, 'the pace of reform had to defer to the quality of reform' (Liu, Mingkang 刘明康 2009, vii). The rapid pace of economic development after the establishment of the socialist market economy made it imperative for the state to develop regulatory institutions to mitigate risks that had emerged in the banking sector. Careful sequencing of reform was vital to ensure that the most urgent risks to the sustainability of China's banking system were addressed. Officials were also mindful of time constraints and limited resources available in implementing banking reforms. The timing of reforms was subject to China's national conditions. The socialist market economy was established only after the planned economy was strengthened to contain cycles of currency and price inflation, which created the conditions necessary for further reform. Similarly, shareholding reform proceeded by virtue of favourable conditions including rising levels of domestic economic growth, strong world markets and deepening foreign exchange reserves. These conditions had not been present a few years earlier in the aftermath of the 1997 AFC, when the state was forced to bail out the banks without instituting any major reform of bank governance. Officials chose to implement reforms that were easier first. Reforms that empowered centrally controlled financial institutions preceded more difficult political reforms such as the centralisation of bank appointments and the widening of People's Bank of China (PBoC) branch areas. In determining the listing order of state-owned banks, officials prioritised those banks with relatively favourable levels of capital adequacy and NPLs.

## The orthodox view of reform and the regulation of markets

The emphasis of the orthodox view of reform on policies of financial deregulation and liberalisation causes it to neglect the role of the Chinese state in constructing a system of market regulation to ensure the stability of the financial sector. Former Federal Reserve Chairman Alan Greenspan has been a notable advocate of the orthodox view during the period of research. In a speech titled 'The Evolution of Banking in a Market Economy', given less than 3 months before the AFC, Greenspan extolled the benefits of self-regulation of markets and suggested '... market-stabilizing private regulatory forces should gradually displace many cumbersome, increasingly ineffective government structures' (Greenspan 1997). Such a view neglects the inherent instability of markets. The increased incidence and severity of financial crises since neoliberal ideas have gained popularity around the mid-1960s caused Charles Kindleberger to label it '... the most tumultuous in international monetary history' due to the increase in cross-border capital flows (Kindleberger and Aliber 2005, 277). Minsky argued that the capitalist financial system was inherently unstable because in good times firms would underestimate the risk of external finance and overestimate future profits (Minsky 1980, 1992). He stated that 'over periods of prolonged prosperity, the economy transits from financial relations that make for a stable system to financial relations that make for an unstable system' (Minsky 1992, 8).

The academic literature has overlooked the development of market institutions that has allowed the Chinese state to harness the power of the market safely and effectively. For example, Shih (2007, 1238) characterises the period between 1998 and 2003 as one of 'reform stagnation' in China's banking sector because, in his view, market reforms following the establishment of the socialist market economy were blocked by the interests of the central political elite. Shih defines reform as policies that increase the efficiency of resource allocation and cites the Washington Consensus policies as examples. According to Shih, reform stagnated because China failed to liberalise interest rates and legalise private banking, which he considers to be 'some of the most important reform measures' (Shih 2007, 1241). The period covered by Shih's article was in fact one of significant institutional development, provoked by the AFC, as policymakers reduced systemic risk and solidified the foundations of the socialist market economy. His article neglects fundamental market-building reforms that occurred in areas such as loan-making and risk management. Similarly, Walter and Howie call the year 2005 the 'end of reform' because, although substantial, the reform that followed was not part of the journey towards a free market system (Walter and Howie 2012, 15). This book argues that Walter and Howie overlook the reforms undertaken by CBRC to strengthen regulation and improve the governance of state-owned banks after listing, reforms which greatly improved the resilience of the banking sector. Studies which focus on bank regulation tend to focus on institutional form ahead of regulatory development, criticising the lack of independence of PBoC and CBRC, suggesting they are not able to maintain a 'market system' as other state organs will intervene when the interests of state-owned banks are compromised (see for example Huang 2010).

## Part II: reform as an evolution of institutions

Contrary to the orthodox view, the development of China's banking system is best described as an evolution of institutions that reflect historical patterns of political and economic organisation in China. China's leaders applied the concept of 'Chinese learning for the fundamental principles, Western learning for practical application' (中體西用 *zhongti xiyong*), in gradually adapting Western ideas and technology within China's traditional political and economic system to modernise the banking sector. China's officials have determined how reform would be implemented. The focus on free market policies in literature holds little explanatory value in describing banking reform given that the Chinese state has not implemented such policies. China did not attempt the 'big bang' approach to market reforms that was observed in Russia and certain Eastern European states. China's policymakers, according to the principles of Deng Xiaoping's Reform and Opening policy, have implemented gradual, experimental reform as if 'groping for stones to cross the river'. Deng's ideas have remained highly influential from the establishment of the socialist market economy until today. In 2012, at a visit of Shenzhen's Special Economic Zone (SEZ) to mark the 20-year anniversary of Deng Xiaoping's Southern Tour, General Secretary Xi Jinping declared his resolve to continue with reform according to the theories and practices of 'Reform and Opening Up' which he considered 'the only route that must be taken to adhere to and develop socialism with Chinese characteristics' (*Xinhua News Agency* 2012). Xi vowed that there would be 'no stop in reform, and no stop in opening up' (*Xinhua News Agency* 2012).

It is argued that historical patterns of political and economic organisation persist in institutions, causing institutions to be path dependent and subject to an evolutionary process of development. According to Hodgson, institutions, defined as 'systems of established and embedded social rules that structure social interactions', are socially constructed and embedded in the country's history, culture and politics (Hodgson 2006, 18). Therefore characterising change in China's banking system as part of a convergence towards 'one ideal, pure market system' in the literature is problematic because China's market system is unique and comprised of its own, historically-specific institutions of governance (Hodgson 2001, 31). In this way institutional analysis rejects the idea of a 'natural economic system' and emphasises the role of institutions in market regulation or governance of financial institutions. Instead of being considered as part of a 'natural economic system', neoliberal policies can be viewed as a consequence of a particular institutional arrangement. In his work *The Great Transformation*, Karl Polanyi stated that since the nineteenth century, 'the road to the free market was opened and kept open by an enormous increase in continuous, centrally organized and controlled interventionism' (Polanyi 2001, 146).

Institutional analysis has previously been applied to demonstrate the influence of historical patterns of political and economic organisation and the lack of convergence towards one model of an economic system. The theoretical foundation for much of this work has been Granovetter's article on the embeddedness of economic behaviour in social relations (Granovetter 1985; see also Whitley 1999; Boyer 2005). Gerlach (1992) details the close relationships between banks, corporate shareholders and business partners in Japan's economy, alliance structures which 'have remained largely enduring even with ongoing financial liberalization and other changes in the political and economic environment of Japanese industry' (Gerlach 1992, xvii). *In The Origins of Nonliberal Capitalism: Germany and Japan in Comparison*, the authors compare the historical origins of these two 'nationally embedded capitalisms' (Streeck and Yamamura 2001, 3). The authors also note the pressure on German and Japanese officials to conform to a liberal economic model:

> the debate on Germany and Japan and their special trajectories (Sonderwege) of capitalist development turned overwhelmingly toward pressures for convergence on American 'best practice,' alleging a compelling need for the two deviant capitalisms to liberalize and disembed economic transactions formerly constrained and facilitated by a national institutional framework.
>
> (Streeck and Yamamura 2001, 4)

In his work on the Danish economy, Ove Kaj Pedersen identifies institutional features that explain how the Danish state has incorporated neoliberal ideas within its economic system to create what he terms a 'negotiated economy' (Pedersen 2006a, 245; see also Pedersen and Kjaer 2001). Pedersen suggests that Denmark's 'long history of lost wars and territories', which instilled 'into the public mind a sense of national vulnerability', was instrumental in the establishment of a common national identity (Pedersen 2006a, 245). He also finds that the existence of a small, centralised ruling elite, along with 'a political culture marked by institutionalized class cooperation', has allowed Denmark to drive national development strategies in the public interest. With respect to the evolution of Denmark's economy, Pedersen too rejects the notion that it should be evaluated according to its degree of conformance with a neoliberal economic system, favouring instead an institutional approach. He states: 'The important lesson of the Danish case … is that the differences between economies are not based on their being more or less liberal, but on the political, economic, organizational, and other mechanisms by which they are coordinated' (Pedersen 2006b, 466).

This book will utilise institutional analysis to answer the following question:

> What factors explain the evolution of China's banking system since the establishment of the socialist market economy?

## Why history matters

### *The overarching goal of reform is rooted in China's pride in its ancient civilisation*

Through the policies of Reform and Opening, Deng Xiaoping wished to see China rise again, to catch up with developed Western nations and claim the benefits of modernity for the Chinese people. China has a proud history as one of the world's oldest civilisations and had the most vibrant and prosperous economy in the world prior to the industrial revolution. As Western countries experienced the industrial revolution, China's economy experienced a decline that was associated with a loss of sovereignty and oppression by foreign powers. These experiences have underlined to Chinese policymakers the importance of economic sovereignty for any programme of modernisation. In a speech made to mark the 30th anniversary of Reform and Opening, Hu Jintao declared that China 'should always put the nation's sovereignty and security above anything else' and that the state was 'determined to deal with Chinese affairs according to China's realities by relying on the strength of the Chinese people' (Hu 2008). Deng's reform vision was highly influenced by time he had spent in advanced nations with modern economic systems such as France, the United States of America and Japan (Vogel 2013). Through Reform and Opening, China opened itself to the ideas, technology and capital of Western countries. These would be incorporated within a Chinese system according to the concept 'Chinese learning for the fundamental principles, Western learning for practical application' (中體西用 *zhongti xiyong*).

In March 2006, current General Secretary Xi Jinping explained the influence of history on China's Reform and Opening policy. He said:

> To understand our dedication to revitalize the country, one has to appreciate the pride that Chinese people take in our glorious ancient civilization. This is the historical driving force inspiring people today to build the nation. The Chinese people made great contributions to world civilization and enjoyed long-term prosperity. Then we suffered over a century of national weakness, oppression and humiliation. So we have a deep self-motivation to build our country. Our commitment and determination is rooted in our historic and national pride.
>
> (Kuhn 2010, 4)

According to economic historian Angus Maddison, prior to the nineteenth century China was the most powerful country in both Europe and Asia. China's GDP in 1820 was 30 per cent higher than Western Europe and its Western off-shoots combined (Maddison 2006, 119). China contributed valuable technological advancements to the world that supported important industries such as shipping, textiles and mining. Merchants were engaged in peaceful trade of exports such as porcelain, tea, silk and textiles, predominantly through South East Asia. Prosperous areas such as the Jiangnan region in Eastern China experienced high levels of urbanisation.

China's century of national humiliation was characterised by military defeats resulting in the loss of territory and the imposition of disadvantageous terms of commercial trade through unequal treaties. China's economy experienced a decline from the 1840s until the birth of new China in 1949. China's defeat at the hands of the British and the French during the Opium Wars in the 1840s forced China to open its borders to traders from the United Kingdom, United States, Japan and twelve other European nations. Treaties were imposed on

China that guaranteed traders jurisdiction over ports and access to Chinese markets at low tariff rates. Foreigners established a large international settlement in Shanghai. Japan imposed its military might over China, taking over control of Korea in the late nineteenth century and Manchuria in the 1930s, and occupying China for 8 years during the Second World War. China's GDP per capita fell 25 per cent between 1820 and 1950 (Maddison 2006, 119).

The modernisation of China's banking system has been a source of great pride for China's leaders. According to a book edited by former Head of Bank of China (BoC) and CBRC Liu Mingkang, which details the history of Chinese banking sector reform since Reform and Opening, reforms have rendered the banking system 'incomparable' to its past forms (Liu, Mingkang 刘明康 2009, 3–4). Before reform, China's banking system was far behind that of Western European nations where financial institutions resembling modern banks had been developed and refined since approximately the end of the sixteenth century. The development of systems and mechanisms to regulate the market economy is considered by Liu to be a 'historical breakthrough' (Liu, Mingkang 刘明康 2009, 2). He considers that these achievements have only been possible because the state has had full responsibility for the development and implementation of strategies for the banking sector.

Due to China's history of oppression by foreign powers, officials were wary of adopting Western ideas and technology in a manner that would undermine China's economic sovereignty or be unsuitable to China's national conditions. Officials incorporated ideas that would enable China to meet reform goals and resisted those that were unsuitable or even harmful. China rejected the neoliberal model promoted by the West that had given rise to a dangerous and insufficiently regulated global financial system. China's officials, though perhaps possessed with less sophisticated understanding of modern banking systems, were able to resist pressure from self-interested large financial conglomerates (often supported by their governments) who advocated for deregulation and the break-up and privatisation of large state-owned banks in order to pursue a strategy of M&A in China's banking sector. This pressure was particularly intense after China signalled its intention to join the WTO and open up its financial sector to foreign firms, at a time when China's large state-owned banks were considered by external observers to be technically insolvent. Minority investment in China's banks by foreign financial institutions was restricted in order to limit the influence of Western ideas on the character of China's banking system while still allowing for the benefits of foreign knowledge and competition.

## Why history matters

### *The bureaucratic system embedded within the banking sector is reflective of China's bureaucratic tradition*

China possesses a unique bureaucratic system that has been historically characterised by a politically united, centrally controlled bureaucracy led by scholar-officials. According to the structure of traditional Chinese society, social class was defined by one's profession with scholar-officials being of a higher social class than that belonging to peasants, artisans and merchants. The influence of officials extended to all aspects of society. China developed and refined its system of bureaucracy over 2,000 years, particularly after the unification of China (Dawson 1964). In the Han dynasty (206 BC–AD 220), Confucianism became the state doctrine. Confucian thought emphasised the idea that rulers govern and maintain legitimacy through virtuous example and serving the interests of society. The rival legalist school remained influential and through it valuable bureaucratic concepts relating to personnel administration and organisation were introduced. A meritocratic system of examination for the entry of scholar-officials into civil service was developed. Over time detailed rules were developed to refine the roles and responsibilities of officials and their place in the bureaucratic structure. Institutions such as the censorate were established to monitor the behaviour officials. Over the sixteen centuries or so which followed, institutions for 'investigation, criticism, advice and complaint' of officials were developed (Dawson 1964, 319).

The party system of governance that is deeply embedded in the banking sector has descended from China's bureaucratic tradition. The Communist Party exerts centralised control through a system of party committees, led by the Central Committee, which is comprised of China's most powerful political leaders. The general direction of state policy for the economy is determined at the level of the Politburo, a small group of party leaders elected by the Central Committee. It is the role of government organs such as the State Council, PBoC and CBRC to execute the vision of party leaders. Within the banking system, each bank has a party committee. Party committees are a vehicle for transmitting the values and ideology of the party to officials. They also serve as a means to monitor and discipline officials, with the Central Discipline Inspection Commission charged with the most serious cases of official misconduct. The Central Organisational Department (COD), which is the party organisation responsible for personnel administration, has taken the leading role in the appointment of senior officials in the banking sector. In the early 1990s it was estimated to control appointments of 5,000 party and government posts, including those of its centrally controlled SOEs (McGregor 2012, 81). Within the banking sector, the COD controls the appointments of the executive board members of its centrally controlled banking institutions, namely the 'Big Four' state-owned banks, Bank of Communications (BoCom), the three policy banks, and the banks of China International Trust Investment Corporation (CITIC) Group and Everbright Group. Even the appointment of CEO for China Minsheng Bank, known as China's first private bank, passes through the COD (McGregor 2012). As in the past, the appointment system facilitates the assessment of officials in different roles, which provides the party with valuable information on which officials are suitable for higher office (Zhang 2012).

Many of China's top bankers identify themselves as officials with a political career within the bureaucratic system rather than as career bankers. As one

CBRC official stated, the ultimate goal of such officials remains higher political office and the chance to contribute to the country. When asked of such motivations, the official in question quoted the Confucian phrase 'a good scholar can become an official' (Interview with CBRC official, 20 March 2015). The career of officials in the banking sector is defined by progression within the bureaucratic system. It is extremely common for officials in China's large state-owned banks to move to and from roles in financial regulatory agencies that report to the State Council (Chen 2013). For example, current Head of the CBRC, Guo Shuqing, was Chairman of China Construction Bank (CCB) from 2005–11. During his career, Guo also assumed the roles of Chairman of China Securities Regulatory Commission (CSRC) and State Administration of Foreign Exchange (SAFE) and was Governor of Shandong Province prior to moving to the CBRC. Officials in the banking sector have an interest in serving the needs of society. Many of the CBRC officials interviewed cited pride in contributing to the development of the banking sector as a major reason for choosing this career path (Interviews with CBRC officials, 10 October 2014–19 March 2015).

The party system of governance within the banking sector was centralised after the establishment of the socialist market economy. This followed a period of decentralisation of economic decision-making within China's bureaucratic system during the early period of Reform and Opening following the success of agricultural reforms in 1978. Agricultural reforms led to the eventual devolution of production decisions from the commune to the household. Industrial reforms, which followed in 1984, transferred control of large industrial plants or enterprises from central industrial ministries to local governments. Relations of production changed as households and industrial enterprises formed contractual relations with the state over production. According to Liu Mingkang, the development of specialised banks proceeded according to the spirit of the contract responsibility system (CRS) employed in industrial reforms (Liu, Mingkang 刘明康 2009). At this time banks did not function as unified enterprises. Branches had their own legal person status that afforded them considerable autonomy. The devolution of power to provincial regions rendered local governments with significant influence over the financial sector. Local party officials held the power to appoint local heads of branches of both the central bank as well as the specialised banks. They pushed central bank and specialised bank officials to lend money to local enterprises. This was not limited to loan-making and included inter-bank and central bank loans.

Centralising reforms of party governance were undertaken to align the incentives of party officials with reform goals relating to financial regulation, credit allocation and monetary policy. After the establishment of the socialist market economy, the party emphasised the duty of officials to maintain financial order and respect national financial regulation. The bureaucratic system was forced to adapt to the unification and commercialisation of centrally controlled financial enterprises. *The PRC Commercial Bank Law*, enacted in 1995, had provided a legal basis for greater autonomy of banks and a single-tier legal person structure was established within the banks. Reform of the personnel system completed in

2003 shifted authority for local appointments of centrally controlled state-owned banks to the COD in Beijing. The role of party organs in controlling appointments and monitoring and disciplining officials has remained a fundamental part of the governance of China's large state-owned banks. It has adapted to the governance changes caused by shareholding reform and the establishment of a basic framework of corporate governance with a board of directors and board of supervisors.

The cohesive nature of the bureaucratic system, particularly since centralising reforms, has proved an effective foil to the excesses of the market. The party system aligns the incentives of officials in banks and regulatory agencies with those of the party core. In this way it has limited the ability of agents in the financial sector to lobby for deregulation or acquisition of Chinese banks by foreign entities. In the banking sector, the desire of officials to serve the interests of society has been expressed through the idea that banks should serve the real economy. This can be seen in the regulation of financial derivatives, for example, which has been limited by the CBRC to 'practical, transparent, and straightforward innovations that serve the fundamental demands of the real economic sectors' (CBRC 2011, 41). While market capitalisation of Chinese banks has surged, the compensation of executives in the financial sector in China remains a tiny fraction of that of their counterparts in the West. China's bureaucratic control of the financial sector has allowed it to rein in the market and use it as a means to achieve public policy goals.

## Why history matters

*The emphasis of officials on stability, which has defined the approach towards regulation of the banking system, can be linked to historical Chinese political thought*

Historically, stability has been a fundamental concern of China's bureaucracy. Successive dynasties struggled to protect the population from fundamental problems of food production, famine and management of water supplies (see for example Chi 1970; Will 1990). The fall of a dynasty not only brought a loss of power to its rulers but also created significant political turmoil. The question of how to rule over Chinese civilisation with stability has been a central goal of scholars of Chinese political thought, such as Confucius, which remain influential today. The weight of this history magnifies the sense of responsibility felt by China's leaders towards the political system and heightens the fear of system disintegration. More recently, China has suffered through periods of instability during both the Republican and Communist eras. Many of the leaders at the 14th Party Congress in 1978 were themselves victims of ideological attacks during the Cultural Revolution and other movements and experienced first-hand the devastating impact of political instability on economic progress. Hu Jintao said of the state's attitude towards reform that 'we are deeply aware that development is the fundamental principle and stability is the fundamental goal. Without stability, we will get nowhere and may even fritter away our past achievements' (Hu Jintao 2008).

The concern for stability is reflected in policy implementation for the banking sector during Reform and Opening. It was magnified by the challenge of economic transition from a planned economy with a banking system that had been severely weakened during the Cultural Revolution. As a supplier of credit to other industries, instability in the banking system had the potential to slow down or derail China's economic reform programme. Consequently, reform of the banking sector has proceeded 'half a step' behind the reform of other SOEs according to one CBRC official (Interview with CBRC official, 10 March 2015). China's officials have viewed markets as inherently unstable and requiring close supervision and regulation. Stability has been prioritised ahead of market discipline and market efficiency. The banking sector has supported struggling SOEs during economic transition in order to maintain social stability. According to one official, loans made to SOEs to maintain social stability were termed 'dumpling loans', as they would ensure workers had money to buy dumplings at Chinese New Year (Interview with government official, 10 October 2014). The most significant failure in the banking sector, that of the Guangdong International Trust and Investment Corporation (GITIC) in 1998, was permitted by officials to mitigate systemic risk, reduce moral hazard and increase the accountability of China's financial institutions.

Since the establishment of the socialist market economy, officials have been concerned with how to regulate the banking system in order to maintain financial stability. In the early stages of its development, the priority was to empower the regulatory system so that it could bring order to the banking sector. The advent of the AFC alerted officials to the danger of NPLs to the stability of the financial system and prompted reforms to create a more resilient financial system, many of which were based on international regulatory standards. China has repeatedly voiced its concern regarding the inability of global financial regulatory institutions to ensure financial stability, most notably after the GFC. Shortly after the crisis Central Bank Governor Zhou Xiaochuan wrote that 'the frequency and increasing intensity of financial crises following the collapse of the Bretton Woods system suggests the costs of such a system to the world may have exceeded its benefits' (X. Zhou 2009). This scepticism has been the major factor for China's relatively slow integration into the global financial system, particularly with respect to its unwillingness to allow free movement of capital and the gradual liberalisation of interest rates. Prior to the GFC, the CBRC improved supervision of the banking system and governance mechanisms of the large state-owned banks, thereby lowering credit risk and allowing banks to build up capital buffers. After the crisis, the CBRC focused on close supervision and interaction with banks to reduce risks that emerged as a result of the crisis in areas such as local government debt and shadow banking.

# Why history matters

*The economic and social instability of Mao's era strongly influenced*
*Deng Xiaoping's desire for a pragmatic approach to reform*
*from 1978*

The pragmatic approach to reform observed after the establishment of the social-ist market economy can be linked to the spirit of Reform and Opening policies. According to Hu Jintao, the Third Plenary Session of the 11th Central Com-mittee in 1978, which marked the beginning of Reform and Opening, 'redefined the Party's ideological line'. The party, following Deng Xiaoping's vision, resolved to 'proceed from actual situations, integrate theory with practice, seek truth from facts, and test and develop truth through practice' (Hu Jintao 2008). This represented a significant departure from the ideological excesses of Mao's era and indeed Deng's pragmatic stance allowed him to navigate through dan-gerous ideological waters as reform proceeded.

While the overall goals for reform in the banking sector were clearly expressed, policymakers did not have a fixed view for how to achieve goals of maintaining financial stability, supporting economic modernisation, transforming SOEs and developing infrastructure. Prior to the establishment of the socialist market economy, the implementation of Reform and Opening policies did not imply the inevitable transition to the market economy. Prior to 1993 there was no commit-ment to the development of a system of market regulation. Rather, policymakers aimed to develop a more scientific and informed planned economy. Policymakers elected to establish the socialist market economy based on the observation that market-based incentives had driven economic growth and improvements in living standards. This shows that the state does not have blind faith in the market. Instead, the state views it as a 'double-edged sword' that has the potential to create finan-cial instability. Wang Dashu, Professor of Public Finance at Peking University and former senior researcher at the Research and Development Centre of the State Council, insisted that China's rapid rate of change, diverse developmental chal-lenges and the imperfect nature of markets have necessitated a strong role for the state (Interview with Wang Dashu, 25 March 2015).

This has led to a pragmatic approach to the regulation of China's banking sector after 1993, as illustrated by Zhou Xiaochuan's comments relating to reform in the financial sector:

> The characteristic of reform in China is to uphold the attitude of 'trial and error', sufficiently respect the practice and treat practice as the only test of truth. ... The approach of progressive reform may make some policies and regulations rather strongly explorative and avoiding to duplicate the statutes of mature markets will probably result in many provisional regulations, but the reality has proved that the overall consequences of Chinese practices are quite positive.
>
> (Lin 2003, 7–8)

As Zhou suggests, reforms in the banking sector were highly exploratory and evolved according to practical results. Successful trials of policy initiatives within particular banks or regions prior to a nationwide roll-out were a feature of China's banking reforms. Important regulations issued by the PBoC and the CBRC were labelled 'provisional' and subject to further revision after implementation. The CBRC has tended to issue comprehensive rules only when a particular area of regulation reaches the end of an exploratory rule-setting process, whereupon previous rules are annulled.

The 'primary task' of each type of financial institution has been to 'keep serving the real economy' (CBRC 2014, 18). There is no one model of financial institution for the banking sector. Each type of financial institution serves a particular purpose based on its characteristics. Accordingly, officials have generally implemented pragmatic reform programs by type of financial institution. China's 'Big Four' state-owned banks, which were carved out of the monobank system to serve large SOEs, were initially specialised banks serving a particular area of the economy. The introduction of shareholding banks helped cultivate a competitive environment for the specialised banks. The urban credit cooperative (UCC) model was established when reform began in order to provide capital to collective enterprises and individual businesses. After UCCs were converted into city commercial banks, exceptions were made to allow banks that had demonstrated superior performance to expand beyond provincial boundaries, according to 'the principle of rewarding good performance' (*China Economic Review* 2006; CBRC 2007, 42). This policy was adjusted when regulators decided that it was necessary to encourage greater specialisation of city commercial banks rather than allow further expansion of a model based on the interest rate spread. In the rural financial sector, the state made significant efforts to re-establish collective financial organisations that had become state-run within the commune system in order to serve rural communities. Although the scale of agricultural development eventually exceeded that of the village unit, the State Council rejected a proposal to merge rural credit cooperatives (RCCs) into a large agricultural bank as it believed the co-operative model would provide a more balanced supply of funding to rural areas. Instead the State Council elected to group RCCs into county-level companies, thereby allowing them to retain their intrinsic nature. Eventual reform of RCCs into commercial banks and rural co-operative banks proceeded according to risk management capability, with some RCCs remaining unchanged (Interview with CBRC official, 12 March 2015).

Foreign banks have been utilised by Chinese policymakers to help develop the domestic banking sector. Foreign banks were utilised as a conduit for foreign and overseas Chinese investors to invest in the SEZs in Southern China in the 1980s. The threat of foreign competition created by the announcement of China's entry into the WTO in 2001 drove improvement in the domestic banking sector. Since WTO restrictions were lifted, foreign banks have provided competition in high-value areas and assisted Chinese companies with overseas expansion in accordance with the 'going out 走出去' policy. Foreign banks, acting as minority investors, assisted the preparation of China's banks for listing on foreign stock exchanges and their engagement in the sector provided vital assurance to overseas investors. Policy banks have carried the burden of policy lending within specific, priority areas of industry, thereby facilitating the commercial transition of the large state-owned banks. China Export-Import Bank, for example, was charged with the task of expanding exports of capital goods, particularly in the electronics sector. The China Development Bank was responsible for domestic infrastructure projects but as SOEs expanded internationally, its mandate expanded significantly. Asset management companies (AMCs), which were established to dispose of NPLs, leveraged this capability and expanded operations to the disposal of bad assets across the entire financial sector. The trust sector has been at the forefront of market-orientated innovation within China's banking sector. In the early reform period, trust companies acted as a 'window overseas' for China by sourcing foreign capital and technology through measures such as the issuance of international bonds and financial leasing. For example in 1980, CITIC used financial leasing to import the first Boeing 747 airplane into China. Today the trust sector is part of a shadow banking system that helps provide credit to marginalised sectors of the economy. In recent years, the trust sector has been an important conduit for commercial banks in the development of China's wealth management sector. The high risks and consequent instability of the trust sector have caused it to be restructured several times of the course of reform, notably during the AFC. The CBRC has elected to standardise the activities of trust companies, establish firewalls and increase transparency in response to growing risk in the shadow banking sector.

China has employed a pragmatic approach to its segregation of financial sectors. By international standards China's regulation of cross-sector activities is strict in order to reduce financial contagion. Commercial banks have been prohibited from engaging in trust, security or insurance business according to the 1995 *PRC Commercial Bank Law* (Loechel and Li 2009). In 2009 CBRC Head Liu Mingkang stated, 'we don't discuss universal banking' (Alreddy 2009). However parent companies of shareholding banks CITIC Group, China Everbright Group and China Merchants Group have been permitted to retain their status as financial conglomerates despite the passing of this law. Subsequently, large state-owned banks have entered the insurance and securities sectors through Hong Kong subsidiaries and in 2004 these exceptions were formally recognised through an amendment to the *Commercial Bank Law*. In 2011, the CBRC reported that pilot programs had been launched for commercial banks investing in other financial sectors according to a best practice operating model and strict performance requirements (CBRC 2011).

## Why history matters

### *It was necessary for the state to actively foster market behaviour and develop market institutions as part of the transition from a planned economy*

The process of fostering market behaviour began before the establishment of the socialist market economy. Deng Xiaoping had the vision of making banks 'real banks' that would allocate capital to projects that supported economic development rather than merely appropriate funds (Du, Hua 杜华 2007, 9). The profit motive was introduced to the banking sector through experimental institutional arrangements such as the CRS. To establish the profit motive, banks and their sub-branches were granted significant autonomy within a highly decentralised system. The results of this policy experiment provided the basis for the commercialisation of specialised banks and the establishment of institutions of monitoring and governance to replace the loss of administrative control. The monitoring institutions include financial regulation, a legal framework of rules, auditing and accounting standards. These institutions have been refined and updated over the period of research. The governance structures of large state-owned banks were unified and strengthened so that banks were more empowered to act according to commercial principles and resist the demands of local governments. Unified governance facilitated the establishment of systems to control market risk, including systems of asset and liability management and loan classification. The CBRC has breathed life into the two-tier board structure established through shareholding reform. The CBRC issued a series of guidelines that defined the responsibilities of management and the board with respect to decision-making processes, the development of mechanisms for risk management and internal control, and the introduction of incentives to stimulate commercial-orientated lending.

The introduction of competition also served to foster market behaviour. The shareholding banks were introduced to drive improvement in specialised banks by creating a competitive dynamic in the banking sector and promoting commercial concepts. Shareholding banks were not restricted by industry and had more flexible human resource structures and more commercially orientated branch networks. China's entry to the WTO created the threat of impending competition from foreign banks, which proved an important stimulus for bank improvement and regulatory development. Chinese policymakers carefully designed WTO regulations to ensure the sustainability of the domestic banking sector. Foreign banks proved an important source of competition in high value areas. The recent establishment of private banks, announced in 2014, represents another initiative to strengthen the role of the market in resource allocation through the introduction of competition.

# References

Alreddy, James T. 2009. 'China Wrestles with Shaping the Future of Shanghai'. *Wall Street Journal*, 18 May 2009. www.wsj.com/articles/SB124259885772428149.

Barth, James R., Gerard Caprio and Ross Levine. 2004. 'Bank Regulation and Supervision: What Works Best?'. *Journal of Financial Intermediation* 13 (2): 205–48. https://doi.org/10.1016/j.jfi.2003.06.002.

Bekier, Matthias M., Richard Huang and Gregory P. Wilson. 2005. 'How to Fix China's Banking System'. *McKinsey Quarterly* 1: 110–19.

Berger, Allen N., Iftekhar Hasan and Mingming Zhou. 2009. 'Bank Ownership and Efficiency in China: What Will Happen in the World's Largest Nation?'. *Journal of Banking & Finance* 33 (1): 113–30. https://doi.org/10.1016/j.jbankfin.2007.05.016.

Bonin, John P. and Yiping Huang. 2001. 'Dealing with the Bad Loans of the Chinese Banks'. *Journal of Asian Economics* 12 (2): 197–214.

Boyer, Robert. 2005. 'How and Why Capitalisms Differ'. *Economy and Society* 34 (4): 509–57.

CBRC. 2007. 'China Banking Regulatory Commission 2006 Annual Report'. Beijing: China Banking Regulatory Commission. www.cbrc.gov.cn/showannual.do.

CBRC. 2011. 'China Banking Regulatory Commission 2010 Annual Report'. Beijing: China Banking Regulatory Commission. www.cbrc.gov.cn/showannual.do.

CBRC. 2014. 'China Banking Regulatory Commission 2013 Annual Report'. Beijing: China Banking Regulatory Commission. www.cbrc.gov.cn/showannual.do.

CBRC. 2016. 'China Banking Regulatory Commission 2015 Annual Report'. Beijing: China Banking Regulatory Commission. www.cbrc.gov.cn/showannual.do.

Chen, Li. 2013. 'National Champions and Industrial Policy in China'. PhD thesis, Cambridge, United Kingdom: University of Cambridge.

Chen, Yougang, Stefan Matzinger and Jonathan Woetzel. 2018. 'Chinese Infrastructure: The Big Picture | McKinsey & Company'. www.mckinsey.com/global-themes/winning-in-emerging-markets/chinese-infrastructure-the-big-picture.

Chi, Ch'ao-Ting. 1970. *Key Economic Areas in Chinese History*. New York: Kelley.

*China Economic Review*. 2006. 'Pushing the City Limits'. 1 May 2006. www.china economicreview.com/node/23628.

Cull, Robert and Lixin Colin Xu. 2003. 'Who Gets Credit? The Behavior of Bureaucrats and State Banks in Allocating Credit to Chinese State-Owned Enterprises'. *Journal of Development Economics* 71 (2): 533–59. https://doi.org/10.1016/S0304-3878(03) 00039-7.

Dawson, Raymond Stanley, ed. 1964. *The Legacy of China*. Oxford, UK: Clarendon Press.

Dobson, Wendy and A. K. Kashyap. 2006. 'The Contradiction in China's Gradualist Banking Reforms'. *Brookings Papers on Economic Activity* 2006 (2): 103–62. https://doi.org/10.1353/eca.2007.0004.

Du, Hua 杜华, ed. 2007. '*Jinrong Gongzuo Wenxian Xuanbian (1978–2005)*' 金融工作文献选编（一九七八——二00五）. Beijing: Zhongguo Jinrong Chubanshe.

Feyzioglu, Tarhan N., Nathan Porter and Elöd Takáts. 2009. 'Interest Rate Liberalization in China'. Working Paper 2009–2171. International Monetary Fund. http://211.253.40.86/mille/service/ers/20000/IMG/000000017525/wp09171.pdf.

Firth, Michael, Chen Lin, Ping Liu and Sonia M. L. Wong. 2009. 'Inside the Black Box: Bank Credit Allocation in China's Private Sector'. *Journal of Banking & Finance* 33 (6): 1144–55. https://doi.org/10.1016/j.jbankfin.2008.12.008.

Fu, Xiaoqing (Maggie) and Shelagh Heffernan. 2009. 'The Effects of Reform on China's Bank Structure and Performance'. *Journal of Banking & Finance* 33 (1): 39–52. https://doi.org/10.1016/j.jbankfin.2006.11.023.

García-Herrero, Alicia, Sergio Gavilá and Daniel Santabárbara. 2009. 'What Explains the Low Profitability of Chinese Banks?' *Journal of Banking & Finance* 33 (11): 2080–92. https://doi.org/10.1016/j.jbankfin.2009.05.005.

Gerlach, Michael L. 1992. *Alliance Capitalism: The Social Organization of Japanese Business.* Oxford, UK: University of California Press.

Granovetter, Mark. 1985. 'Economic Action and Social Structure: The Problem of Embeddedness'. *American Journal of Sociology* 91 (3): 481–510.

Greenspan, Alan. 1997. 'The Evolution of Banking in a Market Economy – Speech at the Annual Conference of the Association of Private Enterprise Education, Arlington, Virginia April 12, 1997'. The Federal Reserve Board. 14 April 1997. www.federalreserve.gov/boarddocs/speeches/1997/19970412.htm.

Greenspan, Alan. 2007. *The Age of Turbulence : Adventures in a New World.* London: Allen Lane.

Hodgson, Geoffrey M. 2001. *How Economics Forgot History: The Problem of Historical Specificity in Social Science.* London: Routledge.

Hodgson, Geoffrey M. 2006. 'What Are Institutions?'. *Journal of Economic Issues* 40 (1): 1–25.

Hu Jintao. 2008. 'Speech at the Meeting Marking the 30th Anniversary of Reform and Opening Up'. *BEIJINGREVIEW.com.cn*, 18 December 2008. www.bjreview.com.cn/learning/txt/2009-04/27/content_192896.htm.

Huang, Hui. 2010. 'Institutional Structure of Financial Regulation in China: Lessons from the Global Financial Crisis'. *Journal of Corporate Law Studies* 10 (1): 219–54.

Huang, Yiping. 2001. *China's Last Steps across the River: Enterprise and Banking Reforms.* Canberra: Asia Pacific Press, Australia National University.

Huang, Yiping, Xun Wang and N. Lin. 2010. 'Financial Reform in China: Progresses and Challenges'. Working Paper. China Macroeconomic Research Center, Peking University, China. http://paftad.org/files/34/07_HUANG_Fin%20Reform_nofig.pdf.

Huntington, Samuel P. 1997. *The Clash of Civilizations and the Remaking of World Order.* New Delhi: Penguin Books India.

IMF. 2017. 'People's Republic of China: Financial System Stability Assessment'. IMF Country Report No. 17/358. Washington, DC: International Monetary Fund.

Jia, Chunxin. 2009. 'The Effect of Ownership on the Prudential Behavior of Banks – The Case of China'. *Journal of Banking & Finance* 33 (1): 77–87. https://doi.org/10.1016/j.jbankfin.2007.03.017.

Kindleberger, Charles P. and Robert Aliber. 2005. *Manias, Panics, and Crashes: A History of Financial Crises.* New Jersey: John Wiley & Sons.

Kuhn, Robert Lawrence. 2010. *How China's Leaders Think: The Inside Story of China's Reform and What This Means for the Future.* Singapore: Wiley.

Kwong, Charles C. L. 2011. 'China's Banking Reform: The Remaining Agenda'. *Global Economic Review* 40 (2): 161–78. https://doi.org/10.1080/1226508X.2011.585056.

Lardy, Nicholas R. 2014. *Markets over Mao: The Rise of Private Business in China.* Washington, DC: Institute for International Economics, US.

Laurenceson, James and J. C. H. Chai. 2001. 'State Banks and Economic Development in China'. *Journal of International Development* 13 (2): 211–25. https://doi.org/10.1002/jid.727.

Law, Daniel and Shaun Roache. 2015. 'Assessing Default Risks for Chinese Firms: A Lost Cause?'. Working Paper WP/15/140. Washington, DC: International Monetary Fund.

Levenson, Joseph Richmond. 1964. *Confucian China and Its Modern Fate*. Vol. 1. University of California Press.

Lin, Changyuan. 2003. 'Financial Conglomerates in China'. https://papers.ssrn.com/sol3/papers.cfm?abstract_id=446840.

Lin, Xiaochi and Yi Zhang. 2009. 'Bank Ownership Reform and Bank Performance in China'. *Journal of Banking & Finance* 33 (1): 20–29. https://doi.org/10.1016/j.jbankfin.2006.11.022.

Liu, Mingkang 刘明康, ed. 2009. *'Zhongguo Yinhang Gaige Kaifang Sanshinian (1978–2008) Shangce'* 中国银行业改革开放30年 (1978–2008) 上册. Beijing: Beijing Jinrong Chubanshe.

Loechel, Horst and Helena Xiang Li. 2009. 'China's Changing Business Model of Banking'. Working Paper No. 010. EU‐CHINA BMT WORKING PAPER SERIES. Shanghai: CEIBS. www.criticaleye.com/insights-servfile.cfm?id=1924&view=1.

Maddison, Angus. 2006. *The World Economy*. Development Centre Studies. Paris, France: Development Centre of the Organisation for Economic Co-operation and Development.

McGregor, Richard. 2012. *The Party: The Secret World of China's Communist Rulers*. London: Penguin Books.

Minsky, Hyman P. 1980. 'Capitalist Financial Processes and the Instability of Capitalism'. *Journal of Economic Issues* 14 (2): 505–23.

Minsky, Hyman P. 1992. 'The Financial Instability Hypothesis'. The Jerome Levy Economics Institute Working Paper, no. 74. http://papers.ssrn.com/sol3/papers.cfm?abstract_id=161024.

Mo, Y. K. 1999. 'A Review of Recent Banking Reforms in China'. *BIS Policy Papers* 7 (90): 109.

Naughton, Barry. 2007. *The Chinese Economy: Transitions and Growth*. Cambridge, MA: MIT Press.

*Nicholas Lardy on Markets over Mao: The Rise of Private Business in China*. 2014. Peterson Institute for International Economics, Washington, DC. www.youtube.com/watch?v=lcu7p2m71B0.

Park, Albert and Kaja Sehrt. 2001. 'Tests of Financial Intermediation and Banking Reform in China'. *Journal of Comparative Economics* 29 (4): 608–44.

Pedersen, Ove Kaj. 2006a. 'Corporatism and Beyond: The Negotiated Economy'. In *National Identity and the Varieties of Capitalism: The Danish Experience*, edited by John L. Campbell, John A. Hall and Ove Kaj Pedersen. Montreal: McGill-Queen's University Press.

Pedersen, Ove Kaj. 2006b. 'Denmark: An Ongoing Experiment'. In *National Identity and the Varieties of Capitalism: The Danish Experience*, edited by John A. Hall, John L. Campbell and Ove Kaj Pedersen. Montreal: McGill-Queen's University Press.

Pedersen, Ove Kaj and Peter Kjaer. 2001. 'Translating Liberalization: Neoliberalism in the Danish Negotiated Economy'. In *The Rise of Neoliberalism and Institutional Analysis*, edited by John L. Campbell and Ove Kaj Pedersen. Princeton: Princeton University Press.

Podpiera, Richard. 2006. 'Progress in China's Banking Sector Reform: Has Bank Behavior Changed?'. Working Paper. International Monetary Fund. http://papers.ssrn.com/sol3/papers.cfm?abstract_id=898732.

Polanyi, Karl. 2001. *The Great Transformation: The Political and Economic Origins of Our Time*. Boston, MA: Beacon Press.

Shih, Victor. 2007. 'Partial Reform Equilibrium, Chinese Style: Political Incentives and Reform Stagnation in Chinese Financial Policies'. *Comparative Political Studies* 40 (10): 1238–62. https://doi.org/10.1177/0010414006290107.

Shih, Victor. 2008. 'Factions and Finance in China'. *Elite Conflict and Inflation*. www.langtoninfo.com/web_content/9780521872577_frontmatter.pdf.

Shih, Victor, Qi Zhang and Mingxing Liu. 2007. 'Comparing the Performance of Chinese Banks: A Principal Component Approach'. *China Economic Review* 18 (1): 15–34. https://doi.org/10.1016/j.chieco.2006.11.001.

Streeck, Wolfgang and Kōzō Yamamura. 2001. *The Origins of Nonliberal Capitalism: Germany and Japan in Comparison*. Ithaca, NY: Cornell University Press.

Vogel, Ezra F. 2013. *Deng Xiaoping and the Transformation of China*. Reprint edition. Cambridge, MA: Belknap Press.

Walter, Carl and Fraser Howie. 2012. *Red Capitalism: The Fragile Financial Foundation of China's Extraordinary Rise*. Revised edition. Singapore: Wiley.

Whitley, Richard. 1999. *Divergent Capitalisms: The Social Structuring and Change of Business Systems*. Oxford, UK: Oxford University Press.

Wildau, Gabriel. 2015. 'World Bank Redacts Report Critical of China Financial System'. *Financial Times*, 3 July 2015. www.ft.com/cms/s/0/23dcc148-2152-11e5-aa5a-398b2169cf79.html#axzz3i8ZdC4jU.

Will, Pierre-Etienne. 1990. *Bureaucracy and Famine in Eighteenth-Century China*. Translated by Elborg Forster. Stanford, CA: Stanford University Press.

Williamson, John. 1989. 'What Washington Means by Policy Reform'. In *Latin American Adjustment: How Much Has Happened*, edited by John Williamson. Vol. 1. Washington: Institute for International Economics. https://edisk.fandm.edu/min/IST-325-Ecuador/What-Washington-Means-by-Policy-Reform.pdf.

World Bank. 2016. 'World Development Indicators'. 2016. http://data.worldbank.org/indicator/NE.EXP.GNFS.ZS?locations=CN.

Xi, Jinping. 2014. *The Governance of China*. Beijing: Foreign Languages Press.

*Xinhua News Agency*. 2012. 'Xi Jinping Vows No Stop in Reform, Opening Up'. 12 November 2012. http://news.xinhuanet.com/english/china/2012-12/11/c_132034269.htm.

Yeung, Godfrey. 2009. 'How Banks in China Make Lending Decisions'. *Journal of Contemporary China* 18 (59): 285–302. https://doi.org/10.1080/10670560802576034.

Zhang, Xiaowei. 2012. 'Why Are the Elite in China Motivated and Able to Promote Growth?'. In *The Role of Elites in Economic Development*, edited by Alice H. Amsden, Alisa DiCaprio and James A. Robinson. Oxford, UK: Oxford University Press.

Zhou, Wubiao. 2009. 'Bank Financing in China's Private Sector: The Payoffs of Political Capital'. *World Development* 37 (4): 787–99. https://doi.org/10.1016/j.worlddev.2008.07.011.

Zhou, Xiaochuan. 2009. 'Zhou Xiaochuan: Reform the International Monetary System'. Bank of International Settlements. www.bis.org/review/r090402c.pdf.

# 2 The search for a modern banking system (800–1990)

The modernisation of China's banking system under Deng Xiaoping's Reform and Opening policy reflected historical patterns of political and economic organisation in China. It should, therefore, not be viewed as an institutional convergence with Western developed nations, as indicated by Walter and Howie, who claim Deng's rise to power 'freed China to take part in the great financial liberalization that swept the world over the past quarter-century' (Walter and Howie 2012, 3). Instead, to quote Hodgson, Reform and Opening policies can be seen as 'path dependent' and 'historically specific' (Hodgson 2001, 3, 4). The historical development of China's indigenous banking system is characterised by a pattern of strong bureaucratic control to regulate market activity, and this pattern has persisted in the evolution of banking sector during the current Reform and Opening period. China had already begun to establish a relatively sophisticated indigenous banking system prior to Western intervention in 1840. The subsequent process of incorporation of Western ideas and technology in China's banking sector can be best understood as occurring according to the concept 'Chinese learning for the fundamental principles, Western learning for practical application' (中體西用 *zhongti xiyong*) (see Levenson 1964). China's leaders strongly associated the decline of China's economy which began in the nineteenth century with foreign intervention and the consequent loss of economic sovereignty. Ever since, officials have sought to restore pride in China's civilisation, a goal which has been predicated on the establishment or maintenance of sovereignty over the financial system. Deng's reform vision was shaped by this historical circumstance, acknowledging in 1978 after visiting Western, industrialised countries that 'the basic point is: we must acknowledge that we are backward … and that we need to change' (Vogel 2013, 218). Furthermore, the emphasis of China's officials on stability was reinforced by the devastating impact of episodes of political instability on China's economy and banking system. The gradual, pragmatic reform approach to reform adopted by Deng reflected this emphasis on stability, along with the desire to remove the harmful ideological excesses of the Maoist period from economic policy. The legacy of the planned economy caused Reform and Opening to be a policy of economic transition. To regulate new forms of economic activity, the state began to establish new forms of institutions to monitor and govern banks and firms and in doing so borrowed from many ideas from Western experience.

## China's indigenous banking system

In traditional Chinese society, China's officials sought to regulate the indigenous financial institutions which had emerged to serve its vibrant economy in order to promote social stability and ensure the welfare of the people. As early as the beginning of the ninth century, the domestic tea trade stimulated the development of an early remittance system for merchants known as *feiqian* or 'flying money'. During the Song dynasty (960–1279), a joint body of sixteen merchant families in Sichuan province established a more sophisticated remittance system using certificates known as *jiaozi*, which were popular among traders in silk and grain (Hu 1988). Ultimately the 'dishonest conduct' of the merchant families, along with failed endeavours in commercial activities, led to a payments crisis at the *jiaozi* money changing shops (Hu 1988, 401). The county government intervened, closing down the *jiaozi* shops and ensuring that merchants were able to receive cash payment for their *jiaozi*, albeit at a 20–30 per cent loss (Hu 1988, 401). The *jiaozi* shops were reopened under the authority of the local government of Yi County in Sichuan, which implemented strict regulations regarding the use of *jiaozi*. The local government unified the value of *jiaozi*, set a quota for their issuance, developed requirements for the holding of cash reserves and set a circulation period of 3 years (Hu 1988).

The evolution of China's indigenous banking system from the eighteenth century can be viewed as part of the emergence of economic patterns of organisation that have been termed 'embryonic capitalism' (Xu and Wu 2000). China's economy had experienced sustained phases of economic development in the late Ming and Qing dynasties which were marked by dynamic changes to patterns of economic organisation including the development of China's banking system. Also associated with this phase of 'embryonic capitalism' were the commercialisation of agriculture, the effective private ownership of land, and the increasing use of wage labour (Xu and Wu 2000). The Shanxi banks and the *qianzhuang* developed relatively sophisticated systems of remittance and credit in response to the growing demand for trade-related financial services (Mann Jones 1972). Shanxi banks provided merchants with remittances services by draft, letter and cheque. This service allowed merchants to spare the expense and risk of travelling with hard currency. Shanxi banks expanded rapidly, particularly in the North of China. By the end of the nineteenth century, there were thirty-two Shanxi banks with 475 branches, with operations in all provinces and frontier regions of China (Cheng 2003, 12). The incorporation of Shanxi banks into China's bureaucratic system as a financial intermediary in transactions between the central and provincial government caused them to function as a 'quasi-government institution' (Mann Jones 1972, 48). The *qianzhuang* were smaller-scale banks that provided services to merchants in the central and Southern coastal areas of China. *Qianzhuang* were typically established by wealthy merchant families. They issued notes and operated as a clearinghouse for merchant transactions. The regulation of *qianzhuang* was achieved largely through banking guilds controlled by merchants, which maintained regional stability of the financial system through control of interest and exchange rates and managing the liquidation of smaller banks (Mann Jones 1972). Susan Mann Jones (1972) finds support in the literature for the argument that *qianzhuang* descended from the money changing shops of the Song dynasty. According to Rawski (1989), China's indigenous financial system 'paralleled that of pre-industrial Europe in its complexity and sophistication' (Peng 2007, 126).

## Foreign intervention and a failed attempt to establish a modern banking system

Foreign intervention, which commenced with the advent of the first Opium war in 1839, undermined the ability of the Chinese state to continue to develop the indigenous banking sector. According to the unequal treaties imposed by the British (and subsequently other countries) on China, the state was unable to subject foreign financial institutions to control or regulation. By the end of the century, nine foreign banks had established a total of forty-five branches in China's treaty ports (Cheng 2003, 18). China's indigenous banks suffered a decline and the financial power of foreign banks quickly rivalled then exceeded that of the Shanxi banks and the *qianzhuang*. According to Eastman (1988, 165), 'thirty-two foreign banks in China and Hong Kong in the early 1930s financed some 90 percent of China's foreign trade'. Foreign bankers' lack of understanding of domestic trade caused them to work through Chinese agents. Foreign banks extended credit to the Chinese government, private enterprises and the *qianzhuang*, while wealthy officials took advantage of their perceived security to make deposits. The Qing government had become dependent on foreign banks for capital, not least to pay war indemnities after suffering defeat at the hands of the Japanese in 1884. From 1884, HSBC had custody of the Imperial Maritime Customs and also managed the salt tax. These were major sources of government revenue (Kynaston and Roberts 2015). Prior to the establishment of China's central bank, HSBC 'acted as financial agent, depository, adviser and underwriter for the Chinese government' (Kynaston and Roberts 2015, 7). Currency issued by foreign banks was preferred to Chinese notes as it held its value better (Eastman 1988).

Chinese officials attempted to develop a modern banking system in the face of this foreign intervention and loss of sovereignty over the banking sector. The state established the Imperial Bank of China, in 1897, and sixteen more banks were established before the collapse of the Qing dynasty. Most were either led by officials or were official-merchant joint ventures, including Daqing Bank (which later evolved into the Bank of China) and BoCom (Cheng 2003). In the Republican era, Chiang Kai-shek advocated state control of private capital and prioritised state ownership of strategic sectors of the economy. According to Chiang, while 'China's destiny formerly … was controlled by foreign imperialists', 'her destiny hereafter … rests in the hands of our [China's] entire citizenry' (Chiang 1947). The banking system expanded even more rapidly during the Republican era, in part aided by the preoccupation of foreign powers with the First World War. By 1925 there were more than 150 modern Chinese banks, most established through private interests (Cheng 2003, 42). The rapid development of the modern Chinese banking system resulted in the declining influence of foreign banks. Chiang's victory over regional warlords in 1927 facilitated the development of national institutions of financial governance. That year the state established a central bank and bureau of financial supervision and issued regulation on the registration and operation of banks. The state reclaimed control over the collection of customs and salt revenues (Kynaston and Roberts 2015). As Chiang's vision suggested, Chinese banks in the Republican era had a strong relationship with the state. Banks extended anywhere between 40 per cent and 70 per cent of loans to government bodies (Eastman 1988, 165). General Manager of BoC, Zhang Jia'ao, confirmed that 'in times of emergency the government can obtain money from the Bank...' (Peng 2007, 74). Peng writes that '...BOC had no choice but to support state enterprises' (Peng 2007, 81). Ironically, Zhang was ultimately removed from his post for not supporting the issuance of government treasury bills in the early 1930s (Peng 2007).

The Second World War and the Chinese Civil War had a devastating impact on economic and financial stability that ultimately derailed efforts to establish a modern banking sector. In what became known as the Banking Coup of 1935, the government gained control of around 70 per cent of China's financial assets, including those of BoC and BoCom, in response to insufficient support by private banks for government economic policy (Eastman 1988; Peng 2007). This did not end efforts to modernise the sector and professional bankers retained significant influence (Cheng 2003). However the Japanese invasion compelled the Nationalist government to appropriate the nation's financial assets to help finance the war effort, ending any attempt to establish a diversified banking system. China's economic and financial systems were highly dysfunctional over this period. Japan occupied China's most economically developed areas including its major ports and industrial areas, which not only deprived the state of important products and services but also caused a dramatic reduction in tax revenue. The puppet regime established by the Japanese also began to issue currency, creating a fractured and highly unstable monetary system. Both the Japanese puppet regime and the nationalists elected to print money for the purpose of creating seigniorage revenue. Their currencies experienced hyperinflation (Hewitt 2007; Yan 2015). The civil war between the Nationalist government and the communist forces continued for 4 years following the surrender of the Japanese. The victory of the communists provided a new opportunity for the stable development of China's banking system.

## Banking within the planned economy system

The semi-colonial and semi-feudal China of the past, which for over a hundred years had suffered from foreign aggression and bullying, was turned into a new and independent socialist China in which the people were the masters.

(Jiang Zemin, speaking of the achievements of Mao and his comrades at the 14th Party Congress (CCP 2011))

Following the founding of new China in 1949, the Communist Party moved to establish clear sovereignty and centralised control over the financial system. A new national-level central and commercial bank, the PBoC, was founded through the merger of banks established in areas controlled by the Communists. The state took measures to unify and stabilise the new currency, the Renminbi, by withdrawing other currencies and reducing inflation. The BoC and BoCom were taken over by the government. The state moved quickly to revoke the special privileges of foreign banks acquired during the Republican era. All but four of the foreign banks exited China and those that remained operated in a very limited capacity. Upon the implementation of the first 5-year plan in 1953, which served to introduce a centrally planned economy based on the Soviet model, the banking system was gradually restructured into a unified and vertically managed system. The PBoC, which reported to the State Council, was at the core of this system. The BoC, which handled foreign exchange and international settlements, was made subordinate to the PBoC. Also subordinate to the PBoC was the Joint-State Private Bank, a merger of over sixty formerly private banks. Other financial institutions include the People's Construction Bank of China, which was subordinate to the Ministry of Finance (MOF) and was responsible for capital investment, and credit cooperatives, which served as banks for communes in the countryside. Within this system, banks were under complete state control and were used by the state to supervise the economic activities of its SOEs (Donnithorne 1967).

Under this system, the banking system was a passive actor in the development of China's economy. The PBoC did not perform the duties of a financial intermediary, namely aggregating savings and allocating capital for investment. Instead, the PBoC allocated capital according to the annual budget set by the MOF and provided working capital for SOEs. 'Savings' were predominantly generated by and 'reinvested' in SOEs, whose provision of a wide range of services to state sector employees and their families reduced the need for private savings. Aside from the relatively few holdings that passed through the RCCs, there was little development of financial assets. Transactions between government entities and SOEs were made through deposit transfers at the central bank and there were strict requirements on state organs and communes to deposit excess currency (Gurley 1976).

The nature of economic relations did not require the banking sector to develop the institutions for loan selection, monitoring and enforcement that were present in Western-style banking institutions. While the PBoC did monitor firms, the purpose was to verify whether firms were implementing the plan correctly. The PBoC was intimately involved with the development and execution of the credit plan that corresponded with the plans for agriculture and industry. The central bank monitored the use of capital and consequent output by firms who were provided production targets by the state. Bank branches were established near industrial sites such as factories or mines. One major problem was the excessive use and misappropriation of working capital. Banks monitored for the use of working capital for fixed asset investment, which was a violation of the plan. From 1959, the state required enterprises to pay interest on working capital loans. The state experimented with other policies to resolve the issue, including channelling funds directly through the MOF and charging the PBoC with supplying above-quota working capital (Donnithorne 1967). As firms held little cash, there existed an incentive to demand greater raw materials than required and hoard these for use in later production cycles or to barter for other goods. Central bank official works would examine firm bank balances and even visit production sites to detect hoarding. Without the aid of market price signals, much energy was devoted by state planning agencies to gathering accurate and timely information about the ever-changing supply and demand of materials (Gurley 1976). The decision of the state to decentralise important functions of the Agricultural Bank of China, a financial institution which had previously been abolished, likely reflected the desire to allow local officials to respond to the needs of producers in a timely fashion (Donnithorne 1967).

Along with the rest of the economy, China's banking system suffered a severe institutional decline as a consequence of the large-scale instability and loss that occurred during the Great Leap Forward campaign (1958–61) and the Cultural Revolution (1966–76). During the Great Leap Forward, the state implemented economic policies that were designed to achieve rapid industrialisation but instead resulted in mass starvation as harvest sizes fell. The banking sector was given licence to extend credit beyond the plan to achieve the state's policy goal, though contradictorily the supervisory powers of banks were 'whittled away' as party committees took over (Donnithorne 1967, 429). The banking sector did not possess the institutional capability to evaluate loans effectively and as a consequence it experienced heavily losses. The turmoil created by the ideologically-driven Cultural Revolution (1966–76) severely damaged the banking system as all functional departments aside from the operations and political departments within PBoC's head office were removed. By 1969, the PBoC had been formally absorbed by the MOF, for whom it provided accounting and payment functions. As an institution, the PBoC had become so weak that its head office was unable to implement financial policies and systems at branch level and lacked a consistent administrative form at district and county levels (Liu, Mingkang 刘明康 2009).

## Reform and opening: banks to become 'real banks'

Deng Xiaoping's desire to modernise China's economy was the inspiration behind the economic reform policy Reform and Opening, which was announced at the Third Plenary Session of the 11th Central Committee in 1978. Deng wanted banks to play an active role in liberating productive forces in the economy. In October 1979, at a meeting convened by Deng to explain his economic philosophy to provincial and city party secretaries, he signalled that banks would now play an active role in allocating capital rather than merely administering the plan: 'Banks must become the lever for the development of the economy and technological innovation, banks must become real banks' (Liu, Mingkang 刘明康 2009, 5). During this speech, Deng bemoaned the failure of the financial system under the plan to allocate capital to profitable projects. To achieve more effective allocation of capital, Deng envisaged an institutional strengthening of the banking system to increase the accountability of capital use by the state: 'Any government entity that wants goods and materials will need to obtain a bank loan and will pay interest on that loan' (Du, Hua 杜华 2007, 9).

While it was clear that the shift in economic policy heralded a far more prominent role for banks in the economy, China's policymakers did not have a predetermined view for how to transform the banking sector and achieve modernisation of the economy. In the words of Deng Xiaoping, the Chinese people had endured unnecessary hardship as a consequence of the 'excessive egalitarianism and ultra-left tendencies', seen most prominently during the Cultural Revolution (Nolan 2004, 8). Deng advocated a new, pragmatic approach to economic reform based on empirical evidence, for which he borrowed the Chinese idiom 'seeking truth from facts'. The implementation of reform in the banking sector would be a highly exploratory process subject to much trial and error, as if 'groping for stones to cross the river'.

## Diversification of the banking sector

The first step towards Deng's vision of the banking system began with the development of a diversified banking sector that grew from the foundations of the planned economy. The bureaucratic structure remained relatively constant, with the State Council and PBoC responsible for implementing the vision of party leaders and developing concrete proposals on reform. A new agency, the State Council's Research and Development Centre, was established in 1980 to act as a 'think tank' and provide policy recommendations. Between 1979 and 1984, the state carved out four large state-owned banks from the PBoC. These were known as specialised banks as the business of each bank was divided by industry. Competition between banks was limited to deposits and new business in the emerging real estate, trust and securities sectors. According to a CBRC official, specialisation was the principal reason for the establishment of the Big Four, as the state sought to address the needs of particular sectors with a specific financial institution, rather than any intention to develop competition between banks (Interview with CBRC official, 10 March 2015). This was a model the state had previously experimented with prior to 1978, establishing and disestablishing both the Agricultural Bank of China and the People's Construction Bank of China on more than one occasion. Indeed, Liu Mingkang stated that the decision to re-establish these banks was 'carried out according to the industrial management concepts of the planned economy' (Liu, Mingkang 刘明康 2009, 9).

The establishment of specialised banks was both a reaction to the new demands on the banking system after the introduction of economic incentives and a reflection of China's desire to transform SOEs, adopt foreign capital and technology, and develop infrastructure. The introduction of incentives represented the first major step of economic transition, with Deng hoping to resolve the 'excessive egalitarianism' of the planned economy that he felt provided no incentive for managers to run enterprises at a profit. The rural and urban reforms that developed incentives also caused the quantity of capital flowing through the banking system to dramatically increase. At the 3rd Plenum of the 11th Party Congress, when China's leaders created incentives for farmers to lift production by raising the prices substantially for production outside of quotas set out in the plan, it was also decided to establish the first specialised bank, the Agricultural Bank of China (ABC). The ABC would support the expected development of household-based production and rural enterprises. Reforms of SOEs, which were announced at the subsequent 3rd Plenum in 1984, endorsed the widespread implementation of the CRS. To enhance incentives, the state compelled enterprises to enter into individual profit-sharing and tax agreements and allowed production above the quota to be sold at market prices. That same year the Industrial and Commercial Bank of China (ICBC) was established to support the economic transformation of urban enterprises. It took over the industrial and commercial business of PBoC. China's opening up led to the rapid development of international trade and a consequent rise in international settlements, causing the State Council to endorse a PBoC report which recommended the BoC split off from the PBoC in 1979. BoC would become a bank that specialised in the management of the country's foreign exchange and foreign trade businesses. Its relationships with the outside world would help facilitate the introduction of foreign capital and technology. CCB, which in its previous forms had been under the supervision of the MOF, became subordinate to the State Council in 1983. It had a mandate to finance construction and investment in fixed assets in order to develop the country's infrastructure.

The PBoC was established as an independent central bank in 1984 as officials struggled to control the allocation of credit and currency in an increasingly monetised economy. The PBoC was given many of the supervisory powers of a regulator in a market economy, though this was problematic while the PBoC retained functions of an operating bank. The PBoC was assigned the responsibility for supervision and audit of all financial institutions, including non-banking financial institutions (NBFIs). The PBoC had the authority to act as the gatekeeper for the entry and exit of financial institutions in the financial sector. The PBoC reported directly to the State Council and held a ministry-level status within the state's bureaucratic hierarchy. Detailed PBoC policy-making was primarily conducted by a council comprised of the PBoC Governor and Vice Governor, the Vice Ministers of the MOF, the State Planning Commission, and the System Reform Commission as well as the Presidents of the specialised banks, though conditional upon the State Council's approval (World Bank 1990).

Strong bureaucratic control over credit allocation continued after the establishment of a pluralised banking system. Loan selection was primarily determined by officials at each administrative level of government. Credit was directed according to the state's mandatory investment plan, which was comprised of projects approved by the State Planning Commission. While interest rates were set by the PBoC, state priority projects received loans at a discounted rate as well as priority access to raw materials. Typically the credit plan would specify the bank responsible for financing each project. Mandatory provincial plans were a subset of the credit plan and the projects chosen were determined by planning agencies, local government and SOEs. In 1990, the World Bank estimated that the central government and local governments each controlled approximately 40 per cent of fixed asset investment, with the surplus comprised essentially of household investment in residential construction (World Bank 1990, 31). The majority of loans were invested in the industrial and commercial sectors. At this time, the relative strength of planning institutions within the China's bureaucratic structure hindered the ability of PBoC to develop regulatory capability. PBoC deputy secretary general Ren Junyin described the institution's relationship with the State Planning Commission as 'not very smooth' (O'Neill 1987a).

## The role of new financial institutions in the development of the banking sector

### *Shareholding banks*

Party leaders had become aware that the structure of the banking system had to change in order to achieve Deng's vision of making banks 'real banks'. In order to develop banks that were truly commercial in nature, it was imperative to cultivate a more competitive environment for specialised banks. Chinese economists had written papers supporting the establishment of shareholding banks and this was formally proposed to the State Council by the State Council Research and Development Centre (Interview with Wang Dashu, former senior researcher at the Research and Development Centre of the State Council, 25 March 2015). Between 1987 and 1988, six shareholding banks were established with a further three entering the sector in 1993 following Deng's Southern Tour. Regional commercial banks were also established around China, particularly in areas such as Shanghai and Guangzhou. The initial capital needed to establish these banks also came from the state, but from diverse sources. Shareholding banks were either controlled through centrally controlled SOE groups, which was the case with CITIC Bank, Everbright Bank and Merchants Bank, local government investment, for example Shanghai Pudong Development Bank, large-scale SOEs (Hua Xia Bank was originally a subsidiary of Capital Steel) or local financial companies as was the case with Fujian Industrial Bank. The activities of shareholding banks were not restricted by industry. According to Liu Mingkang, the arrival of shareholding banks 'introduced a mechanism of competition which promoted the improvement of the overall financial sector and its service level' (Liu, Mingkang 刘明康 2009, 18).

The decision to establish shareholding banks demonstrated a willingness by China's central officials to release some control of the banking system in an attempt to promote its development. On one hand, the decision to develop shareholding banks was a bold decision from the central government. It represented perhaps the most significant step away from the monobank system since reforms began. The shareholding bank model was distinct from that of specialised banks and had the ability to challenge their monopoly over sectors of the economy. Shareholding banks were of a smaller scale and typically had a regional focus under the jurisdiction of local governments. On the other hand, the decision was a pragmatic one by the state that was designed to accelerate the commercialisation of the banking sector without having to fundamentally alter the course of reform. While planning decisions were generally made at a more decentralised level than at specialised banks, the lending activities of shareholding banks remained under the plan and this reform did not fundamentally alter the mechanism by which credit was allocated.

The establishment of shareholding banks 'gradually changed the old supportive banking organisational model to become a real enterprise organisational model' (Liu, Mingkang 刘明康 2009, 22). While shareholding banks were state-owned and had their roots in the planned economy, as newly established financial enterprises they did not have the same level of obligation to provide SOEs with financial support. This comparative lack of 'institutional inertia' allowed them to be relatively dynamic and act more according to commercial principles. While the corporate governance framework of shareholding banks, comprised of a board of directors, board of supervisors and the general meeting of shareholders, was bloated and ineffective, there was at least a clear ownership structure in place through which to monitor managerial performance. While the branch networks of specialised banks conformed to state administrative areas, shareholding banks chose to establish branch networks concentrated in thriving coastal regions such Guangdong and the Yangzte River Delta. From their establishment, shareholding banks instituted flexible employment policies, composed of labour contracts and a salary system with performance objectives upon which promotion and demotion decisions were based, at a time when specialised banks were just beginning to dismantle a system of guaranteed employment and wages. Along with performance incentives, management were also incentivised to reduce risk. Shareholding banks pioneered the early development of systems of risk management and asset liability management. Furthermore unlike specialised banks the governance systems of shareholding banks, with the exception of BoCom and Guangdong Development Bank, were organised according to a one-tier legal person system that greatly assisted in the uniform management of enterprises.

Competition proved an effective instrument for progress for specialised banks, though this was achieved more through the bureaucratic system than by means of a credible competitive threat. Officials in senior positions in the Big Four state-owned banks did not want to 'lose face' when comparisons were made to the performance of shareholding banks. At the time of their establishment, the scale of shareholding banks caused them to be at a significant disadvantage to specialised banks. Indeed even by 1996, 11 shareholding banks had a total of 85,505 staff and 3,748 branches, less than any of the specialised banks (Liu, Mingkang 刘明康 2009, 22). Nevertheless, officials in specialised banks were influenced by exposure to this new model of banking enterprise, which provided a clear path forwards in terms of system change.

### Trust and investment companies

China's trust sector was established to raise capital for the purchase of new technology and equipment from foreign countries to facilitate the modernisation of China's industry. Trust companies raised funds by attracting domestic savings, executing short-term financing and issuing overseas bonds. The NBFI sector in China began in 1979 with the establishment of the first trust company, CITIC, which was founded by Vice Premier Rong Yiren. In 1980 CITIC used financial leasing to import the first Boeing 747 airplane into China and 2 years later issued a 12-year bond in Tokyo for 10 billion Yen, which was China's first bond issued on international markets (Liu, Mingkang 刘明康 2009, 10). Initially trust companies were highly integrated into the bureaucratic structure. Officials at each level of government established trust companies to deliver investment services required after the introduction of profit sharing arrangements under the CRS. This led an explosion of new firms, with 620 trust companies opened by 1982 (Liu, Mingkang 刘明康 2009, 11). In order to establish greater order in the sector, there was a reorganisation of trust companies. That same year, operations of trust companies were restricted to the PBoC or a PBoC-approved specialised bank. Following this reform, control of the trust sector shifted from government entities to branches of the specialised banks. Provincial branches and some city branches of specialised banks established their own trust companies. 454 of the 745 trust companies at the end of 1988 were affiliated with three of the specialised banks, which were the predominant source of funds (World Bank 1990, 13).

The trust sector was a vehicle for policymakers to understand the risks associated with more market-orientated institutions. At a time when credit was tightly controlled under the plan due to vigorous demand, trusts were able to lend a greater proportion of capital to lenders which were outside of the plan and could make loans to enterprises at higher rates with fewer restrictions on loan size and clientele. The greater profits available through arbitrage activities such as selling goods or lending outside the plan incentivised banks and their trust companies to allocate more capital outside the planning system. Between 1986 and 1988 the total assets of trust companies doubled each year (World Bank 1990, 13). Given the perverse incentives, it was no surprise that reports suggested that only half of trust financing and investment activities accorded with government regulations (Pei 1998, 330). The growing leakage from the plan to what was largely unregulated banking activity became a priority issue for the state in 1988 due to the weak state of regulatory institutions (Interview with Wang Dashu, former senior researcher at the Research and Development Centre of the State Council, 25

March 2015). Regulation of the sector had failed to ensure that trust and investment corporations (TICs) and other NBFIs were institutionally adequate or sufficiently capitalised. It was also alleged that trust companies had exceeded their business scope by undertaking the traditional lending and deposit activities of commercial banks (World Bank 1990). Along with TICs, other finance, leasing and credit firms were accused of being 'not well managed and not adequately controlled' because they offer illegally high interest rates and 'divert capital into unauthorised projects and disobey orders from Peking on how funds should be used' (*Reuters News* 1988).

Problems in the trust sector created a resolve within the party to improve systems of regulation in order to contain market risk. In a speech made in August 1989, then Premier Li Peng decried the reckless nature of trusts which had caused the leakage of capital, inappropriately structured investment and created the conditions for 'all kinds of corruption' to occur. However Li pragmatically compared the problems of corruption of China's most market-orientated institutions with that of central government officials. He suggested that in both fields, corruption occurred only in a minority of cases and the key issue was governance of markets, given the 'lax systems and weak management', rather than a problem of the market system itself (Du, Hua 杜华 2007, 95).

### *Foreign banks*

China opened its doors to foreign banks in order to attract foreign capital, technology and ideas. Strict limitations were placed on the operation of foreign banks to maintain sovereignty over the banking system and ensure that new ideas could be adopted in a manner suitable to China's political and economic institutions. Foreign banks were not permitted to undertake RMB business, which would put them in direct competition with domestic banks. Instead regulators encouraged foreign banks to advise foreign firms and facilitate foreign currency investment into SEZs and certain coastal cities. From 1979 informal permission was given to foreign banks to establish representative offices in China. By 1987, 181 representative offices had been opened, by which time 22 foreign banks had opened branch offices in the Shenzhen, Zhuhai and Xiamen SEZs as well as Shanghai. Significant funds had been raised through these branches. For example, to raise funds for the development of energy, transport and raw materials industries, China 'floated 20 bond issues through foreign financial institutions, for a total of 340bn Japanese yen and 400m US dollars in Japan, Singapore and Europe' (*BBC Monitoring Service: Asia-Pacific* 1987).

## Bureaucratic control and decentralising reforms

The party system was at the core of the governance of the banking system, reflecting the historical influence of China's bureaucracy over patterns of economic organisation. Party agencies were responsible for the appointment, monitoring and discipline of officials. Through its system of party committees, the party maintained a strong presence in banking institutions. The decentralisation of China's SOEs that followed Zhao Ziyang's reform of the urban sector in 1984 shifted the control of many large industrial plants and enterprises from central industrial ministries to local party committees. This policy of decentralisation allowed local party officials in provincial regions to gain greater influence over banks and regulators and diminished the power of officials in central ministries. Local officials utilised this enhanced power to advance the economic interests of their home province or region. The key mechanism utilised by local governments to exert influence was their ability to control appointments of local banking and regulatory officials through the bureaucratic system. The local party committee was responsible for the appointment of the top banking officials at regional level, with minimal input from the bank's head office. Control over the appointment of officials was used to push lending to local enterprises. This was made possible by a policy, instituted in 1985, which decentralised the management of specialised bank credit through the allocation of funds at PBoC branch level. Branches also took advantage of the indicative nature of specialised bank plans and the flexibility around loans for working capital (Holz 1992). Local authorities, who wanted funds for projects, were often able to gain access to such funds despite the directives from central party officials, who sought monetary stability and a more sustainable model of economic development. Li Guixian, Governor of PBoC between 1988 and 1993, acknowledged while in office that every bank branch 'had to consciously accept the leadership of the local CCP committee' (Holz 1992, 35).

The governance structure of banks and regulators was highly responsive to decentralising reforms and the increased influence of local party officials. City and provincial bank branches were accorded their own legal status. Control and supervision of specialised bank branches was conducted at the provincial level, demonstrated by the tiny proportion of staff located at banks' head offices. For example, ABC had only 200 staff at its head office from a total number of 350,000 employees at 30,000 branches (World Bank 1990, 6). The appointment powers of local governments had a similar impact on central bank branches and prior to 1988 the PBoC did not have full authority to appoint the managers of its own branch offices (Yang 2004). The activities of local PBoC branches generally deferred to the interests of planning bureaus and local government officials. Local regulators were required to coordinate activities with local Finance and Planning Bureaus and follow the general practices of the relevant local administration. The lack of bureaucratic power limited the ability of the head office of PBoC to exert control over its own sub-branches and ensure their compliance with credit and monetary targets.

PBoC banking supervision was highly decentralised. PBoC headquarters was responsible for the supervision of less than fifty financial institutions, while provincial and local branches together took responsibility for the supervision of over 1,500 financial institutions (World Bank 1990, 93). Supervisory activities were conducted using a bottom-up approach that treated branches as separate entities instead of scrutinising bank activities at an enterprise level. Banking inspections were essentially performed at a branch level rather than at the level of the enterprise, causing the majority of supervisory resources to be located at the lower-level branches. While the central bank had a total staff of over 130,000 staff in 1988, its headquarters along with the Beijing and Shanghai branches each had no more than 30 staff each, despite having supervisory responsibilities over specialised banks in some of the most thriving economic regions in China (World Bank 1990, 4,92).

Policymakers actively encouraged the trend of decentralisation within the banking sector to increase incentives, a policy which was an extension of the thinking behind agricultural and urban reforms. Between 1985 and 1988 the CRS, along with similar decentralising reforms, was trialled in the banking sector. In 1987 ICBC formally established 'the city' as the basic operating unit and 22 per cent of all ICBC branches implemented trials of the CRS. At ABC, trials which gave county branches authority for their accounting practices were implemented at 4,600 branches in 1985. In 1987, wide-ranging reforms of its operating mechanism led to greater autonomy at the unit of the city (or county) through trials of a 'targeted management responsibility system'. ABC was the first and only bank to achieve full implementation of the CRS in 1988, under which it delivered a tax quota that was pre-negotiated with the government in return for the right to retain a proportion of profits above the quota. CCB linked the financial performance of county bank branches with retained earnings and staff numbers and trialled a responsibility system based on fees. In addition to trials of CRS and the targeted management responsibility system within parts of its branch network, it also broadened the scope the contract system to include areas of finance, loan-making and human resources (Liu, Mingkang 刘明康 2009, 16–17). Even the central bank had instituted systems through which branches retained earnings and were responsible for tax payments.

While these reforms increased incentives, the fractured nature of governance created significant problems at branch level. Staff would engage in unsustainable business practices aimed at maximising short-term profits and which created harmful competition between branches. The problem most severe at lower-level branches where a lack of governance caused corrupt practices to develop as well as the violation of financial rules and processes (Liu, Mingkang 刘明康 2009).

Along with problems of governance, the increased autonomy of branches made it difficult for the state to ensure sufficient credit reached heavy industry and other price-controlled sectors where profitability was low. Banks became more reluctant to lend to projects with small returns such as those related to heavy industry and infrastructure in favour of the rapidly expanding light industrial sector. Chinese authorities labelled this phenomenon a 'twisted structure of credit' (World Bank 1990, 33). As this liberalisation of credit expanded, the state actually increased efforts to direct capital to these industries through administrative guidance and implementing credit ceilings on non-priority sectors.

## Establishing institutions of market governance

During the 1980s, the state began to gradually establish institutions that could provide monitoring and governance functions to ensure financial stability as administrative control was reduced. The use of regulation, while secondary to the planning system, was endorsed at the 3rd Plenum of the 12th Party Congress in 1984, while Party leaders approved an economic system that integrated planning and regulation functions at the 3rd Plenum of the 13th Party Congress in 1988.

The development of monitoring and governance institutions was highly dependent on the adoption of ideas from the modern banking systems of developed countries. These ideas were incorporated within China's existing political and economic institutions in a manner that was suitable to China's national conditions. During the 1980s, China consciously began a strategy of learning from the outside. The PBoC developed a strong relationship with leading foreign regulators and banks and regularly sent delegations overseas to interact with and learn from bankers and regulators (Interview with Wang Dashu, former senior researcher at the Research and Development Centre of the State Council, 25 March 2015). Chen Yuan, son of influential Communist leader Chen Yun and Chairman of China Development Bank from 1998 to 2013, recalled a 2-week training programme taken while at PBoC in 1988: 'My classroom was Washington and New York. I visited the Fed, the Treasury, investment banks and commercial banks. They were my teachers. I learned supervision, risk management, payment services, and financial products' (Kuhn 2010, 272). Bank employees also underwent periods of secondment with correspondent banks abroad. The training received in modern management practices was hugely influential in the development of modern banking concepts in Chinese banks.

Monitoring and governance functions were needed to control market risk and promote the development of commercial behaviour within Chinese banks. Simply granting greater autonomy to specialised banks was not sufficient to cause them to act in a commercially sustainable fashion. As part of the state apparatus, specialised banks had an obligation to direct capital to priority projects and support SOEs during economic transition. In keeping with this support, banks would not withhold capital from SOEs who failed to return loans. This effectively provided SOEs with a soft budget constraint. SOEs were unconcerned by the prospect of bankruptcy and endeavoured to obtain as much capital as possible from banks. In many ways their actions resembled the competition for raw materials during the planned economy. Additionally, given the fractured nature of governance, meeting loan targets to regional SOEs was a stronger consideration for banks than profitability.

The state needed to establish new institutions to govern and regulate banks in order to change this culture. Making these new institutions effective, particularly given their early stage of development, was a challenge for the state. This problem was compounded by the fragmented governance structure present in the banking sector, which limited the ability of the state to implement reforms consistently across financial institutions. Furthermore throughout the 1980s the state was simply unable to obtain good information through which to effectively monitor the performance of banks and the SOEs to whom they were supplying capital.

## Financial regulation

The initial establishment of a regulatory framework in the banking sector was a highly explorative process. Policymakers took a pragmatic approach in designing a system of regulation that would control market risk and facilitate the development of a sustainable banking model. In October 1984, Premier Zhao Ziyang established a working group with the aim of empowering the central bank to drive the establishment of a regulatory framework for the banking system. The working group was comprised of officials from the PBoC, the MOF, the State Commission for Reform of the Economic System and the Economic Research Centre of the Council.

The PBoC developed the initial regulatory framework for the banking sector through what one CBRC official described as a 'series of trials' (Interview with CBRC official, 10 March 2015). These occurred within particular geographic areas and where successful were followed by the issuance of provisional, nationwide regulation. The state selected a group of cities (*jinrong gaige shidian chengshi*) that would undertake the initial trials of reform measures in the financial sector. Regulatory trials were coordinated centrally and conferences were held which brought together the relevant stakeholders of reform including representatives of the PBoC, specialised banks and local government. By the time of the fourth conference, held in Dalian in September 1987, the number of trial cities had reached 27 (Holz 1992, 10). In January 1986, the State Council issued the *Provisional Regulations on the Administration of Banks in the PRC*, which was the first comprehensive and unified set of regulations for the banking system. The regulations defined the role of the PBoC as financial regulator, responsible for drafting and implementing regulations, and set out rules for the approval of the establishment and merger of financial organisations and the supervision and audit of operations of financial institutions. It also defined the basic operational scope of financial institutions. In the second half of the 1980s a series of provisional regulations followed for the various types of financial institutions including trust companies (1986), UCCs (1998), and RCCs (1990) (Liu, Mingkang 刘明康 2009).

At this early stage of regulatory development, central bank officials struggled to ensure the effective implementation of regulation. The PBoC did not yet have the capability to utilise the information it gathered in off-site supervisory reports and on-site examinations effectively as part of the bank supervisory process. Furthermore the PBoC's strong focus on credit and monetary policy led it to use information collected to analyse bank liquidity, where applicable, or simply for statistical purposes. The ad hoc nature of regulatory development, which aimed to develop regulatory coverage for each type of financial institution, gave rise to a fragmented coverage of the banking system and regulatory distortions. Additionally, the primary focus of legal development emphasised 'the social and developmental role of banks', prioritising compliance with the national credit plan ahead of important regulatory objectives such as the safety and soundness of financial institutions (World Bank 1990). It became evident that a comprehensive banking law was needed to resolve these issues. China passed its first bankruptcy law in 1986, which legally protected the property rights of creditors in the advent of default, but the mechanisms to enforce this law had not been developed. In practice it was difficult for banks to successfully claim the assets of borrowers in the event of a default as assets were owned by the state and SOEs had a social responsibility to workers and their families. Following the passing of the law a PBoC official pointed out that 'relations between a firm and its local government are too close. The government does not want its own firms to go bankrupt. Bankruptcy will be very hard to implement' (O'Neill 1988).

The ineffective nature of the regulatory framework created a lack of order in the financial sector. The entry and exit of financial institutions to the banking sector was not monitored effectively, while there was often little distinction between the activities of different types of financial institutions despite large variations in their regulatory environments. A World Bank report produced in 1990 suggested there was 'almost a complete overlap' of function between the various types of financial institutions (World Bank 1990, 15). Specialised banks were able to engage in trust business through trust subsidiaries and TICs and finance companies were involved with commercial lending. The lack of compliance with existing regulations compounded the problem. There were state organs that had covert financial firms and enterprises with illegal enterprise banks. Even the central bank was involved in commercial lending. While explicitly forbidden by the authorities, some illegal private banks also emerged. The *New York Times* reported in 1988 that 27 private banks had been established in the city of Wenzhou alone. These banks offered higher interest rates on deposits and loans than the state regulations allowed. While local PBoC officials were aware of this phenomenon, there was no crackdown by authorities, perhaps due to the small scale of activities and limited regulatory resources (Gargan 1988).

The development of financial regulatory capability was stimulated by efforts to deal with the serious problems of governance in the NBFI sector. The PBoC presided over the clean-up of the NBFI sector between 1989 and 1991. The number of financial companies, which had reached over 1000 in 1988, was reduced considerably. The PBoC gave approval for 285 to remain a going concern, closing 792 in 1990. Similarly, the number of trust companies fell from 745 in 1988 to 386 in 1992 (Liu, Mingkang 刘明康 2009, 32). The clean-up tested the auditing capabilities of the PBoC, who conducted investigations into the financial circumstances and operating standards of fifteen national-scale trust companies, along with a large-scale investigation of credit use by financial companies. The PBoC conducted audits of loan limits, loan direction and loan effectiveness and addressed issues problems of unreasonable competition for deposits caused by NBFIs offering excessive interest rates. The clean-up also reinforced the importance of PBoC's role as a gatekeeper to entry and exit into the financial sector. In August 1988, the State Council reiterated that no department could establish a financial institution without first gaining PBoC approval. The clean-up facilitated the development of a concrete policy for the merger and closure of financial companies. It also began a process of separation between specialised banks and trust companies that foreshadowed the formal separation of sectors which was announced in 1994 (Interview with Wang Dashu, former senior researcher at the Research and Development Centre of the State Council, 25 March 2015). Importantly, it was an exercise that stimulated a comprehensive examination of the existing regulations and standardised documents of the PBoC, many of which were discarded. This process allowed the drafting of a comprehensive banking law to begin.

## Risk management

In the 1980s, China's banking system had only a very rudimentary system of risk management. Banks did not have a strong awareness of concepts of risk management and seldom considered credit risk when making loans. Policies relating to management of credit risk were relatively undeveloped at Chinese banks. Internal bank documents tended to focus on the response to non-repayment of loans rather than the events preceding it. Documentation detailed written procedures for loan rescheduling, visits to borrowers to prevent default of loans, loan collection and the taking possession of collateral. Due to the absence of policies relating to allocation of loans, there was a lack of consistency within specialised banks with regards to policies for loan structure and pricing, loan to collateral ratios, borrower information and concentration of credit within borrowers, sectors and geographic areas. Specialised banks lacked a clear system of lending authority and consequently it was difficult to establish accountability for lending decisions. Staff lacked the required training in credit analysis or accounting to evaluate loans effectively. Furthermore there was no separation of loan-making and loan assessment that would have added much-needed accountability to the loan-making process.

It was not normal practice for banks to write-off loans, even when it was felt that it was no longer possible to make any further recovery. This general practice is evidenced by the requirement of State Council approval for write-offs above RMB 100,000 (World Bank 1990, 94). There was no adequate general loan loss provision and no provision for specific loans where a loss in the value of assets had been identified. As of 1988, the MOF had an upper limit on loan provisions of 0.01 per cent or 0.02 per cent in effect, depending on the sector where the loan was made. Early loan classification systems were highly limited. There was little information available on NPLs as banks did not attempt to classify loans by quality.

Asset and liability management, which would provide a mechanism by which to control capital utilisation and address areas of the potential liquidity and interest rate risk, was not practised by Chinese banks in the 1980s. Furthermore, Chinese banks did not yet have a system of key financial indicators by which to monitor and assess the performance and risk of branch operations. Consequently, banks were not aware of their performance relative to competitors, nor did they possess a clear understanding of their own risk profile.

## Auditing

Western forms of auditing had not existed in the planned economy era and consequently the priority in the 1980s was to establish a basic framework for auditing practices. There was a lack of trained and experience staff at all levels of audit, principally because there were few qualified accountants.

Following the PBoC's National Disciplinary Inspection Audit Work Meeting in 1985, it was decided to establish a new, independent structure of audit within the PBoC. This event signified the beginning of its on-site examination system. By the end of 1985 there were audit departments in all provincial-level branches and branches in 258 of the 284 city-level branches (Liu, Mingkang 刘明康 2009, 31). In July 1985 the PBoC issued the *PBoC Audit Work Provisional Regulations*, which was the first attempt to define the regulatory principles for audit of the different types of financial organisations. Later the PBoC issued detailed instructions on working procedures including rules and the standardisation of practices relating to the incentive system, and procedures for communication with specialised banks. While by the end of 1986 there were only 2,500 auditors, this marked an increase of over 1,000 from the year before (Liu, Mingkang 刘明康 2009, 31). The capability of PBoC audit gradually improved and by 1992 a unified system of off-site assessments and risk monitoring audits was developed. By this time, loan quality and financial policy audits had also been conducted for each type of financial organisation. The PBoC issued detailed rules for the resolution of violations discovered by audit and for audit reporting methods in 1989 and 1992 respectively (Liu, Mingkang 刘明康 2009).

The lack of capability of internal audit within specialised banks compelled the PBoC audit system to bear the responsibility of basic tasks such as the verification of transactions within specialised banks. Unlike the PBoC, banks had not established a parallel structure for internal audit and auditors reported directly to branch managers. This impaired auditor independence. Compounding this problem was the bottom-up audit structure in which higher branch levels relied on lower levels for self-audit. Staff shortages were chronic. As of 1988, PCBC employed approximately 1,000 auditors at provincial level to audit around 10,000 offices (World Bank 1990, 64). The inconsistent implementation of CRS-style reforms created variable practices across specialised banks. For example, county-level branches formed an accounting unit for ABC but not for PCBC (World Bank 1990). Specialised bank branches had not yet implemented standardised reporting methods and or a unified system for the verification of financial reporting. There was a divergence in audit frequency across branches.

China's accounting firms found it difficult to provide the state with meaningful and accurate information regarding bank performance and the level of NPLs. The MOF did not permit international firms to operate in China and Chinese accountancy firms typically had their origins in the state finance bureaus. The lack of political independence of Chinese accounting firms caused them to serve merely as a 'rubber stamp' for the state (Interview with PWC Partner David Wu, 3 April 2015). An awareness of international accounting practices had been built up over the 1980s, with the MOF having translated annual volumes of International Accounting Standards and International Financial Reporting Standards. However China's own accounting standards were also lenient. They did not yet comply with the 'generally accepted accounting principles' (GAAP) and fundamental practices such as the write-down asset losses and bad debts, making loan loss provisions or valuation of assets at 'lower of cost or market' had not been established (World Bank 1990). Accounting firms also remained more concerned about verifying if capital was spent according to the plan than with enterprise performance (Interview with former PWC China accountant Paul Gillis, 30 March 2015).

The National Audit Office (NAO) was established in 1983. Staff numbers increased from 28,600 in 1985 to 63,000 in 1989 as a nationwide branch network was established (Yang 2004, 280). In the 1980s its mission, to undertake audits of SOEs and provided a check on other levels of audit, was compromised by its low administrative ranking relative to the departments it audited.

## Human capital

The development of the necessary human capital to implement new institutions of governance was also a priority within the banking sector. For obvious reasons, the generation of China's officials that were in office at the beginning of Reform and Opening were simply not familiar with the operational concepts of a more active and commercial banking system. In 1989, Premier Li Peng contrasted workers in China's banking system with their counterparts from the 1950s, commenting that while the complexity of banking operations had increased, the level of skills and training of workers had regressed. The urgency of the problem was such that he even suggested an extension of the retirement age to allow bankers from the Republican era to remain at their posts (Du, Hua 杜华 2007).

Many of the entry-level staff came from occupational schools that were operated and staffed by the specialised banks. Students enrolled in these schools for what was normally the last 3 years of middle school. The Shanghai Municipal NanHu Bank Vocational School, which commenced operations in 1982, was associated with ICBC. Its teachers were allocated from ICBC's *jinrongzhigongdaxue* 金融职工大学. While the school taught specialist banking classes, its graduates typically began work at the counter. There were a fixed number of students that entered the school each year. Each of these students was promised a job with ICBC upon graduation (Interview with Chen Chengyou, former President of Nanhu Bank Occupational School, 25 April 2015).

The World Bank deemed training in the banking sector to be sufficiently comprehensive as to 'meet the needs of current banking practices'. The ICBC operated a total of 100 educational institutions at the end of the 1980s (World Bank 1990, 79). In addition to occupational schools, specialised banks also had an affiliation with training institutes. Mrs Chen Chengyou, President of Nanhu Bank Occupational School from 1982 to 2000, estimated that over 90 per cent of her students enrolled in tertiary education while working in the banking sector as a recognised qualification was a prerequisite for further career development (Interview with Chen Chengyou, 25 April 2015). The sector itself was constantly evolving and adopting new concepts and practices of modern banking.

The system of guaranteed employment at specialised banks began to be dismantled during the second half of the 1980s in line with practices already employed at shareholding banks. Specialised banks introduced trials of recruitment systems of cadres that were more competitive in nature as well as fixed-term appointments and employee contracts. There were early attempts to develop performance incentives.

## Increasing burden on banks

During this initial period of regulatory development, the banking sector found itself taking an increasing share of the burden of SOE transition. The shift to loan-based funding was accelerated by decentralising fiscal reforms that pushed the central government to use the banking system to finance important national infrastructure projects. The share of bank financing in fixed investment projects rose from 12.7 per cent in 1981 to 20.3 per cent in 1988, while budgetary financing fell from 28.1 per cent to 9 per cent over the same period (World Bank 1990, 32). This had a direct effect on the profitability of SOEs. Fiscal subsidies decreased from RMB 50.7 billion in 1985 to RMB 33.7 billion in 1996 in a growing economy as SOEs were forced to rely more on bank loans (Lardy 1998, 37). Price reform throughout the decade both increased input costs for state firms and removed a barrier from competition. Over this period the number of loss-making SOEs continued to expand with one third of medium or large-scale firms reporting a loss by 1995 (Lardy 1998, 39). The challenges faced by SOEs affected profitability and consequently the ability of SOEs to repay loans. This decline in profitability caused almost a corresponding increase in NPLs and a decline in the financial health of China's banks. In 1987 Dai Xianglong, who was Vice President of ABC at that time, estimated that bad loans made by ABC totalled over RMB 40 billion with approximately 15 per cent of its business customers having financial and management issues that made them unsuitable customers (O'Neill 1987b). The total number of bad loans was estimated by a PBoC official to be RMB 57 billion (O'Neill 1988). Bank capital declined from 9.8 per cent of assets in 1985 to 7.75 per cent in 1989 (World Bank 1990, 65).

## Conclusion

The evolution of China's banking system under Reform and Opening should not be viewed simply as institutional convergence with the banking systems of Western developed nations. While there were elements of convergence in the initial establishment and development of China's regulatory framework, there is strong evidence of a persistence of historical patterns of political and economic organisation. The purpose of the Reform of Opening policy, to modernise China's economy, stemmed from a desire to restore pride in Chinese civilisation after the humiliation of military defeat and the subsequent loss of economic sovereignty that had undermined China's efforts to build a modern banking system. As a consequence, officials regarded the sovereignty over the financial system as imperative. While China opened its doors to attract foreign capital, technology and ideas, it placed strict limitations on the operations of foreign banks and did not permit international auditing firms to operate in China. The fundamental role of the party system in the appointment, monitoring and discipline of officials in the banking sector reflects a pattern of strong bureaucratic control seen in the development of China's indigenous banking system, the modern banking system of the Republican era and the administrative banks of the planned economy. The state actively managed the gradual transition of China's banking sector from the planned economy. The state developed a pluralised banking sector and released some control of the financial system to promote the development of an enterprise organisational model. Specialised banks, carved out from the financial sector of the planned economy, retained a dominant position in the sector with around 75 per cent of assets at the end of the 1980s (World Bank 1990, 6). As in the past, stability was a central concern for China's officials. While credit was still allocated predominantly through the planning system, the state developed institutions to provide monitoring and governance functions in order to control market risk and promote the development of commercial behaviour in Chinese banks. Officials incorporated ideas from the modern banking systems of developed countries. Early systems of financial regulation and audit were established in a pragmatic and exploratory fashion that reflected both a desire for stability and a deliberate departure from the ideological excesses of the Maoist period. Prior to the establishment of the socialist market economy, China's regulatory framework was at an early stage of development. As a consequence, officials struggled to ensure that regulation was effective. There were many challenges including the lack of bureaucratic power of the PBoC, the decentralised nature of banks and regulatory institutions, the focus on meeting objectives of the plan, the lack of a comprehensive banking law, the inability of auditors to provide high-quality information regarding bank performance to the state, and a general lack of understanding of concepts of risk management and market regulation. The lack of financial order that resulted created a resolve within senior party officials such as Premier Li Peng to improve systems of regulation to better contain market risk.

# References

*BBC Monitoring Service: Asia-Pacific*. 1987. 'Foreign Banks and Bond Issues'. 7 October 1987. http://global.factiva.com/redir/default.aspx?P=sa&an=bbcfe00020011204dja700 67a&cat=a&ep=ASE.

CCP. 2011. 'Full Text of Jiang Zemin's Report at 14th Party Congress'. *Beijing Review*, 29 March 2011. www.bjreview.com.cn/document/txt/2011-03/29/content_36 3504.htm.

Cheng, Linsun. 2003. *Banking in Modern China: Entrepreneurs, Professional Managers, and the Development of Chinese Banks, 1897–1937*. Cambridge, UK: Cambridge University Press.

Chiang, Kai-shek. 1947. *China's Destiny and Chinese Economic Theory*. London: Dennis Dobson.

Donnithorne, Audrey. 1967. *China's Economic System*. London: Allen & Unwin.

Du, Hua 杜华, ed. 2007. '*Jinrong Gongzuo Wenxian Xuanbian (1978–2005)*' 金融工作文献选编 （一九七八——二00五）. Beijing: Zhongguo Jinrong Chubanshe.

Eastman, Lloyd E. 1988. *Family, Field and Ancestors: Constancy and Change in China's Social and Economic History, 1550–1949*. New York: Oxford University Press.

Gargan, Edward. 1988. 'Wenzhou Journal; 3 Chinese Bankers Full of Nonrevolutionary Zeal'. *New York Times*, 5 August 1988. http://global.factiva.com/redir/default.aspx?P=sa&an=NYTF000020050427dk85006hx&cat=a&ep=ASE.

Gurley, John G. 1976. *China's Economy and the Maoist Strategy*. London: Monthly Review Press.

Hewitt, Mike. 2007. 'Hyperinflation in China, 1937–1949'. *The Market Oracle*, 22 May 2007. www.marketoracle.co.uk/Article1068.html.

Hodgson, Geoffrey M. 2001. *How Economics Forgot History: The Problem of Historical Specificity in Social Science*. London: Routledge.

Holz, Carsten. 1992. *The Role of Central Banking in China's Economic Reforms*. Ithica, NY: East Asia Program, Cornell University.

Hu, Jichuang. 1988. *A Concise History of Chinese Economic Thought*. Beijing: Foreign Languages Press.

Kuhn, Robert Lawrence. 2010. *How China's Leaders Think: The Inside Story of China's Reform and What This Means for the Future*. Singapore: Wiley.

Kynaston, David and Richard Roberts. 2015. *The Lion Wakes: A Modern History of HSBC*. London: Profile Books.

Lardy, Nicholas R. 1998. *China's Unfinished Economic Revolution*. Washington, DC: Brookings Institution.

Levenson, Joseph Richmond. 1964. *Confucian China and Its Modern Fate*. Vol. 1. Berkeley and Los Angeles, CA: University of California Press.

Liu, Mingkang 刘明康, ed. 2009. '*Zhongguo Yinhang Gaige Kaifang Sanshinian (1978–2008) Shangce*' 中国银行业改革开放30年 (1978–2008) 上册. Beijing: Beijing Jinrong Chubanshe.

Mann Jones, Susan. 1972. 'Finance in Ningpo: The "Ch'ien Chuang", 1750–1850'. In *Economic Organization in Chinese Society*, edited by W. E. Willmott. Stanford, CA: Stanford University Press.

Nolan, Peter. 2004. *China at the Crossroads*. Cambridge, UK: Polity Press.

O'Neill, Mark. 1987a. 'China's Central Bank Struggles to Play Proper Role'. *Reuters News*, 18 December 1987. http://global.factiva.com/redir/default.aspx?P=sa&an=lba00 00020011205djci006j1&cat=a&ep=ASE.

O'Neill, Mark. 1987b. 'China Banks Threatened By Rising Tide of Bad Debts'. *Reuters News*, 31 December 1987. http://global.factiva.com/redir/default.aspx?P=sa&an=lba00 00020011205djcv008pn&cat=a&ep=ASE.

O'Neill, Mark. 1988. 'China's Banks Face Ideological Minefield'. *Reuters News*, 17 May 1988. http://global.factiva.com/redir/default.aspx?P=sa&an=lba0000020011203dk5h01 m64&cat=a&ep=ASE.

Pei, Minxin. 1998. 'The Political Economy of Banking Reforms in China, 1993–1997'. *Journal of Contemporary China* 7 (18): 321–50. https://doi.org/10.1080/1067056980 8724318.

Peng, Yuanyuan. 2007. *The Chinese Banking Industry: Lessons from History for Today's Challenges*. London: Routledge.

Rawski, Thomas G. 1989. *Economic Growth in Prewar China*. Berkeley and Los Angeles, CA: University of California Press.

*Reuters News*. 1988. 'China Banks Losing Business to Dubious Competitors'. 10 August 1988. http://global.factiva.com/redir/default.aspx?P=sa&an=lba0000020011203dk8a02 h50&cat=a&ep=ASE.

Vogel, Ezra F. 2013. *Deng Xiaoping and the Transformation of China*. Reprint edition. Cambridge, MA: Belknap Press.

Walter, Carl and Fraser Howie. 2012. *Red Capitalism: The Fragile Financial Foundation of China's Extraordinary Rise*. Revised edition. Singapore: Wiley.

World Bank. 1990. 'China: Financial Sector Policies and Institutional Development'. A World Bank Country Study PUB-8415. Washington, D.C.: World Bank.

Xu, Dixin and Chengming Wu, eds. 2000. *Chinese Capitalism, 1522–1840*. Translated by C.A. Curwen. 2000 edition. Basingstoke, UK: Palgrave Macmillan.

Yan, Xun. 2015. 'In Search of Power and Credibility: Essays on Chinese Monetary History (1851–1945)'. PhD thesis, London: The London School of Economics and Political Science (LSE).

Yang, Dali. 2004. *Remaking the Chinese Leviathan-Market Transition and the Politics of Governance in China*. Stanford, CA: Stanford University Press.

# 3 Building a banking regulatory system for the socialist market economy (1990–96)

At the establishment of the socialist market economy, China's policymakers implemented reforms that created a platform for the development of a more standardised and rigorous system of banking regulation that was aimed at ensuring financial stability and mitigating market risk. While China incorporated Western ideas and technology subsequent to the establishment of the socialist market economy, it did so selectively. China chose not to implement policies of financial liberalisation and deregulation, which were now becoming established regulatory policy in Western developed countries such as the United States and had strongly influenced policies in other developing countries. Walter and Howie's statement that 'in the 1990s, China's domestic reforms followed a path of deregulation blazed by the United States' fundamentally mischaracterises the reform process (Walter and Howie 2012, 3). This chapter demonstrates that banking reforms were path dependent and subject to an evolutionary process of development. General Secretary Jiang Zemin maintained Deng's pragmatic approach to reform, saying (with regards to the socialist market economy): 'the criterion for judging the success or failure … is whether it helps develop the productive forces of socialist society, strengthen the overall capacity of the country and improve the people's living standards' (CCP 2011). The decision to establish a socialist market economy, announced at the 3rd Plenum of the 14th Party Congress in November 1993, reflected the success of early market reforms in facilitating modernisation of the economy. By 1995, China's gross national product was more than four times higher than in 1980 and the country's already substantial investment in infrastructure continued to grow. Living standards had improved markedly and the population of the poor had decreased by 20 million since the end of the 1980s (State Council 2006). Regulatory reforms in the banking sector were a direct response to the inability of the state to maintain macroeconomic stability and mitigate market risk during periods of rapid economic development. The *Commercial Bank Law* and *Central Bank Law* became guiding documents for exploratory reforms in the banking sector. Reforms to strengthen the governance of state-owned banks reflected their growing importance in determining capital allocation as SOEs became increasingly autonomous. Jiang Zemin affirmed the country's desire to maintain economic sovereignty and build a stronger country: 'Modern Chinese history and the realities of the present-day world show that so long as a country is economically backward, it will be in a passive position, subject to manipulation by others' (CCP 2011).

## Inability to ensure economic stability

As China's economy grew in the late 1980s, it became evident that the state did not possess the tools to provide stability to the economy at the macro-level. The central bank, which lacked both unified governance and political strength, was not sufficiently strong to effectuate macro-economic control of the economy, particularly given the high degree of influence of local government over credit allocation. According to Holz, 'the lack of an endogenous mechanism restraining the volume of credit and cash in circulation turned out to be a major factor in the cycle of monetary over-investment characteristic of the PBC' (Holz 1992, 149). There was excess demand for credit, which was hotly contested by local authorities within the planning system and also through the rapidly expanding interbank market which more than quadrupled in size between 1991 and 1993 (Pei 1998, 331). A CBRC official, at the time an employee of ABC, estimated that approximately 60–70 per cent of decision-making by PBoC and bank local branches in 1993 reflected local government wishes, with the remaining 30–40 per cent reflecting the wishes of their respective head offices (Interview with CBRC official, 10 March 2015). The President of the People's Construction Bank, Zhou Daojiang, revealed the lack of control over credit, saying 'when local governments and enterprises have money, they invest as they like, and you can hardly do anything about them' (Thomson 1987). The pattern of over-investment, predominantly in fixed assets, caused China to suffer from a shortage of capital. Total investment in fixed assets between 1991 and 1995 grew at an annual rate of 22.9 per cent, far in excess of the 4.1 per cent growth rate recorded in the previous period (State Council 2006). The state budget fell into deficit and cash in circulation ballooned as the state resorted to printing money to fund projects. PBoC Deputy Secretary General Ren Junyin revealed the gravity of the situation, saying that 'the money in our country each year is not enough to cover our priority projects. Because capital is short, everyone comes to the banks … [for funding]' (O'Neill 1987).

The deficiencies in macroeconomic control led to cycles of inflation that in turn had a serious impact on economic stability. These were exacerbated by the constant increase in wages and salaries along with reform of the dual track price system, which had begun in some commodities. During the first cycle of inflation, inflation rates reached just under 20 per cent in 1988 and rumours of further price increases caused 'panic buying' of all types of consumer goods and a rapid depletion of bank savings (World Bank 1990; Holz 1992, 129). Retail sales across the country in the first half of 1988 were 25 per cent higher than in the corresponding period of the previous year (*Reuters News* 1988b). In Harbin the problem was particularly serious. Between 25 July and 27 July, RMB 12.5 million was withdrawn from banks, constituting the worst bank-run in new

China's history. Sales at the city's biggest department store were 200 times above average in July 1988. By 28 July there were no televisions, tape recorders, refrigerators, washing machines, rice cookers and carpets left in the city (*Reuters News* 1988a). During the second cycle of inflation, deepening reform of the price system compounded issues of monetary expansion. In 1992, the price of grain rose around 50 per cent in most provinces as a large pilot programme for free grain markets began. According to an article in *China News Digest* (27 December 1993), the continuation of such price rises in the following year precipitated social unrest and rioting in rural areas as farmers vented their frustration, prompting Jiang Zemin to express the need to 'take forceful measures to maintain social and political stability' (as cited in Blecher 2009, 82).

The government was unable to direct credit to the parts of the economy that needed it most. Problems in rural areas were exacerbated by the inability of specialised banks, particularly ABC, to provide the necessary funds for state purchase of agricultural goods. Specialised banks simply did not have enough reserves at the time of harvest and the PBoC was reluctant to expand the money supply any further to assist. According to a PBoC official interviewed by the *Farmers Daily* newspaper, the PBoC was only prepared to loan ABC a total of RMB 1.5 billion in 1989 despite RMB 26 billion being needed to meet payments in full, causing half the farmers selling grain and oilseeds to be paid in IOU notes (*Reuters News* 1989). Premier Li Peng himself pointed out the contradictory nature of an economy in which fixed asset investment and consumption rates continued to rise but farmers could not receive the economic support promised by the state (Du, Hua 杜华 2007, 93). Instead of supporting farmers, the banking sector was directing capital to speculative areas of the economy such as coastal real estate and the stock market. Deng Xiaoping's message of continued economic reform during the Southern tour bolstered the spirits of such investors. The number of real estate developers rose from 3,000 at the beginning of 1992 to 20,000 just 18 months later, with the investment bubble particularly severe in parts of Hainan, Guangdong and Guangxi. Incredibly, the GDP of Hainan grew by a whopping 41.5 per cent in 1992 (Zarathustra 2011). Such speculation was alarming for the state, whose investigations determined that speculative investments totalled more than RMB 100 billion, diverted primarily from the interbank market at high interest rates (Pei 1998, 337). A CBRC official stated that speculation in real estate was a major contributing factor behind the failure of Hainan Development Bank which was liquidated in 1998 after the housing market cooled down (Interview with CBRC official, 11 March 2015).

## Implementation of 'control and rectification' policy

In the face of this lack of macroeconomic control, the state attempted to bring stability by tightening the reins on the planning system. Indeed in the years prior to the 1993 reforms, China actually strengthened the planned economy model of allocating credit. The state broadened the credit plan in 1989 so as to include NBFIs and slow the growing leakage of funds from the planning system.

Investment funds were funnelled to trust companies, which were less restricted in their investment activities. While outside the plan, trust companies had also been able to take advantage of arbitrage opportunities available due to the dual pricing system and the restrictions on interest rates in the traditional banking sector.

At the same time, the state implemented a dramatic programme of austerity through a tight control of credit and government investment within the parameters of the plan. The PBoC also raised both its lending rate to banks and the required reserve ratio. There was a stricter administration of the credit plan with priority given to essential goods and projects. Regulations banned loans that were outside the plan or related to non-manufacturing construction projects or speculative activities, as well as loans made to companies that were unprofitable or held large inventories (*Financial Times* 1989). The austerity policy was particularly devastating for small private and collective enterprises, many of whom were forced into bankruptcy as a result (*Xinhua News Agency* 1989). The policy was known as *zhilizhengdun* or 'control and rectification', with its principal goal being the stabilisation of prices, a strong agricultural harvest and a reduction in the imbalance between supply and demand (Du, Hua 杜华 2007, 92).

The state's decision to tighten control over the banking sector using tools of the planned economy was not an indication that the state wished to revert back to a planned system. On the contrary, the decision to slow down the economy was made in order to bring about the necessary economic conditions for further reform to take place. Premier Li Peng explained that 'the motive for the current 'control and rectification' measures remained the improved implementation of Reform and Opening policies' (Du, Hua 杜华 2007, 92). Stability was an overriding principle that superseded any push for market reform. The 'control and rectification' policy achieved a certain degree of success. Speaking to PBoC officials, Vice Premier Yao Yilin praised their 'great achievements' in achieving price stabilisation (Du, Hua 杜华 2007, 97). Indeed by 1990, inflation levels had dropped to only 3 per cent (World Bank 1990, 37).

However ultimately economic stability could not be delivered within China's transitional economy merely by using the old tools of the plan, and would instead require the development of a new set of tools to regulate the economic activity of enterprises and financial institutions that were becoming progressively more autonomous. Stricter control of the plan naturally impacted more on SOEs who relied directly on the plan for funding than on other enterprises, even though this was not the intention of the policy. In the first quarter of 1989, while SOE production fell substantially, there was a large increase in production from town and village enterprises and collective enterprises. Similarly, levels of consumption and infrastructure construction continued to rise (Du, Hua 杜华 2007). The adverse, unintended effects of tightening left the state no choice but to provide emergency funds for SOEs (*Xinhua News Agency* 1989). Measures under 'control and rectification' could only control provision of capital within the plan and in particular capital for centrally controlled projects. At local levels, local governments held the last say on the allocation of capital. The state's success in achieving greater control over credit and prices was short-lived. Following Deng's Southern tour, investment euphoria returned and inflation levels rose even further than before, reaching almost 25 per cent (World Bank 2016).

The 'control and rectification' policy also had other unintended effects on the economy. Within the environment of tight credit, a phenomenon of debt chains between enterprises known as 'triangular debt' appeared. It is estimated that between 1991 and 1992 triangular debt amounted to as much as one third of total bank loans (Guan 2013). While the high levels of debt created a liquidity issue among enterprises, the PBoC's attempts to resolve the issue through capital injections were unsuccessful. This is because both parties to the debt were often unwilling to see the debt paid. Debtors wished to delay payment to remain afloat, while creditors were also unwilling to receive payment if it would have to be used to repay bank loans. Both parties preferred to wait for government support to solve their financial issues. This issue required a complex solution that was achieved by the PBoC at the end of 1992 through clearing the debts of large-scale, fixed asset investment projects which were situated at the start of the debt chain (Liu, Mingkang 刘明康 2009).

## Lack of financial order

The lack of economic stability was both created and compounded by a lack of order in the financial sector that reflected the lack of a robust system of regulation. This problem became known in the industry as the 'the three disorders' – disordered financing, disordered establishment and approval of financial organisations and disordered financial operations (Liu, Mingkang 刘明康 2009, 39). Disordered financing referred to the use of the interbank market by banks to bypass the credit plan, as well as the leakage of funds from specialised banks to their trust companies at each level, along with the consequent allocation of funds within the trust sector, all of which were highly unregulated despite attempts to bring them under the plan. Entry of financial institutions was not regulated effectively and many state organs and enterprises, as well as private firms, had established illegal financial institutions. The fractured governance structure of the PBoC did not allow it to implement a consistent policy on entry of financial institutions. A survey of the establishment of 648 TICs, conducted between 1995 and 1996, found that 249 were granted approval by PBoC branches that did not have the requisite authority (Pei 1998, 330). The final issue, the disorder of financial operations, referred to the trend of rising NPLs and reduced capital adequacy within banks. Policies to develop economic incentives through the decentralisation of banks had inhibited the development of strong governance mechanisms that could prevent violations of financial rules and processes and instances of corrupt practices (Liu, Mingkang 刘明康 2009). The fractured governance structure of banks also limited the ability of policymakers to drive improvements in credit risk management. Implementation of a consistent asset and liability management policy, for example, would require the development of unified financial enterprises with a singular governance structure. A further cause of operational disorder was imperfections in bank supervision. The problem of triangular debt, for instance, had been due in large part to a lack of robust bank supervision and audit procedures that allowed enterprises to open settlement accounts and receive loans from multiple banks.

## Reform measures

The establishment of the socialist market economy in 1993 represented an evolutionary step in (and not a departure from) China's historical patterns of political and economic organisation. China's leaders envisioned the development of a market system that would reflect the historical priority for economic and financial stability. Party institutions of governance would adapt to this market system and officials would remain deeply embedded within the banking sector. Deng Xiaoping emphasised that the end goal of reform, the revitalisation of China's economy, was more important than the means used to achieve it:

> Capitalism and socialism have no direct bearing on the planned economy and the market economy … Planned economy and market economy are both economic measures. Socialism's real nature is to liberate productive forces, and the ultimate goal of socialism is to achieve common prosperity …
>
> (Ash 1992, 456)

Deng re-emphasised the importance of continuing Reform and Opening policies for the purpose of economic modernisation:

> If we do not uphold socialism, do not carry out reform and opening, do not develop the economy, and do not try to improve the people's livelihood, then there will only be the road to ruin. This basic line should be valid for 100 years and must not be shaken …
>
> (Ash 1992, 456)

The decision to establish an improved system of market regulation had been foreshadowed by the increasing acknowledgement of the state of the role of regulation alongside planning processes at the 3rd Plenums of 1984 and 1988.

China's policymakers did not have a fixed view on how to develop a market system and reform measures in the banking sector were a pragmatic response to the problems facing China's banking sector. In early 1993, the basic principles of reform were developed through consensus at a meeting of China's leading finance professionals and academics. These experts agreed that a stronger, more independent central bank was needed to effectuate effective macro-economic control and develop a more standardised and rigorous system of financial regulation. It was hoped that these measures would 'ensure a stable financial order and the healthy development of financial operations' (Liu, Mingkang 刘明康 2009, 40). These experts concluded that, despite remarkable progress in the banking sector, Deng's vision to make banks 'real banks' or autonomous entities capable of efficient allocation of capital had not yet been realised. To achieve this, it was recommended that the governance of China's state-owned banks be unified and strengthened so that banks could act as autonomous, commercial financial enterprises capable of managing market risk. The unification and empowerment of the PBoC and state-owned banks would provide a platform for the development of institutions to provide monitoring and governance functions necessary in the socialist market economy (Liu, Mingkang 刘明康 2009). It would also counter the excessive influence of local government on bank branches that had been partly to blame for economic overheating and the consequent macroeconomic instability.

At the National Financial Work Meeting, Zhu revealed the blueprint for the transformation of specialised banks to state-owned commercial banks (SOCBs). This commercialisation process was necessary to empower banks to bear the responsibility of allocating capital efficiently and managing market risk as SOEs gradually became more independent from central industrial ministries and the planning system as a result of economic reforms announced at the 3rd Plenum of the 14th Party Congress. According to these reforms, SOEs would develop horizontal linkages between firms or plants to build large enterprise groups and then be subjected to a process of corporatisation by means of shareholding reforms and listings to develop modern enterprises. In 1991, 55 large business groups were selected to take part in the first group of trials (Sutherland 2001). Corporatisation of firms signalled a transition from the profit sharing arrangements with the state through the CRS in favour of more autonomous governance. SOCBs had the responsibility of providing capital to SOEs during this transition. To facilitate the commercialisation of SOCBs, the central bank established policy banks to reduce the policy burden. SOCBs would now operate autonomously and bear the responsibility for profits and losses as well the burden of market risk. These reforms effectively released banks from the constraints of their specialised industries. One CBRC official, who began his career at ABC in 1993, noted the focus of the bank at that time on entering the cities (Interview with CBRC official, 10 March 2015). To mitigate market risk, SOCBs would institute systems of asset and liability management. It was also decided that banks would abide by the 1988 Basel Capital Accords with respect to policies of risk-weighting assets and loan assessment to address the issue of credit risk.

On Christmas Day 1993, the State Council issued 'The Decision Regarding Reform of the Financial System'. The state pursued two main strategies in order to strengthen the central bank and the newly autonomous SOCBs. The first strategy was to establish laws and regulation that would legitimise their enhanced role within the banking system by clearly and transparently defining their roles and responsibilities. *The Law of the PRC on the PBoC*, passed in March 1995, empowered the central bank as regulator of the financial sector. With regards to banking supervision, it gave the central bank the authority to establish and implement regulation, determine the entry, exit and operational scope of financial organisations, and supervise, inspect and audit financial organisations (*Law of the People's Republic of China on the People's Bank of*

*China* n.d.). *The PRC Commercial Bank Law*, also passed in 1995, defined the rules for establishment or termination of commercial banks, as well as their organisational form and management structure (along with *the PRC Company Law*) and the scope of business operations. The *Commercial Bank Law* asserted the autonomy of SOCBs, who would 'make their own decisions regarding their business operations, take responsibility for their own risks, [and] assume sole responsibility for their profits and losses…' and 'conduct business operations without interference from any unit or individual'. The *Commercial Bank Law* also guaranteed protection of the law in recovering the principal and interest of loans when due. The law had a clear emphasis on the development of systems of risk management and its first clause identified the goal of improving asset quality as a key objective (*'Law of the People's Republic of China on Commercial Banks'* n.d.). Despite their increased autonomy, SOCBs would continue to support reform goals of economic modernisation, infrastructure development, the transformation of SOEs and improvements in social welfare. According to the law, banks would 'conduct their business of lending in accordance with the needs of the national economic and social development and under the guidance of the industrial policies of the State' (*'Law of the People's Republic of China on Commercial Banks'* n.d.). In order to minimise the risks of financial contagion, the *Commercial Bank Law* formally segregated the banking sector from other financial sectors. As a consequence, commercial banks would no longer be permitted to engage in security, insurance and trust activities. The second strategy was to unify these institutions to strengthen governance. PBoC business operations were placed under centralised management and branches became agents of head office rather than stand-alone branches. Decentralising, CRS-inspired profit retaining and tax payment systems employed at PBoC branches were abolished. China's SOCBs were gradually transformed into unified financial enterprises. The organisational concept of a one-tier legal person commercial bank, predicated on the ultimate control of capital management at head office level, was developed and strengthened. SOCBs developed systems of centralised capital management and restructured important operating functions such as accounting under a vertical organisational structure. This unification, which was implemented in large part between 1994 and 1995, made it possible to drive systemic improvements through the SOCBs.

These banking reforms created greater opportunities for China to selectively adopt Western ideas and technology to suit China's reform programme. Since Reform and Opening, China had been very open to learning from other countries. According to a former PBoC official, committees had been established within the financial sector and beyond to facilitate relationships with foreign experts including academics and banking professionals (Interview with current Ministry of Commerce official, 29 March 2015). China's officials had established regular dialogue with financial experts and executives from Wall Street in order to gain knowledge about how the financial systems of developed countries were operated and regulated (see for example *Toronto Star* 1986). Senior executives from international banks such as Goldman Sachs and Bank of America had consulted with the state on the management of risk by financial institutions. With the establishment of the socialist market economy, China paid greater importance to international standards of financial regulation, as evidenced by its adoption of the 1988 Basel Accord. The state was able to refer to examples of international best practices to understand how best to regulate the banking system.

Officials chose to adapt Western ideas to develop a system of close regulation and supervision of China's banks. This was in sharp contrast with the process of deregulation and liberalisation that was occurring in the West at this time. According to Johnson and Kwak, it was in this decade that 'Wall Street translated its growing economic power into political power and when the ideology of financial innovation and deregulation became conventional wisdom in Washington on both sides of the political aisle' (Johnson and Kwak 2010, 89). Johnson and Kwak further argue that 'the 1990s witnessed the final dismantling of the regulatory system constructed in the 1930s' in the United States as 'leading policymakers from Alan Greenspan on down chose to rely on "self-regulation" of financial markets' (Johnson and Kwak 2010, 89). Ideas from the West strongly influenced the financial policy of developing countries and China's officials were extremely nervous about the increased risk to global stability created by the deregulation of financial systems. Jiang Zemin's explicit reference to the crises which occurred in Mexico (1994), Russia (1998), Turkey (2000) and Argentina (2001) in his speech at the National Financial Work Meeting in 2002 demonstrates that officials paid close attention to the growing dangers of the global financial system, even beyond the Asian region (Du, Hua 杜华 2007). China's officials selectively adopted Western ideas that would enhance the stability of China's banking system. The new systems of asset and liability management employed by China's banks utilised a number of simple ratios to ensure that the timing, quantity and structure of assets and liabilities corresponded in order to improve asset safety and liquidity (Liu, Mingkang 刘明康 2009). CBRC Head Liu Mingkang would later comment that regulators were reliant on 'a set of simple, useful and effective ratios, limits and targets, modeling those used by some developed markets in the past and were later abandoned by themselves during the frenzy [of] innovation and deregulation' (Liu 2010). Jiang Zemin affirmed that while 'there are a great deal of areas that are undoubtedly worth studying', it remained that 'drawing lessons from foreign experience must start from the actual situation in our country' (Du, Hua 杜华 2007, 150, 151).

Policymakers also sought to adapt Western technology to China's banking system. One senior banker, employed by what is known today as the Bank of Beijing, recalls that offices made the transition from written work to computer systems in 1994–95 (Interview with Yao Libao, Head of Personal Loan Service Centre, Guangdong Development Bank, 9 October 2014). The construction of the electronic interbank system was achieved in 1995 with technical assistance from the World Bank and covered 250 large or medium-sized cities ('Almanac of China's Finance and Banking 1996' 1996). Prior to its launch, Jiang Zemin spoke vividly about the impact of financial satellite communication networks on

Western banking systems, and how it would enable the use of ATMs and credit cards. Jiang also emphasised its impact on financial stability, such as how it would enhance the supervisory power of the PBoC and reduce corruption (Du, Hua 杜华 2007). Western technology would become progressively more integrated within China's financial system. ATM networks in China would ultimately become highly reliant on Intel processors and Microsoft software, while the computer systems of China's tier 1 state-owned banks would depend on technology belonging to IBM and HP (Nolan 2013).

## Bureaucratic control and market regulation

Market regulation required the full support of the officials in China's bureaucratic system in order to become effective. Newly established regulatory agencies such as the central bank did not have the political power that resided within planning ministries and local governments. As a consequence early systems of market regulation had lacked legitimacy. While Premiers Zhao Ziyang and Li Peng supported the development of market regulation, neither Chen Muhua nor Li Guixian (Governors of the PBoC from 1985–88 and 1988–93) had been members of the Politburo, let alone the Standing Committee. The new importance vested in the banking regulatory system caused China's leaders to appoint Vice Premier Zhu Rongji as Head of the central bank in July 1993. According to Zhu, the 'chief problem' was the lack of commitment by officials to the institutions that governed the banking sector. Officials 'were not handling affairs strictly according to the directives of the Central Committee and State Council or the banking regulatory framework' (Du, Hua 杜华 2007, 179). Zhu emphasised that establishing financial order required Party officials at all levels to take on board policies of the banking sector, to 'stick to the Party's path at all times and not waver' (Du, Hua 杜华 2007, 183). Zhu put his political weight fully behind new regulations, promising that banks must take them seriously or risk investigation. Zhu had a brash style and officials feared him, not only because of the potential consequences for their political careers, but also because he was not afraid to publicly humiliate those with whom he was unsatisfied.

Along with Zhu Rongji, many of the officials posted to the PBoC would have an important influence over the development of the banking sector in the years ahead. These were career bureaucrats who were rotated between bureaucratic posts at the central bank, CBRC, commercial banks and to political positions beyond the sector according to the needs of the party leadership. These officials had a strong understanding of their responsibilities as leaders in the banking sector. Most officials had been sent down to the countryside during the Cultural Revolution and experienced the consequences of political and economy instability first hand. Each felt a heavy weight of responsibility to ensure the stable development of the banking sector and contribute to the revitalisation of Chinese civilisation. Zhu's Vice Governors at the PBoC were Wang Qishan, Dai Xianglong, Zhou Xiaochuan and Chen Yuan. Wang Qishan, who worked at the

*Shaanxi* museum prior to studying history at Northwest University in Xi'an, would later become a key figure in mitigating the effects of the 1997 AFC and now presides over Xi Jinping's anti-corruption campaign. Dai Xianglong became Head of the central bank after Zhu Rongji's departure in 1995, though Zhu maintained a strong interest in the sector as Vice Premier. Current PBoC Head Zhou Xiaochuan was appointed Head of the central bank in 2002. Chen Yuan was Chairman of the China Development Bank between 1998 and 2013. These officials, subject to the leadership of the party centre, had a strong influence over the direction of reform. China's officials did not have a sophisticated understanding of modern banking systems but were open to learning from the West while avoiding the dangers of a deregulated financial system. They gradually became more familiar with concepts of market regulation as reform progressed. Zhu Rongji and Chen Yuan had received their education in economics, while Dai Xianglong was trained in financial accounting. Neither of Zhu's predecessors as Premier (Zhao Ziyang and Li Peng) or as Head of the PBoC (Chen Muhua and Li Guixian) had any formal training in economics.

The immediate focus for officials was to bring order to the financial sector. Financial order was a key policy objective for senior party leaders in the Central Committee and Zhu Rongji had been advised that 'if we do not resolve to turn around the current financial chaos, and repress inflation, it could lead to large fluctuations in the economy and we could lose an excellent opportunity to develop' (Du, Hua 杜华 2007, 179–80). It was significant that at his closing speech at the National Financial Work Meeting in July 1993, Zhu's announcement of three new provisional regulations designed to return order to the banking sector preceded any discussion of market-based reforms. The regulations attempted to address the lack of order by putting a stop to illegal short-term loans, preventing deposit wars and prohibiting banks from funnelling money out of the planning system. PBoC lending was centralised and interbank markets were suspended below the level of head office (Du, Hua 杜华 2007). Zhu's measures to increase control on credit ultimately reduced inflation levels from a peak of 24 per cent in 1994 to 8 per cent in 1996 while economic growth rates remained relatively stable (World Bank 2016). According to the Almanac of China's Finance and Banking, restoring price stability was a top priority of party leaders ('Almanac of China's Finance and Banking 1996' 1996). Zhu's ability to restore financial order and control inflation likely contributed to his eventual promotion to the position of Premier in 1998.

## 'Groping for stones' – subsequent institutional development in the banking sector

The *Commercial Bank Law* and the *PBoC Law* became guiding documents for the pursuit of a highly exploratory process of regulatory development whose ultimate goal was the stable development of the banking sector.

The unification and empowerment of the central bank allowed it to actively develop systems of internal control. The resources invested in audit of financial institutions increased considerably between 1993 and 1997. In 1997 the PBoC invested over 1,000,000 working days in the audit of 28,310 financial organisations (Liu, Mingkang 刘明康 2009, 64). Over this time audits became more varied and specialised as audit capability increased. The increase in the volume of PBoC's audit load compelled the development of related financial regulations, systems of communication and policies to correct and punish violations. In 1997 a series of audit rules were published relating to PBoC methods of conducting supervisory audits as well as principles of internal control within financial organisations (Liu, Mingkang 刘明康 2009). The NAO, strengthened by the *1994 Audit Law*, provided a valuable check on PBoC activities. In 1994, when the NAO discovered a significantly higher number of short-term loans in its audit than claimed by the PBoC, Zhu Rongji ordered the PBoC to dispatch five work teams to branches to resolve the issue (Yang 2004).

The PBoC developed strict regulations relating to the establishment and operation of financial institutions. It was charged with enforcing the segregation of financial sectors as according to the *Commercial Bank Law*. The PBoC managed the split of SOCBs from TICs and the removal of security trading operations from NBFIs. It developed detailed regulations that defined the limits of commercial bank activities. Segregation of financial sectors was successfully achieved by 1997. The greater empowerment of the PBoC as a gatekeeper to the financial sector led to the discovery of a number of financial institutions that had been established illegally or whose operations violated financial regulations. The State Council published a cautionary example relating to the Economic Reform Committee of Lanxi City, Zhejiang Province who allowed three local financial institutions to be established without PBoC approval in 1994 and 1995. Financial operations of these institutions were not conducted prudently or according to regulation. Loan and deposit rates of these organisations were 90 per cent and 50 per cent higher respectively than PBoC limits. The risky nature of loans created an extraordinary total of RMB 23 million of NPLs and a bank run by depositors ensued. What made this case more serious was that the local government attempted to solve this problem without PBoC assistance, resorting to using funds from the local SOCB branch and UCCs to cover their tracks. The local government also planned to hide NPLs within the UCCs. To demonstrate the seriousness of this issue the relevant Lanxi City local government entities, along with the local PBoC branch, were investigated to determine criminal responsibility (State Council 国务院 1996). In June 1995, the NPC Standing Committee issued a law for the purpose of defining criminal punishments for the violation of financial order, which came into effect immediately. The law provided significant weight to the efforts of PBoC head office in establishing financial order. This is evident in one notice issued by the PBoC relating to the emergence of illegal private money houses where the illegal nature of this activity is emphasised with a clear reference to the relevant clause of the *Commercial Bank Law* (PBoC 人民银行 1996).

The unification and strengthening of SOCB governance provided a platform for the development of systems of risk management. The implementation of systems of asset and liability management introduced the concept of managing assets and liabilities to reduce credit and liquidity risk. It also pushed the utilisation of performance indicators that could identify risk such as ratios relating to capital adequacy or loan structure. In 1994, the PBoC issued a notice requiring the gradual implementation of asset and liability management for commercial banks. The issuance of this notice came at the end of several years of exploratory trials, led by ICBC. ICBC commenced trials in 1988 in selected branches in Guangdong, Shandong and Ningbo and gradually expanded these trials, achieving full implementation in some provinces by 1992. In 1993, PBoC permitted ICBC to attempt full implementation of asset and liability management. The learnings accumulated during this process provided a basis for the implementation of systems of asset and liability management at other SOCBs (Liu, Mingkang 刘明康 2009). The implementation of the 1988 Basel Accord provided a stimulus for the evaluation of assets according to their risk profile, the increase of capital adequacy according to international standards and the improvement of systems of loan assessment. The banking system employed a basic four-tier system of loan classification that had been instituted by the MOF in 1988. Within this constraint, SOCBs experimented with new forms of credit risk management and developed initial procedures for the assessment, monitoring and evaluation of loans (Liu, Mingkang 刘明康 2009).

Gradual and pragmatic reforms of other financial institutions were implemented in order to ensure financial safety, serve the real economy and develop mechanisms of competition. Three policy banks, China Development Bank, The Export-Import Bank of China and the Agricultural Development Bank of China were established to facilitate the transition of specialised banks to SOCBs and, importantly, to provide the state with the institutional capability to finance important state projects which had been lacking, notably in the construction and agricultural sectors. Shareholding banks continued to show the way for the Big Four with achievements in areas such as asset and liability management drawing acclaim from international bankers (Liu, Mingkang 刘明康 2009). Despite the strict segregation of financial sectors CITIC, Everbright and China Merchants Groups were allowed to retain their status as financial conglomerates. In the RCC sector, the PBoC took over supervisory activities from ABC to drive regulatory improvement. The RCC model needed to change as the scale of agricultural development now well exceeded the level of the village. According to a CBRC official, the concept of a large-scale RCC bank was mooted, but ultimately it was considered to be unsuitable for the developmental needs of rural communities (Interview with CBRC official, 12 March 2015). Ultimately it was announced by the State Council in 1997 that RCCs would be grouped at the county level in an effort to retain the organisational characteristics that could allow greater participation in finance at the local level. In order to subject UCCs to a higher degree of risk management, it was decided they would be transformed into city commercial banks. The activity of foreign banks was allowed to evolve outside of the SEZs. The restriction of foreign bank activity within SEZs was removed by the PBoC in 1996. Between 1993 and 1997 the total number of foreign financial institutions and total assets had both tripled (Huang, Wang and Lin 2010, 35). Tentative trials of foreign banks conducting RMB business were held in Shanghai.

## Build-up of risk in the banking sector

The level of risk in the banking sector increased after the establishment of the socialist market economy because the development of institutions to mitigate market risk lagged behind the expansion of market-led economic activity. Prior to the AFC, China's economy grew rapidly and SOCBs, reformed into autonomous and commercialised enterprises, had significantly greater responsibility for allocating capital. However the process of commercialisation of SOCBs between 1994 and 1997 was described by policymakers as 'not thorough' (Liu, Mingkang 刘明康 2009, 47). Former Vice Chairman of PBoC's auditing department, Wang Jun, cited 'the widespread lack of credit culture within SOCBs' as one of the principal concerns (Liu, Mingkang 刘明康 2009, 71). To compound matters, the development of systems of financial regulation was at an early stage. These systems were not yet able to control the level of market risk in the banking sector effectively. This resulted in the poor performance of the banking sector and a build-up of credit risk in the years leading up to the AFC. In 1993, early PBoC audits of 175 financial enterprises determined that these enterprises did not have sufficient capital and that loan quality was poor (Liu, Mingkang 刘明康 2009, 65). Not only had none of the Big Four banks reached the Basel I standard of 8 per cent minimum capital ratio, levels of capital adequacy were actually in decline. NPLs of the Big Four increased from 20.4 per cent to 32.2 per cent between 1994 and 1998 according to the relatively lenient four-tier system of loan classification (Liu, Mingkang 刘明康 2009, 77, 78). Profits at the

*Table 3.1* Declining capital adequacy ratios of the four specialised banks, 1990–96

|  | 1990 | 1991 | 1992 | 1993 | 1994 | 1995 | 1996 |
|---|---|---|---|---|---|---|---|
| **ICBC** | | | | | | | |
| Adjusted | 5.48 | 5.35 | 5.13 | 6.57 | 5.7 | – | – |
| Core | 4.5 | 4.3 | 3.8 | 4.07 | 3.33 | 2.98 | 2.55 |
| **ABC** | | | | | | | |
| Adjusted | 7.49 | 6.41 | 5.5 | 4.1 | 6.95 | – | – |
| Core | 5.2 | 4.5 | 3.8 | 2.74 | 3.5 | 3.31 | 2.72 |
| **BOC** | | | | | | | |
| Adjusted | 6.72 | 6.69 | 6.31 | 5.35 | 7.37 | – | – |
| Core | 4.3 | 4.1 | 3.7 | 3.44 | 4.13 | 4.77 | 4.69 |
| **CCB** | | | | | | | |
| Adjusted | 8.72 | 7.4 | 6.32 | 4.79 | 4.31 | – | – |
| Core | 5.9 | 4.9 | 4.4 | 3.21 | 2.81 | 2.32 | 2.13 |

Source: Pei 1998, 335.

Big Four banks had fallen alarmingly from RMB 34.3 billion in 1992 to just RMB 5.1 billion in 1996 (Pei 1998, 333). The lack of strong governance and weak regulatory supervision in the banking sector also provided an environment for other financial institutions such as TICs and shareholding banks to engage in risky behaviour. According to insiders at Guangdong Development Bank, the total value NPLs at the bank had risen to close to RMB 100 million by the end of the 1990s (*www.people.com.cn* 2006). There was rapid growth in speculative investment, particularly in the stock market and real estate market. The heavy international borrowing of international trust and investment corporations (ITICs) and Chinese companies with a presence in Hong Kong, often for the purpose of such speculative investment, would later pose a threat to China's economic stability during the AFC.

The combination of more autonomous banks and the weak nature of early regulation created the conditions for a high level of operational risk. According to the 1996 Chinese Banking Almanac, 'the number of serious crimes was on the rise' ('Almanac of China's Finance and Banking 1996' 1996). The Almanac reported that a range of financial crimes had been discovered in which there had been clear violations of financial rules. As operations of banks became more autonomous, crimes had become harder to detect. Foreign exchange operations had become a notable target for such fraud. Often violations would be left unreported in banks' accounts. Violations of financial procedures by banks often resulted in the use of funds for speculative areas of the economy such as the stock market and the real estate sector. Instances of large-scale fraud generally only came to light from the late 1990s as bank systems of internal control improved.

SOCB workers had not yet been able to comprehend and adapt new concepts required for the development of a strong credit culture. Managers at SOCBs lacked familiarity with modern management concepts and as a result SOCBs continued to function in the mould of an administrative department. SOCB staff were also unfamiliar with new concepts of risk management designed for commercial banks. The state of organisational reforms within SOCBs reflected the notion that the development of commercial concepts was at an early stage. While in recent years SOCBs had 'broken the iron rice bowl', systems of human resources were relatively underdeveloped. Banks had signalled their intention to restructure branch networks to reflect commercial principles but large-scale restructuring and consolidation of branch networks had yet to occur.

There had not been the fundamental shift in the economic relations between SOCBs and SOEs needed for banks to manage credit risk effectively. This was due to the early stage of SOE enterprise reform, which contributed to the build-up of risk in SOCBs. Corporatisation of SOEs through shareholding reform and listing had been conducted in an experimental fashion in selected industries and was not fully endorsed by the state as a reform measure until 1997. The process of corporatisation was complicated by ongoing bureaucratic intervention and welfare responsibilities (Ma 2010). While the *Commercial Bank Law* had required the mandatory establishment of a board of supervisors to monitor bank performance, more substantial governance reforms in SOCBs would occur subsequent to that of other SOEs due to the high priority given to stability in the banking sector. SOEs did not treat relations with SOCBs as that between two commercial entities. An official who worked at ABC during that time remarked that there was undoubtedly a culture of non-repayment among SOEs that persisted regardless of their commercial circumstances (Interview with CBRC official, 10 March 2015). In many ways the borrowing behaviour of SOEs still reflected a 'selfish departmentalism', with some companies aiming to obtain financial resources without giving real consideration to their financial circumstances or ability to repay loans (Liu, Mingkang 刘明康 2009, 46). SOCBs continued to support SOEs during this phase of economic transition. Declining SOE profitability, which had fallen from 25 per cent at outset of reform to just 6.5 per cent by 1996, had a negative impact on bank balance sheets (Lardy 1998, 47, 48).

Reforms in the banking sector that aimed to develop a robust system of market regulation and improve the capacity of banks to manage risk were at an early stage. The gradual roll-out of a standardised set of reform measures for credit risk occurred in the years following the announcement of the socialist market economy. SOCBs had to first trial and then become familiar with new systems. One important reform, the separation of loan-making and loan assessment within the decision-making hierarchy of SOCBs, was not rolled out in a standardised form across SOCBs until 1997. Such systems often still lacked legitimacy. PBoC Vice Governor Dai Xianglong remarked that while the standardised implementation of asset and liability management constituted a 'good start', there were 'many leading comrades who did not place enough importance on this work'. Dai also noted that bank workers needed time to learn how to this new system correctly (Liu, Mingkang 刘明康 2009, 48). Newly introduced systems of regulation were still in their infancy and needed further strengthening and improvement. The four-tier loan classification system that was fundamental to the assessment of credit risk in the banking sector was overly simple. It focused only on whether the loan was overdue and did not consider loan quality or risk, or the relationship between the repayment of the loan's principal and its interest. A former employee of one of the Big Four banks remarked that systems of internal control were poor around this time (Interview with CBRC official, 10 March 2015). A new accounting law had been established according to international standards, but it did not include the requirement for banks to hold loan loss provisions due to the poor financial circumstances of China's banks. International auditors had recently begun operations in China by means of joint-venture partnerships. Audits of China's non-financial SOEs by international accounting firms were vital to the success of their international initial public offerings (IPOs), which began in Hong Kong after 1993. The first international audit in the banking sector did not occur until prior to the 2002 listing of Bank of China (Hong Kong), a subsidiary of the Bank of China.

While newly established laws had unified and strengthened the central bank and centrally controlled commercial banks, the fragmented nature of party governance undermined these reforms. As one CBRC official pointed out, the influence of local governments and ministries continued to cause SOCBs to continue to allocate loans to SOEs that were not commercially viable (Interview with CBRC official, 17 March 2015). While from 1994 PBoC had the authority to vet appointments of SOCBs branches at Vice Governor level or above, appointment powers for the local branches of SOCBs remained in the hands of local party committees (Heilmann 2005; Liu, Mingkang 刘明康 2009). Reforms to widen PBoC provincial boundaries to reduce the influence of local governments, discussed at the 3rd Plenum of the 14th Party Committee, had not yet been implemented. The introduction of centralising reforms had become a priority for officials, as signalled by tax reforms in 1994. Such reforms would further strengthen market-based institutions in the banking sector.

## Conclusion

The banking reforms implemented at the establishment of the socialist market economy reflected the desire of policymakers to develop a stable banking system that would strongly promote economic development and modernisation. The high priority placed by China's policymakers on financial stability in the gradual, pragmatic construction of its regulatory system led China's officials to avoid policies of deregulation and financial liberalisation which had become the political consensus in the United States and were being adopted by many developing countries. Reforms instead entailed an evolution of historical patterns of political and economic organisation. Officials in China's bureaucratic system were urged that a core party of their duty was to maintain financial order and respect financial regulations. While there was a strong level of engagement with foreign experts, Chinese officials adapted the knowledge and technology acquired in a selective manner in order to develop a system of close regulation and supervision that had been forgotten by the West. Reforms empowered the PBoC to establish a stronger and more standardised system of regulation. Through the unification and strengthening of governance systems, the governance of China's large state-owned banks was transformed into an enterprise model. These reforms provided the platform for a highly exploratory process of regulatory development designed to contain market risk. Regulatory developments included the development of PBoC audit systems, the segregation of financial institutions, improved control of entry and exit of financial institutions, and the implementation of systems of asset and liability management in SOCBs. China's banking sector experienced an increase in risk because the development of institutions to regulate market risk could not keep up with the rapid pace of economic growth. SOCBs had low levels of capital adequacy and high rates of NPLs due to the lack of a strong credit culture, the unfamiliarity of staff with modern risk management techniques, the duty to support SOEs in economic transition, the fragmented nature of party governance and the lack of sufficiently robust market regulation. Upon the advent of the AFC, the high rate of NPLs would become an immediate systemic risk that would drive a new phase of regulatory development.

## References

'Almanac of China's Finance and Banking 1996'. 1996.

Ash, Robert F. 1992. 'Quarterly Chronicle and Documentation'. *The China Quarterly*, 130: 454–91.

Blecher, Marc. 2009. *China Against the Tides: Restructuring through Revoution, Radicalism and Reform*. 3rd edition. New York: Continuum.

CCP. 2011. 'Full Text of Jiang Zemin's Report at 14th Party Congress'. Beijing Review, 29 March 2011. www.bjreview.com.cn/document/txt/2011-03/29/content_363504.htm.

Du, Hua 杜华, ed. 2007. *'Jinrong Gongzuo Wenxian Xuanbian (1978–2005)'* 金融工作文献选编 （一九七八——二00五）. Beijing: Zhongguo Jinrong Chubanshe.

*Financial Times*. 1989. 'New Regulations Ban Loans'. 20 October 1989.

Guan, Qingyou. 2013. 'What Three Waves of Debt Crisis Have Taught China'. *CaiXin Online*, 18 March 2013. http://english.caixin.com/2013-03-18/100502730.html.

Heilmann, Sebastian. 2005. 'Regulatory Innovation by Leninist Means: Communist Party Supervision in China's Financial Industry'. *The China Quarterly* 181 (1): 1–21.

Holz, Carsten. 1992. *The Role of Central Banking in China's Economic Reforms*. East Asia Program, Cornell University.

Huang, Yiping, Xun Wang and N. Lin. 2010. 'Financial Reform in China: Progresses and Challenges'. Working Paper. China Macroeconomic Research Center, Peking University, China. http://paftad.org/files/34/07_HUANG_Fin%20Reform_nofig.pdf.

Johnson, Simon and James Kwak. 2010. *13 Bankers: The Wall Street Takeover and the next Financial Meltdown*. New York: Vintage Books.

Lardy, Nicholas R. 1998. *China's Unfinished Economic Revolution*. Washington, DC: Brookings Institution.

*Law of the People's Republic of China on Commercial Banks*. n.d. China.org.cn. www.china.org.cn/english/DAT/214824.htm.

*Law of the People's Republic of China on the People's Bank of China*. n.d. China.org.cn. www.china.org.cn/business/laws_regulations/2007-06/22/content_1214826.htm.

Liu, Mingkang 刘明康, ed. 2009. *'Zhongguo Yinhang Gaige Kaifang Sanshinian (1978–2008) Shangce'* 中国银行业改革开放30年 (1978–2008) 上册. Beijing: Beijing Jinrong Chubanshe.

Liu, Mingkang. 2010. 'Keynote Speech at Asian Financial Forum: Chinese Bankers Carry Hopes for Future Balances'. China Banking Regulatory Commission, 20 January , 2010. www.cbrc.gov.cn/EngdocView.do?docID=2010012011DA7AE6925E5D48FF76107FF744C800.

Ma, Shu Yun. 2010. *Shareholding System Reform in China: Privatizing by Groping for Stones*. Cheltenham, UK: Edward Elgar.

Nolan, Peter. 2013. *Is China Buying the World*. Cambridge, UK: Polity.

O'Neill, Mark. 1987. 'China's Central Bank Struggles to Play Proper Role'. *Reuters News*, 18 December 1987. http://global.factiva.com/redir/default.aspx?P=sa&an=lba0000020011205djci006j1&cat=a&ep=ASE.

PBoC 人民银行. 1996. '"Zhongguo Renminyinhang Guanyu Qudi Siren Qianzhuang de Tongzhi 中国人民银行关于取缔私人钱庄的通知" [PBoC Notice Regarding the Prohibition of Private Money Houses]'. Chinabaike.com, 7 July 1996. www.chinabaike.com/law/zy/bw/gw/zgyh/1362434.html.

Pei, Minxin. 1998. 'The Political Economy of Banking Reforms in China, 1993–1997'. *Journal of Contemporary China* 7 (18): 321–50. https://doi.org/10.1080/10670569808724318.

*Reuters News*. 1988a. 'China Has Worst Bank Run Since 1949 in Harbin City'. 15 August 1988. http://global.factiva.com/redir/default.aspx?P=sa&an=lba0000020011203dk8f02 i01&cat=a&ep=ASE.

*Reuters News*. 1988b. 'China Raises Interest Rates to Try to Curb Inflation'. 16 August 1988. http://global.factiva.com/redir/default.aspx?P=sa&an=lba0000020011203dk8g02 jkh&cat=a&ep=ASE.

*Reuters News*. 1989. 'Millions of Chinese Farmers Face Payments by IOU'. 1 June 1989. http://global.factiva.com/redir/default.aspx?P=sa&an=lba0000020011129dl6103brr& cat=a&ep=ASE.

State Council 国务院. 1996. 'Guowuyuan Bangongting Guanyu Zhejianglanxishi Feifa Chengli Jinrongjigou Bing Yinfa Jidui Shijian de Tongbao 国务院办公厅关于浙江省 兰溪市非法成立金融机构并引发挤兑事件的通报 [Notice of the Office of the State Council Regarding Zhejiang Lanxi City's Illegal Establishment of Financial Institutions and Triggering of a Bank Run]'. Gov.cn. www.gov.cn/zhengce/content/2010-11/12/content_2419.htm.

State Council. 2006. 'The 8th Five-Year Plan (1991–1995)'. Gov.cn, 5 April 2006. http:// english1.english.gov.cn/2006-04/05/content_245691.htm.

Sutherland, Dylan. 2001. 'Policies to Build National Champions: China's "National Team" of Enterprise Groups'. In *China and the Global Business Revolution*, by Peter Nolan, 67–140. New York: Palgrave Macmillan.

Thomson, Robert. 1987. 'Report on China Masses Get Message to Buy Bonds'. *The Globe and Mail*, 6 April 1987. http://global.factiva.com/redir/default.aspx?P=sa&an=g lob000020011118dj4600j98&cat=a&ep=ASE.

*Toronto Star*. 1986. 'Top Bankers from China Meet Wall St. Stock Giants'. 11 November 1986.

Walter, Carl and Fraser Howie. 2012. *Red Capitalism: The Fragile Financial Foundation of China's Extraordinary Rise*. Revised edition. Singapore: Wiley.

World Bank. 1990. 'China Macroeconomic Stability and Industrial Growth under Decentralized Socialism'. World Bank.

World Bank. 2016. 'World Development Indicators'. 2016. http://data.worldbank.org/ indicator/NE.EXP.GNFS.ZS?locations=CN.

*www.People.com.cn*. 2006. Review of '*Guangfahang "Yuhuochongsheng"* '广发行"浴 火重生 [*Guangdong Development Bank's Rebirth from the Fire*], by Tianhang 李天行 Li, 17 November 2006. http://finance.people.com.cn/GB/8215/74587/74591/5066886. html.

*Xinhua News Agency*. 1989. 'Chinese Banks to Grant 100 Billion Yuan in Loans'. 23 November 1989. http://global.factiva.com/redir/default.aspx?P=sa&an=xnews0002001 1130dlbn003q3&cat=a&ep=ASE.

Yang, Dali. 2004. *Remaking the Chinese Leviathan-Market Transition and the Politics of Governance in China*. Stanford, CA: Stanford University Press.

Zarathustra, W. 2011. 'China: The Forgotten Real Estate Bubble Of The 1990s'. *Business Insider*, 23 March 2011. www.businessinsider.com/china-the-forgotten-real-estate-bubble-in-1990s-2011-3.

# 4    Reducing systemic risk in the socialist market economy (1997–2002)

Within the orthodox view of Chinese banking reform, the period since the AFC has been described as one of 'reform stagnation' (Shih 2007, 1238). For proponents of this view, the state should have implemented neoliberal policies to reform China's banking system. The reform measures chosen by the state after the crisis did not accelerate convergence towards the neoliberal model. As a consequence, these measures were deemed 'evasive manoeuvres' and its policies 'inaccurately labelled reform' (*The Wall Street Journal Europe* 1998; Shih 2007, 1241). It is argued that the orthodox view mischaracterises reform in this period because it neglects the influence of historical patterns of political and economic organisation. These historical patterns can explain the fundamental concern of officials for financial stability, the bureaucratic system embedded in China's banking sector and the importance placed on financial sovereignty. Stability was the overriding reform principle as the AFC alerted Chinese officials to the dangers of integration into an under-regulated and dangerous global financial system and the immediate systemic risk posed by the high levels of bad loans to China's banking system. During interviews, a CBRC official pointed out that while each stage of banking reform inevitably posed challenges, the priority for officials was to avoid a big disaster that could derail the reform process (Interview with CBRC official, 10 March 2015). China's officials resolved to mitigate the immediate systemic risk brought to light by the crisis. The party followed the traditional practice of sending a trusted party cadre from Beijing to the provinces to resolve potential instability, with Wang Qishan sent to Guangdong to resolve the province's financial problems and lead negotiations with international creditors. There were reforms to the party's model of governance of the banking sector. A new party body, the Central Financial Work Committee (CFWC), was established to promote financial stability by enhancing central bureaucratic oversight of the banking sector. The response to the crisis also defined the direction of regulatory development. Policymakers progressively incorporated more international best practices into banking regulation. To improve credit risk management, an internationally recognised five-tier system of loan classification based on the United States system was introduced. Measures for the recapitalisation of China's SOCBs and disposal of NPLs were implemented with reference to Basel requirements of capital adequacy and international case studies such as the

United States savings and loan crisis. Global accounting and investment banks participated and advised upon the liquidation and restructuring of troubled enterprises. The direct impact of the crisis on China's financial system also led to the vast restructuring of China's NBFI sector. Navigating this process of restructuring, while also strengthening regulation to reduce future risk, enhanced regulatory capability and increased the accountability of financial institutions. Officials maintained sovereignty over China's banking sector despite intense pressure from foreign financial institutions and their governments who lobbied for the dismantling of the state-led model and greater foreign control of financial assets. This was confirmed by the decision reached at the Second National Financial Work Conference to list the Big Four state-owned banks as whole entities, thereby allowing the state to retain control. In an interview, a CBRC official attributed the protection of the banking sector from external influences, along with the suppression of private banking during this period, to the need for stability (Interview with CBRC official, 12 March 2015).

## The AFC and the dangers of the global financial system

Chinese officials at the core of the party system such as Zheng Bijian, former member of Central Committee and Executive Vice President of the party school, felt that the fundamental cause of the crisis was a dangerous and insufficiently regulated global financial system. Zheng commented that the AFC 'has presented to the world in sharp relief and in a tempestuous way a series of deep-rooted problems and major trends of the world economic situation' and Western countries had promoted financial liberalisation in developing countries while failing to ensure the stability and resilience of their economies in the face of external shocks (Zheng 2011, 67). The countries that were worst affected by the AFC (namely South Korea, Indonesia, Thailand, Malaysia and the Philippines) had been willing participants in the neoliberal, globalised financial regime led by the United States and United Kingdom, which had abandoned capital controls in the 1970s. According to the Reserve Bank of Australia, private capital flows into these Asian economies had increased fivefold in the years leading up to the crisis. Net private capital inflows of almost US$100 billion into these five countries in 1996 had by 1997 become a net outflow of US$12 billion (Stephen Grenville 1998). The sudden reversal of short-term international capital flows, due in large part to speculative attacks against the Thai Baht and other currencies, forced a cycle of currency devaluation in the region.

The crisis alerted officials to the dangers of premature integration into the global financial system and defined the attitude of policymakers towards the future opening of the capital account as one of extreme prudence and caution (Liu, Mingkang 刘明康 2009). It was the lack of exposure to the volatility of short-term international capital flows, rather than the strength of China's banking system, which prevented the crisis enveloping China. In fact a report published by Moody's in June of 1998 confirmed that 'China has long had, by most measures, by far the weakest banking system among major Asian countries' (Harding

1998). China's relative weakness implied a far greater vulnerability to the dangers of financial liberalisation. Famed currency speculator George Soros commented that 'if the Chinese renminbi had been convertible, the Chinese banking system would have collapsed' (Nolan 2008, 108). China's imposition of capital controls had largely prevented exposure to the risk of sudden capital withdrawal. Second, China's exposure to foreign debt, and particularly short-term foreign debt, was much lower relative to countries worst affected by the crisis. Its ratio of foreign borrowing to GDP of 15 per cent was lower than each of South Korea (28 per cent), Malaysia (38 per cent), Indonesia (51 per cent) and Thailand (60 per cent). Similarly, the level of China's short-term debt did not leave it as vulnerable to capital withdrawals. The ratio of China's short-term external debt to foreign reserves was 24 per cent while in the cases of Thailand, Indonesia and South Korea this ratio well exceeded 100 per cent (Sheng 2009, 282).

While a meltdown of the banking system and the collapse of the currency had been averted, China did not escape from the crisis unscathed. There was a significant impact, as companies and financial institutions that had operations in Hong Kong had significant exposure international capital markets. There were two main groups who were affected, namely the 'red chips' (Chinese companies listed on the Hong Kong Stock Exchange (HKSE)) and the international trust and investment companies. When the crisis hit, these companies and financial institutions suddenly found it difficult to meet bond and interest payments to international lenders. The payments crisis threatened the stability of the financial systems of the mainland and also Hong Kong, which had returned to China in the early stages of the crisis. In the mainland there was a real threat of financial contagion. The payments crisis had already began to affect vulnerable, small-scale domestic financial institutions in Guangdong, such as UCCs and rural financial associations, and threatened to spread across China (Nolan 2008). In Hong Kong, mainland companies affected by the crisis played an important role in the Hong Kong economy, to the extent that their failure would threaten the stability of the Hong Kong stock market.

In October 1998, the Hong Kong dollar came under attack from international currency speculators, forcing the intervention of the Hong Kong government, while there had also been rumours of a devaluation of the RMB (Liu, Mingkang 刘明康 2009). Having only regained Hong Kong from the British a few months earlier, the state desperately and ultimately successfully defended the Hong Kong currency against speculators, stopping the cycle of devaluations that had swept across Asia since the crisis began. Similarly the state chose not to devalue the RMB. While there had been some fear that devaluations in the region would cause China to become less competitive as a trading partner, ultimately the state elected not to devalue the RMB in order to bring calm to global financial markets.

# The AFC as a driver for domestic reform

> The Asian Financial Crisis has made us determined to resolve these problems according to their root cause, and we cannot hesitate any longer.
>
> (Vice Premier Zhu Rongji (Du, Hua 杜华 2007, 262))

Chinese officials did not view this crisis solely as the outcome of exposure to a volatile international financial system. According to Liu Mingkang, the crisis could be traced back to a 'concealed banking crisis' in the region and healthy domestic banking systems, such as those present in Singapore and Hong Kong at the time of the crisis, could have prevented or substantially reduced the impact of the crisis (Liu, Mingkang 刘明康 2009, 71). Instead the crisis left the banking systems of the Asian countries affected in a substantially weakened state with a greater number of bad debts and a lower net worth. In March 1998 Wang Jun, Deputy Director of the PBoC's audit department, summarised the learnings that China could take from the weaknesses of the banking systems of the affected Asian countries which had allowed capital inflows to contribute to speculative bubbles and increased enterprise debt. According to Wang Jun, banking systems in Asia suffered from an unhealthy credit culture, through which high rates of NPLs had emerged. Given the high level of bad debt within China's banking system, the crisis made officials aware of how vulnerable it was. China's Minister of Finance at the time of the crisis, Xiang Huaicheng, stated that 'the AFC has offered us a useful lesson. We did not realise before how serious a problem bad loans could be' (Harding 1998).

As the issues present in these countries were even more apparent in China's banking system, the crisis informed the thinking of officials with regards to a programme of domestic banking reform aimed at strengthening regulation and reducing credit risk. The problem of excessive NPLs was acknowledged by Chinese officials to be the biggest threat to its stability. In May 1998, PBoC Governor Dai Xianglong estimated the ratio of NPLs to be at 20 per cent of total bank loans, though he acknowledged that the four-tier loan classification system employed at the time systemically underestimated credit risk (*Reuters News* 1998). International ratings company Moody's consider the NPL rate to be 'much worse than even the most pessimistic of the official indications', and was perhaps as much as 40–50 per cent (Kynge 1998). External observers deemed the sector to be technically insolvent (Liu, Mingkang 刘明康 2009). The vulnerability to credit risk was exacerbated further by insufficient regulation, primarily weak accounting standards and loan provisioning methods which failed to ensure sufficient allowance for credit risk (Liu, Mingkang 刘明康 2009). While East Asian and South East Asian countries had failed to rigorously enforce the standards of the American five-tier loan classification system, China had yet to transition from a more basic system developed by its MOF in 1988. This system was only concerned with whether loans were overdue. It failed to give an accurate indication of whether these loans where likely to be repaid and did not provide any guidance with respect to the risk of loans which had yet to reach maturity.

China's loan classification system therefore did not provide reliable information on the quality or risk of loans in the banking system. As with other Asian countries, China's banks tended to put too much emphasis on loan collateral or guarantees in assessing loans, and insufficient emphasis on the cash flow which would make repayment of the loan possible.

After the crisis officials were aware that reducing credit risk would also require the improvement of accounting and auditing standards, the augmentation of loan provisions and the imposition of a harder budget constraint on SOEs. Weak accounting provisions allowed banks to delay recording non-payment of loan principal and interest in China before 1997 for up to 3 years, a limit greater than the Asian countries and far exceeding international standards of 3 to 6 months (Liu, Mingkang 刘明康 2009, 75). More generally, the fact that China's banks and many corporate lenders had not been subject to an audit by international accounting firms contributed to the lack of accurate and transparent information relating to bad loans. China's loan provisioning system at the time of the crisis was extremely inadequate. Total loan provisions in 1996 only accounted for 1 per cent of all loans and, due to the inadequacies of the loan classification system, provisioning failed to take into account the potential risks of loans yet to be repaid. China lagged well behind these Asian countries with respect to the write-off of loans. Prior to 1995 the PBoC had set a ceiling on the classification of bad loans at 2 per cent, while Wang Jun revealed that limiting loan write-offs had become standard government practice (Lardy 1998, 115; Liu, Mingkang 刘明康 2009). The banking system's support for SOEs had not only created a soft budget constraint but made it problematic for banks to determine when a loan was non-recoverable. Indeed banks would often continue to attempt recovery of the small proportion of 'bad loans' it had written off, even in the rare case that there were suitable loan provisions.

## The first national financial work meeting

The State Council called a National Financial Work Meeting in November 1997, in the midst of the crisis, with the goal of mitigating immediate systemic risk posed by the crisis and developing a medium-term plan to make the financial sector stronger and more resilient. At the meeting, Vice Premier Zhu Rongji reaffirmed the State Council's faith in the policy direction of the political centre, the Central Committee, praising the achievements of the financial sector in supporting the economy and raising living standards (Du, Hua 杜华 2007, 262). In his speech, Zhu reflected that the financial system was not suited to the sharp pace of economic reform and development and that the historical burden of transition from the socialist economy, principally the transformation of its SOEs into profitable and efficient enterprises, weighed heavily on the banking sector. The resolution passed by the Central Committee and State Council at the National Financial Work Meeting represented a continuation of the existing reform path. It called for deeper reform of the financial system to bring order to the banking sector and reduce risk. The key areas of concern were reducing the amount of bad loans and resolving the issues of the NBFI sector. Other priority issues included identifying and resolving financial crime, which had become a more serious issue as autonomy of financial institutions had increased since 1993, as well as improving internal control and bringing order to the financial sector.

## Immediate measures to reduce the level of NPLs

The recapitalisation of SOCBs and the stripping of NPLs were undertaken with clear reference to international standards and practices that were adapted to suit Chinese conditions. In March 1998, the National People's Congress (NPC) approved a plan by the State Council to inject RMB 270 billion into the banking system, at the time equivalent to 4 per cent of China's GDP. The state was making an investment in the long-term survival and future transformation of its state-owned banking sector, despite its weak state. The capital injection did not in itself establish a mechanism through which to improve allocative efficiency of capital or risk management. Officials had a responsibility to deliver future reform which was a both meaningful and sustainable in order to justify this cost to society. The justification for the precise amount of this capital injection was the state's desire for the banking system to accord to international standards of capital adequacy as set out in the first Basel Accord, which China had adopted in 1994. To fund this recapitalisation, the deposit-reserve ratio was reduced from 13 per cent to 8 per cent to free up sufficient capital. SOCBs utilised the extra capital to each purchase a Special Purpose Treasury Bond which was then lent back to the banks, effectively as a capital injection. The purpose of the capital injection was to raise the core capital and supplementary capital of China's large state-owned banks to the Basel requirements of 4 per cent and 8 per cent of risk-weighted assets respectively. That these banks had not yet been subjected to an audit by international accounting firms and had weak loan classification standards increased the risk and uncertainty surrounding the ultimate impact of this reform.

After resolving the urgent need of recapitalisation, the next objective in the reform process was to lower the rate of NPLs of the large state-owned banks. To reduce the quantity of NPLs held by the Big Four, the state established four AMCs, each tasked with absorbing and disposing of the NPLs of one of the Big Four banks. In designing a model for the purpose of carving off NPLs, China again looked outward for international case studies. Zhu Rongji instructed high-ranking PBoC officials to consult with staff from the Resolution Trust Company, an AMC which assisted with the resolution of the United States savings and loan crisis between 1989 and 1995 (Kuhn 2010). It is likely that officials also examined the successful use of a state-owned AMC in Sweden to help resolve its banking crisis during the early 1990s. According to then Vice Governor of the PBoC, Liu Mingkang, the state ultimately selected a state-owned model of AMCs as the combination of China's undeveloped legal framework and the conflicts of interests between commercial banks and AMCs would pose a greater risk if private companies were involved (Kuhn 2010).

Between April 1999 and October 1999 the Cinda, Huarong, Great Wall and Orient AMCs were established to dispose of the NPLs of CCB, ABC, ICBC and BoC respectively. NPLs valued at a total of RMB 1.4 trillion were transferred to the AMCs the following year, including RMB 100 billion from China Development Bank. According to official estimates, this immediately reduced the NPL rate among the Big Four banks by 10 per cent (Liu, Mingkang 刘明康 2009, 80). Given the huge scale of the NPL problem, the state had little choice but to fund the AMC purchase of NPLs almost entirely through the issue of AMC bonds, purchased by the Big Four state-owned banks for RMB 858 billion. This method, which deviated from international practices, was selected as it provided China the means to fund the removal of NPLs from the banking system. There were obvious drawbacks. While the NPLs of the large state-owned banks were removed from their books, the banks remained exposed to these assets through their AMC bond. In 2000 the AMCs officially took on the bad loan portfolios from the Big Four. The AMCs paid face value for the loans at a total of US$170 billion, despite the impaired nature of the loans. This provided valuable capital to the banks but left the AMCs with a virtually impossible task with respect to loan recovery. In short, the state's lack of financial means, along with the lack of institutional capacity, caused it to find a pragmatic method to shift this historical burden of NPLs to specialised entities. Given these obstacles, the state would need to adopt the approach of 'groping for stones to cross the river' in finding a long-term resolution to the NPL issue.

The stripping of NPLs removed a historical burden from the large state-owned banks, providing them with a 'clean slate' and creating a more level playing field within the banking sector. The NPLs of state-owned banks were a consequence of their role in providing financial support for the transition of SOEs and the development of public infrastructure. Liu Mingkang reported that the leaders of the state-owned banks emphasised this historical legacy in the creation of bad loans. According the Presidents of the Big Four, the bad loans were 'caused not by our mismanagement but by loans required by the state and imposed on us' (Kuhn 2010, 266). This responsibility had adversely impacted the development of a credit culture in state-owned banks. With this burden removed, regulators would push the development of an improved credit culture within banks and hold top bank officials accountable for the creation of future bad loans. At a news conference, PBoC Governor Dai Xianglong revealed that with the improved asset quality following NPL disposal, there was an expectation that the commercial performance of banks would improve so that further government bailouts would be unnecessary: 'I consider the establishment of the asset-management companies as the last dinner for the state-owned commercial banks' (Brown 2000).

## SOE reform as a removal of the historical burden

Reform of the SOE sector, while not complete, had also helped relieve the banks of some of the policy burden. Since the early 1990s, the state had adopted a strategy of creating a modern enterprise system by carving assets from ministries and instituting modern forms of corporate governance. By the end of the 1990s, the state had established 120 centrally controlled enterprise groups and transferred their administrative function to bodies that were subsidiary to the State Economic and Trade Commission (Wu 2004, 156). Shareholding reform and listing of SOEs had proceeded rapidly since the mid-1990s. While not complete, the development of a modern enterprise system, the separation from administrative function, and the discipline of external shareholders all pushed more commercially-orientated behaviour within SOEs.

One important aspect of these reforms was the downsizing of the SOEs. According to Naughton, almost 50 million workers lost their jobs in the state sector from 1993–2004, with more than half of the layoffs occurring between 1996 and 1999 (Naughton 2007, 186). The trimming of surplus labour reduced the state's burden to support SOEs, much of which was offered through policy loans from the banking sector. The banking sector also benefitted directly from downsizing. A large-scale, systematic rationalisation of the branch networks of the Big Four was carried out from June 1998 by the PBoC. Mergers and closures of bank branches were implemented according to ratio between staff numbers and deposits (except in the case of ABC). Branches that were superfluous to the hierarchical structure were consolidated. Between 1998 and 2002, the Big Four closed approximately 55,000 branches, which represented a third of their combined organisational network, laying off more than 550,000 workers in the process (Liu, Mingkang 刘明康 2009, 79). While the reform of the SOE sector remained a work in progress, the development of the modern enterprise system had reduced the policy loan burden on the banking sector and enhanced the ability of centrally controlled SOEs to act as more independent and commercially viable enterprises.

## Reform to regulate the market

After the AFC, China's officials wanted to establish a more robust regulatory system to mitigate market risk. The decision to develop a system of close supervision and regulation of financial institutions caused China to take a different path to that of Western developed countries which had implemented policies of deregulation and financial liberalisation. The PBoC played a leading role in the initial development of this regulatory system. While the *Commercial Bank Law* and *Central Bank Law* had provided guidance for the initial development of the banking regulatory system, this was a highly exploratory process which was at an early stage. The central bank steadily issued provisional regulations after the enactment of these laws in 1995. Following the National Financial Work Conference, the regulatory responsibilities of the PBoC in the securities and insurance sectors were devolved to specialist regulatory agencies. The PBoC head office was then reorganised into divisions according to type of banking or NBFIs. In 2001 the PBoC issued a number of comprehensive, though provisional, regulations targeted at specific types of financial institutions as a result of this exploratory process (Liu, Mingkang 刘明康 2009).

As part of this process, the PBoC gradually constructed a risk management system which according to Liu Mingkang 'began to shift the core of financial regulation from regulatory compliance … towards regulation according to law and risk' (Liu, Mingkang 刘明康 2009, 105). Between 1998 and 2002 the PBoC developed and improved its on and off-site evaluation systems, regulatory reporting system, and statistics and information management systems. These formed the basis of its risk assessment activities. Following the initial reforms of the PBoC structure, much work was done to ensure there was accountability for regulatory activities at the various levels of each bank, from head office to branch level. Within this more robust regulatory structure, there were a range of complementary rules and regulations that were established in order to change the credit culture within Chinese banks. These efforts to develop a more comprehensive regulatory structure provided a platform for fundamental reforms which, as they took hold, would greatly enhance the capacity of all Chinese banks to manage credit risk. Provisional rules instructing on the recognition of NPLs, the further standardisation of reporting procedures for bank NPLs and the investigation of branches of the large state-owned banks with particularly high rates or quantities of NPLs provided a strong signal to bank officials of the PBoC's intent to deal with the NPL problem (Liu, Mingkang 刘明康 2009).

Wang Qishan, the official charged with resolving the financial problems in Guangdong during the crisis, stated that 'the 1997 Asian financial crisis helped us gain a deeper understanding of the need to establish principles for commercial credit in accordance with international practices' (Chen 1999). The introduction of an internationally recognised five-tier system of loan classification, based on the United States system and which better reflected loan quality and the risk of non-repayment, was perhaps the most important of these reforms. Up to this point, the loan classification system had essentially recorded the extent to which the principal of the loan was overdue. The new system required staff to grasp an entirely new definition of credit risk and develop an understanding of the quality and risks of new and ongoing loans, with particular attention paid to the financial circumstances of the borrower. The decision to implement the new loan classification came after extensive consultation with international organisations such as international accounting and advisory firm Price Waterhouse Coopers (PWC). While PWC recommended wide-ranging reform of bank prudential supervisory systems, the state decided that initially the banking system could only cope with the introduction of the new loan classification system (Interview with David Li, Beijing Senior Partner, PWC, 3 April 2015). Trials commenced from May 1998 in Guangdong and included all commercial banks. The PBoC announced that from 2002 comprehensive implementation of the five-tier loan classification would begin. Another fundamental reform was the standardisation of the credit approval process. According to a director of a national-level commercial bank, prior to this reform there was very little separation between the processes of loan-assessment and loan-making. To make a loan, a loan officer would simply require the approval of his or her supervisor (Interview with Yao Libao, Director of Personal Credit, Beijing Branch, Guangdong Development Bank, 9 October

2014). The lack of a standardised process with robust checks and balances on loan officer decision-making created the potential for error or corruption to occur. As part of the new credit approval process, loan assessment committees were instituted at the branch level. This system was first trialled within ICBC in 1995 and a unified client credit authorisation system was rolled out across the banking sector in 1997 (Liu, Mingkang 刘明康 2009).

The combination of asset stripping and regulatory measures appeared to have a significant impact on the NPL problem and 2001 marked the first year when the total amount of NPLs and the NPL rate both decreased. Between 2001 and 2002, according to the five-tier loan classification system, the official NPL rate decreased from 31 per cent to 26.1 per cent (Liu, Mingkang 刘明康 2009, 80). However as previously stated, the problem of bad loans was more serious than these official figures suggested as rigorous systems of NPL reporting and recognition were still under development. The meagre loan provisions of the large state-owned banks caused them to remain technically insolvent.

## Clean-up of the NBFI sector

The party moved urgently to address the financial chaos in Guangdong province that had been exposed by the AFC. The rise of economic fortunes in the province, following Deng's Southern tour in 1992, had spurred speculative investment, particularly in real estate and stock markets. Guangdong's financial institutions were able to offer a higher return on domestic capital, particularly in the NBFI sector where illegal high interest rates were offered to attract capital from across the country. International investors also wanted to be part of this growth story, particularly given the state's record of bailing out troubled firms. Forty ITICs, located at various levels of government, along with the 'red chip' companies listed in Hong Kong (and other Chinese 'window' companies with a presence in Hong Kong) had borrowed heavily from international commercial banks. The debt of ITICs registered with SAFE had reached US$18 billion by the end of the 1990s. The advent of the AFC had burst the speculative asset bubbles and many financial institutions were in severe financial trouble, especially those suffering from corruption and poor management. The problems of financial institutions which had borrowed abroad quickly spread to other parts of the NBFI sector such as the urban and rural cooperatives, which were also heavily leveraged. The difficulties in Guangdong were perceived in Beijing as a failure of party leadership to ensure stability and financial order in the province. According to *South China Morning Post*, the province was seen as 'a kingdom unto itself, the key reason being "the sky is high and the emperor is far away"' (*South China Morning Post* 1998). The party leadership in Beijing transferred trusted party cadres to the Guangdong provincial party committee. Wang Qishan, former Vice Governor of PBoC under Zhu Rongji and then Governor of CCB, was appointed Executive Vice Governor of Guangdong in charge of financial affairs. Wang would work under newly appointed Governor Li Changchun, and with Xiao Gang, the former Assistant to PBoC Governor Dai Xianglong and new Head of PBoC's Guangdong branch.

Wang Qishan had to find a middle path which balanced the economic instability created by closure and bankruptcies with this potential threat of future systemic risk. At the beginning of the crisis, it is estimated that the international debts of TICs and red chips represented 60 per cent of China's foreign exchange reserves (Nolan 2008, 107). The huge scale of financial debts relative to China's financial capabilities made an easy resolution of these financial difficulties impossible. International creditors expected the troubled ITICs and firms to receive the backing of the Chinese state, which had been loath to allow its firms to fail in the past. A full bail-out of all the institutions implicated in the crisis, while perhaps desirable, would have greatly diminished China's foreign exchange reserves and threatened the stability of the financial system in the face of future systemic threats. Two of the troubled entities were of particular importance to the Guangdong economy. The first was GITIC, which was an investment vehicle wholly owned by Guangdong province. According to Wang Qishan, GITIC's foreign debt accounted for 80 per cent of the foreign debt of Guangdong's ITICs (*China Securities Bulletin* 1999a). The other was Guangdong Enterprises (GDE), a conglomerate involved primarily in import processing, assembly and export and which also functioned as the effective 'window company' for the Guangdong provincial government. Five of GDE's companies were listed on the HKSE. In October 1998, provincial officials announced the closure of GITIC. Three months later officials confirmed that GITIC would be liquidated, a decision that shocked foreign creditors. Wang Qishan announced that signs of corruption would be followed up, stating that 'some high-level managers are under legal investigation' (*China Securities Bulletin* 1999b). In October 1998, the Guangdong provincial government announced its intention to restructure GDE, through which investors would take a loss. Wang Qishan stated that he felt a 'great responsibility' in the case of GDE, given its contribution to 'the overall economy of Guangdong province' and the impact its failure might have on the economy of Hong Kong, which he described as a 'potential earthquake' (*South China Morning Post* 1999). The case of GDE demonstrated that the state prioritised the rescue of firms whose survival was important for financial stability and whose contribution to the real economy was significant.

The decision not to fully bail out GITIC and GDE caused a shift in the relationship between Chinese companies and the state, which also had a profound impact on international creditors. In prioritising the stability of the financial system, the state had demonstrated that enterprises and NBFIs no longer had the unconditional support of the state and would be allowed to fail in some circumstances. This was a big step in the transition of SOEs, particularly in the financial sector, in becoming more autonomous and responsible for financial performance. International creditors, which had previously benefitted from implicit government support despite lending at commercial rates, were outraged by the change in policy stance. Indeed a contingent of bankers from Hong Kong met with Zhu Rongji, unsuccessfully seeking assurance that the Guangdong provincial government would facilitate the repayment of loans (Guyot 1999). One creditor of the Ningbo ITIC said of the foreign creditors: 'Many of these companies don't realize, or they don't care, that the country's financial system is at stake' (Chang 1999). The liquidation of GITIC, which caused international creditors to lose around US$3 billion, created an important precedent for future negotiations of other ITICs with international creditors and for the restructuring of enterprises such as GDE (Nolan 2008, 113). Meeting with GDE's creditors during negotiations, Wang Qishan stated that 'what we need is to fairly and equally bear the responsibility' of GDE's insolvency (Guyot 1999). He was careful to point out the low rate of recovery if GDE were to be liquidated following unsuccessful negotiations (*South China Morning Post* 1999). With this strong stance, the state was able to come to an agreement with international creditors, who agreed to a total loss of US$2.12 billion with the provincial government injecting assets worth a total of US$2.01 billion (Nolan 2008, 117).

The restructuring, closure and bankruptcies that the crisis provoked provided another important stimulus for reform. In 1999, the State Council approved a plan for a PBoC-led clean-up of the trust sector which advocated the closure of insolvent or high-risk trust companies. This marked the third major restructuring of the trust sector since reform began. Reforms also focused on standardising the scope and practices of trust companies. Despite the separation of sectors in 1993, commercial banking and securities operations remained prevalent with trust companies. In 2001, the PBoC confirmed its intention to close 151 of the 239 ITICs in China, with the remaining 88 to be merged into 60 trust companies (Brown 2001). The trust companies that were not closed were required by regulators to undergo a reregistration process. The closures and separation of trust companies' securities business were completed by the end of 2002 (Liu, Mingkang 刘明康 2009, 86). Regulators also implemented large-scale restructuring programmes in the urban cooperative, rural cooperative and rural finance association sectors. Merger of troubled cooperatives with better performing financial institutions was undertaken in a pragmatic manner, with closures made where it was not practical. Where suitable, RCCs were upgraded to city level to better reflect the new patterns of economic activity. As in the case of the AMCs, these activities also provided regulators with important experience dealing with troubled assets. Restructuring methods were predicated on an extensive, nationwide process of verification of assets and assessment of capital, conducted by the PBoC. In the cases of GITIC and GDE in particular, the appointment of international firms indicated the state's emphasis on achieving resolution in a transparent fashion, utilising internationally recognised practices, rather than attempting to resolve matters internally. International accounting giant KPMG acted as liquidator for GITIC. Its investigations shed light on the widespread corruption and mismanagement that had occurred. KPMG leveraged its vast international experience, advising the government on how best to meet the interests of individual depositors and the other stakeholders involved. International investment bank Goldman Sachs worked closely with the Guangdong government to develop a plan for GDE's restructuring. Upon announcement of the plan, Wang Qishan noted that it 'clearly demonstrates our determination to establish an independent, efficient and commercially viable enterprise

through a commercial restructuring in accordance with international practices'
(Gasper 1999).

The process of restructuring and closure of NBFIs post-AFC cemented the
role of regulation in China's transitional economy and reduced future moral
hazard. At a speech at the Fortune Global Forum in 1999, Wang Qishan confirmed the new emphasis on the use of 'laws to minimize or eliminate moral
hazards in financial activities' (Chen 1999). Wang Qishan stated that legal monitoring and supervision of all financial activities, including those of government
bodies, was imperative. That there was much progress to be made was evident to
all. The restructuring, bankruptcy and closure of financial firms still lacked a
comprehensive legal framework. In the absence of a bankruptcy law that was
specific to financial institutions, the GITIC bankruptcy had proceeded according
to the *1989 Enterprise Bankruptcy Law*. The order of repayment to depositors
and international and domestic creditors in the event of restructuring had also
not been standardised (Xie 1999). While it was a work in progress, the discon-
tinuation of unconditional support for SOEs and adoption of internationally
recognised restructuring methods had greatly enhanced the stature of the socialist market economy.

## Bringing fraud to light

The governance of China's large state-owned banks was placed under increased
scrutiny after the AFC. Investigations revealed cases of fraud and corruption by
senior banking officials which were on such a massive scale that they threatened
the stability of China's economy (Nolan 2017). According to a CBRC official,
the large-scale fraud occurred during this period as a result of a combination of a
market-driven economy and a lack of robust systems of internal control (Interview with CBRC official, 10 March 2015). In May 2000, Li Fuxiang, the official
in charge of China's foreign exchange reserves, was under investigation for his
conduct at BoC and SAFE when he took his own life. According to reports,
'questions over what happened to billions in "missing" reserves remain
unanswered to this day' (Kynge 2002). In 1998, the combined total of foreign
exchange and the trade surplus was US$89 billion but foreign reserves increased
by just US$5.1 billion. In 1999, the combined total was US$76 billion and
reserves grew by only US$9.72 billion. Capital flight, which was estimated at
US$35–40 billion by academics, accounted for only part of the discrepancy
(Kynge 2002). In 1999 the Chairman of Everbright Bank, Zhu Xiaohua, was
detained by party officials and accused of taking bribes in exchange for approv-
ing more than RMB 800 million worth of loans (Sheng and Gao n.d.). Zhu had
been in charge of China's foreign exchange reserves prior to the appointment of
Li Fuxiang. In 2003 Wang Xuebing, former Head of both BoC and CCB, was
sentenced to 12 years for receiving millions of dollars of bribes and accepting
improper gifts such as luxury watches (McGregor 2003a). Li Fuxiang, Zhu
Xiaohua and Wang Xuebing had all been 'close associates' who 'spoke excellent
English and had cultivated relationships with many of the world's top bankers'

(Kynge 2002). Liu Mingkang, a banker with BoC and subsequently a PBoC official, was appointed by the party as the Head of Everbright Bank in 1999 and BoC in 2000 in response to the corruption scandals that had engulfed both banks. Liu Mingkang promised that he and his new colleagues would take 'firm action against irregularities' (McGregor 2002). In 2002, Liu revealed that an internal audit had uncovered the theft of at least US$483 million over the course of 7 years by five BoC officials at the bank's branch in Kaiping, Guangdong. The five co-conspirators took advantage of a time lag within the bank's internal united finds system to transfer funds into personal accounts and eventually move it out of China via Hong Kong (Lu, Long and Zhang 2005). In an interview, PWC Partner David Wu said that fraud on such an enormous scale was only possible due to the lack of robust accounting practices at Chinese banks during the 1990s (Interview with PWC Partner David Wu, 3 April 2015). Cases of fraud would later provide a stimulus for the introduction of regular audits of banks by international auditors and the upgrading and centralisation of IT systems to reduce operational risk.

## Improving party governance

The lack of stability in China's financial sector was considered by party officials as not only a problem of insufficient regulation, but also of weak party governance. According to a senior CBRC official, it was Premier Zhu's frustration with the lack of order in the financial sector that caused him to establish a new party body in 1998, the CFWC, whose purpose was to strengthen this governance in order to promote the 'safety, efficiency and stability' of the financial system (Heilmann 2005). The official suggested that Zhu was motivated to create this new organisation, led by Zhu's Vice Premier Wen Jiabao, because it afforded Zhu with greater control and influence over the reform process than if he were to work through existing party organisations (Interview with CBRC official, 11 March 2015). Wen would play a central role in the reform of the banking sector from this time until his retirement in 2012.

One key issue for the CFWC to examine was the excessive influence exerted by local government on the allocation of credit, particularly with respect to the Big Four state-owned banks. While the unification of the governance systems of these banks and development of regulation had somewhat eroded the influence of local governments in the allocation of credit, local party committees had retained control over appointments for banking officials at regional levels. According to Heilmann (2005), the major achievement of the CFWC was the implementation of reforms which centralised control of appointments for the Big Four. This was realised through the establishment of new party committees at the sub-national level for the Big Four banks. These party committees took over control of local appointments of the Big Four from local party committees. The strengthening of party governance in this manner was not fundamentally in opposition to the trend of regulatory development. The CFWC did not interfere with the business decisions of the state-owned banks. On the contrary, it complemented regulatory development by reducing the ability of local government to exert influence over the allocation of capital and undermine the standardisation of bank practices. In 1998, the same year that the CFWC was established, the PBoC began a reorganisation of its branches from thirty-two provincial branches to nine super-provincial branches. The goal of this major restructure of China's central bank, responsible for regulation of commercial banks, was consistent with the newly created party organisation's objective to reduce pressure on its branches from local governments.

The dissatisfaction of party leaders with party oversight of banking officials led to the CFWC taking control of some of the responsibilities for the appraisal and appointment from the COD. The CFWC was charged with the appraisal and appointment of senior executives in centrally controlled financial institutions from deputy bureau level to vice-ministerial level, including the Big Four, BoCom, the three policy banks, the four AMCs, CITIC Group, Everbright Group, as well as the central bank. While this reportedly created some tension between the COD and the CFWC, the two organisations worked closely together (Interview with government official, 10 October 2014). For example, the CFWC worked with the COD on the appointment and supervision of supervisory board members. It also assumed responsibilities for the appointment of secretaries for the CCP Discipline Inspection Committees of centrally controlled banks.

The activities of the CFWC highlighted the importance of party governance within the financial system. The party had an active presence within the financial sector, with party officials located within every banking institution, responsible not only for personnel control but also with instilling management with the values and ideology of the party. In response to the rise of regulation and decline of administrative planning, the importance of party institutions had not suffered a decline. Instead, they had evolved and adapted to the changing nature of corporate governance in banks. In 2002, when the CFWC was disestablished, its appointment responsibilities returned to the COD. During the period of CFWC's existence, the COD had retained responsibility for ministry-level appointments for centrally controlled organisations. Its reach even extended to the appointments of top executives of Minsheng Bank, which though majority owned by non-SOEs, was of a scale which required it to sit within the same structure of party governance.

While some of the functions of the CFWC and COD could be compared to that of an investor, the governance of state-owned assets was undeveloped and the state had not yet established a firm policy direction. The fundamental work of the State Owned Assets Management Bureau *guoyouzichan guanliju*, which operated as a vice ministry-level organisation under the MOF until 1998, was to reappraise the value of stocks and enterprises (Sun, Tao 孙弢 2012). In 1998 responsibilities for the management of financial assets were divided between two companies established by the MOF. One was responsible for financial SOEs and the other for non-financial SOEs. This reform step foreshadowed later attempts by the state to create the institutional capacity for the management of assets belonging to financial institutions, including those in the banking sector.

## WTO entry as a threat and an opportunity

China's impending accession to the WTO was of particular significance to China's banking sector due to its high level of protection from foreign competition. Entry to the WTO would require China's economy to become more highly integrated with the global economy. The final weeks of arduous negotiations, which had begun with GATT 13 years earlier, related in large part to the access of United States and European firms to China's financial sector. In April 1999 United States President Clinton had rejected an earlier 'liberalisation offer' from Zhu Rongji, at least in part due to lack of access to the banking sector (de Jonquieres 1999). 'The banking sector ... had enjoyed the highest levels of protection and would be most affected' by WTO entry, according to Chinese Newspaper *Southern Weekend*, making it 'the biggest danger zone' for the state (*The Banker* 2002).

The impending entry of foreign financial institutions created an atmosphere of deep fear and uncertainty among banking executives in China, who described it as 'the wolf is coming!' (Interview with current Ministry of Commerce official, 10 April 2015). In contrast, international bankers were in a buoyant mood at the prospect of China opening the banking sector to foreign competition. The large international financial conglomerates were vastly superior to Chinese banks in scale, employee productivity, technology and asset quality. For example the profits of Citigroup in 1999 were US$9.9 billion, which was twenty times that of China's largest bank ICBC, whose profits totalled US$498 million (Wu 2001, 826). The superiority of foreign financial institutions was such that a rapid increase in market share following the lifting of restrictions appeared inevitable. A former commercial banker revealed in an interview that while Chinese bankers did not subscribe to some of the more radical predictions of foreign takeover of the sector, there was nonetheless strong concern that liberalisation of the sector would pose a risk to their bank or their own employment security (Interview with current Ministry of Commerce official, 10 April 2015). While more moderate estimates of foreign bank growth by *Southern Weekend* and Standard Chartered both rejected any scenario in which foreign banks possessed both the ability and regulatory space to dominate the banking sector, these estimates still predicted foreign banks would make a rapid impact. *Southern Weekend* predicted a rise in market share for foreign banks from 2 per cent to 20–30 per cent in just 10 years (*The Banker* 2002). Standard Chartered released a report in 1999 which estimated a compound growth rate of 40 per cent per annum for foreign banks, and forecasted a more conservative 8 per cent share of the market for foreign banks by 2010 (*The Asian Wall Street Journal* 1999).

Despite this threat, China's entry to the WTO was viewed by China's policymakers as a means to promote reform during the period of relative economic uncertainty following the crisis. China's chief WTO negotiator Long Yongtu's statement regarding the pressures of the WTO accord on the economy that 'a nation cannot develop and become strong without a sense of urgency and a sense of crisis' had particular resonance in the banking sector (Kynge 1999). In an interview, UBS investment banker David Chin reported that during this time the senior management of China's banks would urge employees to implement reforms expeditiously due to the fear of impending competition from foreign banks (Interview with David Chin, UBS, 4 November 2015). Thus the Schumpterian concept of 'an ever-present threat' from foreign financial institutions with different organisational methods and use of more sophisticated technology became a driving force for change in the banking sector (Schumpeter 1994, 85).

Ultimately the terms agreed for China's entry to the WTO allowed for the gradual liberalisation of the financial sector to foreign competition. The successful conclusion of bilateral trade negotiations with the United States in November 1999 removed a major obstacle to China's accession to the WTO, which was achieved 2 years later. Under WTO terms, foreign banks could immediately undertake foreign exchange operations for Chinese banks and residents while local currency business with Chinese enterprises could occur within 2 years of accession. There was a commitment to remove restrictions relating to the establishment of foreign banks and branches within 5 years. Restrictions on foreign banks conducting local currency business with individuals were gradually removed, starting with trial cities Shenzhen, Shanghai, Dalian and Tianjin at the time of WTO entry. Each year a new group of trial cities was added until restrictions were removed completely after 5 years.

WTO entry provided a stimulus for regulatory development and the entry of foreign banks changed the landscape of the banking sector. WTO requirements would provide an impetus for the standardisation of China's banking rules and regulations. Chinese regulators had the challenge of incorporating these requirements while relying upon the country's regulatory experience to date and being responsive to changes in national conditions. WTO entry pushed the development of regulations for foreign financial institutions which would accord with the WTO rules and the Basel Accord while new, detailed regulations were issued in 2002 for foreign financial institutions (Liu, Mingkang 刘明康 2009). With the entry of foreign banks, competition would no longer be limited to loans and deposits which made up the vast majority of business for Chinese banks. The central bank moved quickly to enact regulation which provided approval and guidelines for the development of consumer credit operations, along with fee and commission products. These were applicable to all commercial banks. Reforms which reduced the responsibility of SOEs for the provision of employee homes and other items were an important precondition for the expansion of this market. The PBoC developed new rules on consumer lending for home mortgages in 1998 and for automobiles and general lending for individual consumption in the following year. Provisional rules for the use of fee-related products such as bills of acceptance, guarantees, financial derivatives and commission securities business were enacted in 2001. The ratio of non-interest income in bank revenue increased as a consequence. In 2003 ICBC President Jiang Jianqing revealed that the year-end volume of consumer credit would be RMB 400 million, equivalent to 16 per cent of the loan portfolio, after being at 'almost zero' in 1999 (Kynge and McGregor 2003). To encourage sales of new products, banks pushed improvements in customer service and developed incentivised sales teams to create demand for emerging products. Chinese banks partnered with international technology and payment companies such as Visa, who issued over a million international cards in 2003 (McGregor 2003b). The number of credit cards in China rose exponentially, reaching approximately 25 million by 2003, and there was enormous potential for growth in the future. The impetus provided by WTO entry created a new range of products which became an importance source of revenue growth for banks henceforth.

## Sovereignty of China's banking sector

Western banks, supported by their governments, international financial organisations and Western media, placed relentless pressure on officials to open up the banking sector. These outsiders to China's banking system were supported by a significant number of Chinese bankers, often working for foreign financial institutions. The pressure became particularly acute after the announcement of China's entry into the WTO and prior to the confirmation of a detailed plan of shareholding reform. At this critical juncture in reform, these banks sensed an opportunity to influence the reform process and gain control over China's valuable financial assets. The deregulation of the global financial services industry had precipitated a sharp rise in the mergers and acquisitions of financial institutions, particularly since the 1990s. This allowed for the development of large financial conglomerates such as Citigroup, JP Morgan Chase, Deutsche Bank and UBS. These financial conglomerates had gained a foothold in many countries around the world through cross-border M&A, and there was a growing consensus that China was the next major prize. Senior executives from these financial conglomerates, typically backed by their home country governments, lobbied intensely for the lifting of rules which blocked their access to the financial sector. The chief executives of the top investment banks all visited Beijing in late 2003 to lobby for access to domestic financial markets (Guerrera 2003). For a time Goldman CEO Hank Paulson was rumoured to visit China more than five times a year as part of his company's lobbying efforts (Guerrera and McGregor 2004).

Citigroup employees were perhaps the most vocal about their company's desire to establish itself in China's domestic banking sector through a strategy of M&A. In 2002, Citigroup Chairman Sandy Weill confirmed this priority, stating 'we put China as the top country on our list as to where we want to put our energies and invest our assets in the future'. Gaining control of the best assets in the domestic banking sector was the ultimate objective. Gary Clinton, Citibank's head of global relationship banking for Asia, further explained that 'the real opportunity will come when we can deal local currency with local consumers' (*China Securities Bulletin* 2002). Chairman Sandy Weill provided his vision of neoliberal reform path leading to a privatised and deregulated Chinese economy supported by international financial conglomerates: 'Over the next decade or next two decades, China is going to need hundreds of billions of dollars of foreign capital to privatise and develop the tens of thousands of companies that will grow and prosper in this country' (*China Securities Bulletin* 2002).

At this time, the international financial community was extremely confident that it knew what was best for the future of China's banking sector. The argument was made that without greater involvement of foreign financial institutions, China's banking sector would collapse. It was asserted by Western banks and the media that the stripping of NPLs was merely a stop-gap measure and that the China's banking reform model was failing. Merrill Lynch economist Shawn Xu considered the issue of bonds to AMCs as 'a largely superficial exercise' as the capital raised fell far short of that required to ensure capital adequacy, while Goldman Sachs economist Shan Li asserted that 'if you don't have a mechanism to ensure that these kinds of bad loans don't recur, you will run back into the same problems very quickly' (Lindorff 1998). This negative outlook was reinforced by the perception that AMCs were unable to resolve bad debt after the protracted nature of negotiations with international financial institutions regarding the sale of bad debt, despite it being offered at a fraction of face value. A report in 2001 from international ratings agency Fitch had confirmed that despite these measures China's banking system remained insolvent and required further capital injections (Beckerling 2001). Clean-up of the sector was viewed as beyond the state's capability. Standard and Poors calculated the cost of restoring the banking system to health at a massive US$518 billion, equivalent to 43 per cent of China's GDP in 2002, while Goldman Sachs put the cost at between 44 and 68 percent of GDP (*BusinessWeek: Magazine* 2002; *The Economist* 2003). One external commentator speculated that WTO entry could lead to a 'vicious downward spiral of credit contraction leading to business failures' as depositors withdrew funds from state-owned banks in urban areas, causing these institutions to become 'insolvent' as foreign banks assumed control of financial assets (Woo 2003, 7). Another predicted that the cost of recapitalisation, coupled with China's looming accession to the WTO, meant that China's banks were 'doomed' (Chang 2001, 142–43).

Critics of China's banking system advocated for the breaking up of large state-owned banks to facilitate privatisation and the introduction of foreign competition. While this was couched as a policy recommendation for a more open and competitive banking model, there was a clear irony given the massive size and market power of the international financial conglomerates pressing for market access. A *Wall Street Journal* article published in October 1998 and entitled 'A Chinese Model?' summarised the prevailing view that reform measures were inadequate while the financial sector continued to support its SOEs and that greater private ownership was required. The state's policy response to the AFC was deemed as 'evasive manoeuvres' that were 'self-defeating' and the economy would benefit significantly if 'the government cleared obstacles out of the way of the private sector and directed bank credit away from the state behemoths' (*The Wall Street Journal Europe* 1998). According to an editorial in the *Financial Times*, resolution of problems in the financial sector required the Communist Party to 'surrender control over the commanding heights of much of the economy' and introduce foreign competition to provide much needed discipline (*Financial Times* 2001). Goldman Sachs Asia Managing Director Fred Hu wrote that 'speedy resolution of NPLs and recapitalization … inevitably puts pressure on China's fiscal position (but) it is time for a 'Big Bang' substituting the piece-meal measures taken so far for a more aggressive, more comprehensive and accelerated reform strategy' (*Dow Jones International News* 2002). In 2003, Cit-igroup advised that China should 'tear apart the big four banks into relatively small units in order to switch on the process of bank reform', saying that 'if the big four are not broken up soon they will face bankruptcy'. Citigroup's Chief Economist for the Asian region, Yiping Huang, confirmed that this was a 'neces-sary step' in China's economic transition (Huang 2002).

## The second national financial work meeting

China's top officials rejected the discourse of Western-educated bankers and aca-demics at the Second National Financial Work Meeting, convened in February 2002 to determine the future direction of reform. In his speech General Secretary Jiang Zemin articulated the party view that the overall aim of this discourse was to further the power of Western nations and their financial institutions, stating that 'developed Western countries have already made control of international finance a strategic measure for global control'. Jiang cited the view expressed in Hunting-ton's book *Clash of Civilisations* that control and operation of the international financial system, hard currency and international capital markets were all strategic objectives for Western civilisation (Du, Hua 杜华 2007, 454). Despite the weak nature and small scale of the financial sector at the time, China steadfastly refused to relinquish sovereignty over the financial sector. If the state allowed foreign control over the financial sector, its ability to implement policies for the continued growth and development of the Chinese state would be severely compromised. When questioned about China's insistence on retaining control of its banks during this period, a CCB official responded, 'would America allow its banks to be taken over?' (Interview with CCB official, 10 March 2015).

It was nevertheless 'fully acknowledged at the highest policymaking level' of the party that there was a need for comprehensive reform of China's SOCBs (Liu, Mingkang 刘明康 2009, 82). Jiang announced that 'a fundamental trans-formation of the mechanism' in the banking sector would occur through share-holding reform. Shareholding reform would not break up the banks and listing of the banks as whole entities, controlled by the state, would instead provide 'an important exploration of effective forms of public ownership' (Du, Hua 杜华 2007, 458). Jiang indicated that, once completed, shareholding reform would provide a path to listing of SOCBs. Reform would be a gradual, transformative process. Wang Lianzhou, Vice Director of the NPC's finance and economic committee, said of the reform measures: 'There's no way China can reform all at once, so we have to move deliberately and carefully' (Lindorff 1998).

Although China's policymakers chose a different path from that advocated by Western financial institutions and their governments, they continued to be very open to ideas from external sources. David Chin, a banker at UBS, reported that he met and advised many levels of the state apparatus around this time. At the level of the State Council he met with the Premier Zhu and Vice Premiers Huang Ju and Li Langqing to discuss high-level policy objectives. He also met with PBoC for more detailed discussions of financial reform. According to Chin, officials were searching for case studies from abroad which could be applied to Chinese conditions (David Chin, email message to author, 18 January 2016). Besides their lobbying activities, Western financial institutions also provided consultancy services in the hope of securing future business, the most lucrative being assisting with the IPO of one or more state-owned banks. In 2002, the international accountancy firm PWC was one of the foreign firms engaged by the Chinese state to develop a road map of banking reform. The road map covered three major areas, namely finance, operations and accounting. Partner David Wu reported that the Chinese state did not have a concrete idea of how shareholding reform in the sector would proceed, and that the advice of international firms made 'a significant contribution to reform' (Interview with PWC Partner David Wu, 3 April 2015).

In contrast with the market-liberalising reforms advocated by the West, the Second National Financial Work conference had a clear focus on enhancing the stability of the financial system, strengthening regulation and developing a greater resilience to external threats. Indeed for Jiang Zemin, the strengthening of financial regulation was the 'priority among priorities' (Du, Hua 杜华 2007, 456). There was a sense that although China had now developed a regulatory framework, its mechanisms, such as the use of law and rules, had not contributed sufficiently to the development of ordered financial markets and the reduction of systemic risk. Liu Mingkang pointed in particular to the need to transform the culture of regulation in the financial sector from one of approval to one of active regulation of financial enterprises and markets (Liu, Mingkang 刘明康 2009). For Jiang Zemin, healthy and stable economic development depended on having a financial sector with 'solid foundations' to serve the real economy (Du, Hua 杜华 2007, 454). Jiang repeatedly emphasised the crucial need for China to mitigate financial risk and avoid financial crisis. It was evident that China's leaders had observed the dangers of the global financial system, particularly with respect to developing countries. Jiang pointed not only to the experiences of South East Asian nations in the AFC but also to the 1994 Mexico peso crisis, the IMF bailout of Brazil in 1999, the 2000/01 banking crisis in Turkey and the Argentine financial crisis of 2001 (Du, Hua 杜华 2007). It was imperative that China learned from the difficulties experienced by these countries.

## Conclusion

After the AFC, the party's concern for financial stability drove measures to mitigate risk which centralised party governance of the banking sector, reduced the level of NPLs and led to the development of a more robust regulatory system which adhered more closely to international standards. In the development of its banking regulatory system, China's officials had chosen a path that was very different from that taken by Western developed countries such as the United States which were pursuing policies of deregulation and financial liberalisation. The state viewed the market as a double-edged sword. While increasing the role of market forces in the economy had led to rapid economic growth, it had also produced high levels of speculation, poor governance of financial institutions and serious cases of financial crime, all of which had led to major financial instability. As such, policymakers selectively incorporated Western ideas about regulation which would help mitigate financial risk. At the Second National Financial Work Meeting, Jiang Zemin re-emphasised that the strengthening of financial regulation remained the highest priority for policymakers. Officials strived to learn not only from their own recent experience, but also those of other developing countries that had suffered recent financial crises. China's officials were able to resist pressure from Western bankers, supported by their governments and the media, to open up the banking sector to foreign competition. This occurred despite the weak state of China's banking sector, which was characterised by poor governance and high rates of NPLs. It was evident that the large international financial conglomerates were far superior to Chinese banks by any number of measures. The international financial community was confident it knew what was best for China's banking sector and advanced an argument that China needed to break-up and privatise its large state-owned banks and introduce foreign competition in order to save the sector from collapse. It is argued that China's past loss of economic sovereignty and oppression by foreign powers, which had contributed to the decline of China's economy after 1840, served as a reminder to officials of the risks of losing financial sovereignty. China's officials chose to maintain control of the country's future reform path and prevent Western control of its banking sector. In his management of the restructuring of GDE and bankruptcy of GITIC, Wang Qishan prioritised the country's financial stability ahead of the interests of international creditors, while also reducing the future moral hazard of SOEs. At the Second National Financial Work Meeting, China's officials announced their decision to implement shareholding reform and listing of the banks as whole entities in 'an important exploration of effective forms of public ownership' (Du, Hua 杜华 2007, 458). The state rejected proposals to break-up the banks or allow foreign banks to acquire control of domestic banking assets. This decision reflected the willingness of the party to transform the state-owned banking sector through engagement with international financial markets and external stakeholders, in much the same way as it had pursued reform of other SOEs over the previous decade. While reform excluded mass privatisation, this was not a rejection of market-orientated reform. Jiang Zemin proclaimed the goal of reform to be 'under the conditions of developing the socialist market economy, for the market to have a fundamental role in the allocation of resources' (Du, Hua 杜华 2007, 453). Improving national conditions would provide the basis for more fundamental reforms of bank governance and regulation which would greatly improve the safety and soundness of the banking sector going forward.

## References

Beckerling, Louis. 2001. 'China's Banking System Insolvent Warns Rating Agency'. *South China Morning Post*, 31 October 2001. www.scmp.com/article/361629/chinas-banking-system-insolvent-warns-rating-agency.

Brown, Owen. 2000. 'China to Step up Reform Of Banks as WTO Looms'. *The Asian Wall Street Journal*, 21 January 2000, sec. *Asian-Pacific News*.

Brown, Owen. 2001. 'China Will Shut Bulk of Trusts and Merge Remaining Entities'. *The Asian Wall Street Journal*, 17 July 2001, sec. *Asian-Pacific News*.

*BusinessWeek: Magazine*. 2002. 'Commentary: Are China's Banks Caught in Quicksand?'. 24 November 2002. www.businessweek.com/stories/2002-11-24/commentary-are-chinas-banks-caught-in-quicksand.

Chang, Gordon G. 1999. 'Time to Get Tough'. *Far Eastern Economic Review*, 29 July 1999.

Chang, Gordon G. 2001. *The Coming Collapse of China*. New York: Random House.

Chen, Qide. 1999. 'Financial Legislation Crucial for Integration'. *China Daily*, 30 September 1999. http://global.factiva.com/redir/default.aspx?P=sa&an=chndly0020010903dv9u000de&cat=a&ep=ASE.

*China Securities Bulletin*. 1999a. 'Guangdong Rules out GITIC Restructuring'. 10 March 1999. http://global.factiva.com/redir/default.aspx?P=sa&an=chsecb0020010903dv3a0006w&cat=a&ep=ASE.

*China Securities Bulletin*. 1999b. 'Former GITIC Managers under Official Probe-Weekly'. 11 March 1999. http://global.factiva.com/redir/default.aspx?P=sa&an=chsecb0020010903dv3b00079&cat=a&ep=ASE.

*China Securities Bulletin*. 2002. 'Citibank Opens to Chinese, Eyes Yuan Bonanza'. 25 March 2002. http://global.factiva.com/redir/default.aspx?P=sa&an=chsecb0020020325dy3p00003&cat=a&ep=ASE.

*Dow Jones International News*. 2002. 'China Bank Reform Cost Estimated at $373B: Goldman Sachs'. 11 December 2002. http://global.factiva.com/redir/default.aspx?P=sa&an=dji0000020021211dycb000kz&cat=a&ep=ASE.

Du, Hua 杜华, ed. 2007. *'Jinrong Gongzuo Wenxian Xuanbian (1978–2005)'* 金融工作文献选编 （一九七八——二00五）. Beijing: Zhongguo Jinrong Chubanshe.

*Financial Times*. 2001. 'Editorial Comment – China's Banks'. 15 May 2001. http://global.factiva.com/redir/default.aspx?P=sa&an=ftcom00020010715dx5f003z8&cat=a&ep=ASE.

Gasper, Don. 1999. 'GDE Strikes Deal with Creditors, Hongkong Standard'. *Hong Kong IMail*, 17 December 1999. http://global.factiva.com/redir/default.aspx?P=sa&an=hkstd00020010906dvch0012k&cat=a&ep=ASE.

Guerrera, Francesco. 2003. 'Wall Street's Drive to Scale the Great Wall – Banking'. *Financial Times*, 10 December 2003.

Guerrera, Francesco and Richard McGregor. 2004. 'Goldman Sachs Breaches China's Great Wall of Rules'. *Financial Times*, 10 August 2004.

Guyot, Erik. 1999. 'Chinese Province Unveils Proposal To Revamp Firm'. *The Wall Street Journal*, 26 May 1999, sec. International.

Harding, James. 1998. 'Survey – Tighter Controls Increase the Pain'. *Financial Times*, 16 November 1998.

Heilmann, Sebastian. 2005. 'Regulatory Innovation by Leninist Means: Communist Party Supervision in China's Financial Industry'. *The China Quarterly* 181 (1): 1–21.

Huang, Yiping. 2002. 'Is Meltdown of the Chinese Banks Inevitable?'. *China Economic Review* 13 (4): 382–87.

Jonquieres, Guy de. 1999. 'International – China "Seeking Better Deal on WTO"'. *Financial Times*, 11 September 1999.

Kuhn, Robert Lawrence. 2010. *How China's Leaders Think: The Inside Story of China's Reform and What This Means for the Future*. Singapore: Wiley.

Kynge, James. 1998. 'Asia-Pacific – China Considers Debt Restructuring Methods'. *Financial Times*, 16 July 1998.

Kynge, James. 1999. 'World News – Trade – WTO Entry "May Cause Banking Crisis"'. *Financial Times*, 17 November 1999.

Kynge, James. 2002. 'Banker's Fall Highlights China's Missing Funds'. *Financial Times (FT.com)*, 16 January 2002. http://global.factiva.com/redir/default.aspx?P=sa&an=FTC MA00020051015dy1g009pk&cat=a&ep=ASE.

Kynge, James and Richard McGregor. 2003. 'Paranoia Is Weapon of Choice against China's Banks – Beijing's Leaders Have Decided on Innovative Ways…' *Financial Times*, 24 November 2003.

Lardy, Nicholas R. 1998. *China's Unfinished Economic Revolution*. Washington, DC: Brookings Institution.

Lindorff, Dave and Kathryn Hanes. 1998. 'Can Zhu Rongji Save China's Banks?'. *Global Finance*, 1 May 1998.

Liu, Mingkang 刘明康, ed. 2009. *'Zhongguo Yinhang Gaige Kaifang Sanshinian (1978–2008) Shangce'* 中国银行业改革开放30年 *(1978–2008)* 上册. Beijing: Beijing Jinrong Chubanshe.

Lu, Lei, Xueqing Long and Jiwei Zhang. 2005. 'Trial of Former Banker Reveals Banking Loopholes'. *Caijing Magazine*, 22 August 2005. http://english.caijing.com.cn/2005-08-22/100013834.html.

McGregor, Richard. 2002. 'Bank of China Admits $483m Missing'. *Financial Times (FT.com)*, 15 March 2002. http://global.factiva.com/redir/default.aspx?P=sa&an=ftcom000 20020317dy3f0005w&cat=a&ep=ASE.

McGregor, Richard. 2003a. 'Top Chinese Banker Jailed'. *Financial Times*, 11 December 2003.

McGregor, Richard. 2003b. 'Credit Comes Cold Calling in Shanghai: Sales People Are Touring Chinese Office Blocks Touting Credit Cards. Richard McGregor Reports'. *Financial Times*, 29 December 2003.

Naughton, Barry. 2007. *The Chinese Economy: Transitions and Growth*. Cambridge, MA: MIT Press.

Nolan, Peter. 2008. *Integrating China: Towards the Coordinated Market Economy*. London: Anthem Press.

Nolan, Peter. 2017. Unpublished Manuscript.

*Reuters News*. 1998. 'China Sizes up Its Bad Bank Debt Problem'. 6 May 1998. http://global.factiva.com/redir/default.aspx?P=sa&an=lba0000020010925du5605yq7&cat=a&ep=ASE.

Schumpeter, Joseph Alois. 1994. *Capitalism, Socialism and Democracy*. London: Routledge.

Sheng, Andrew. 2009. *From Asian to Global Financial Crisis*. Cambridge, UK: Cambridge University Press. www.langtoninfo.co.uk/web_content/9780521134156_front matter.pdf.

Sheng, Xue and Zhan Gao. n.d. 'The Zhu Xiaohua Case: A Window into Chinese Hardball Politics'. The Jamestown Foundation. www.jamestown.org/programs/chinabrief/single/?tx_ttnews%5Btt_news%5D=3533&tx_ttnews%5BbackPid%5D=192&no_cache=1.

Shih, Victor. 2007. 'Partial Reform Equilibrium, Chinese Style: Political Incentives and Reform Stagnation in Chinese Financial Policies'. *Comparative Political Studies* 40 (10): 1238–62. https://doi.org/10.1177/0010414006290107.

*South China Morning Post*. 1998. 'Regional Regulators Map out Alternative Routes to Riches and Debt'. 23 October 1998. http://global.factiva.com/redir/default.aspx?P=sa&an=scmp000020010926duan0077p&cat=a&ep=ASE.

*South China Morning Post*. 1999. 'I Hope the Nightmare Ends'. 26 May 1999. http://global.factiva.com/redir/default.aspx?P=sa&an=scmp000020010910dv5q00rh9&cat=a&ep=ASE.

Stephen Grenville. 1998. 'The Asia Crisis, Capital Flows and the International Financial Architecture'. 21 May 1998. www.rba.gov.au/speeches/1998/sp-dg-210598.html.

Sun, Tao 孙弢. 2012. 'Hewei "Zhongguan Jinrong Qiye?" "何谓'中管金融企业?"' [What Is the Meaning of "Centrally Controlled Financial Enterprises"]'. *Jinrong Shijie* 金融世界, 28 July 2012. http://fw.xinhua08.com/a/20120728/1005589.shtml.

*The Asian Wall Street Journal*. 1999. 'Foreign Lending in China Expected to Grow'. 31 December 1999.

*The Banker*. 2002. 'Supplement – China – Welcoming the World – The Optimism Surrounding China's Entry into the World …' 1 May 2002. http://global.factiva.com/redir/default.aspx?P=sa&an=bkna000020020510dy5100004&cat=a&ep=ASE.

*The Economist*. 2003. 'Banking on Growth'. 16 January 2003. www.economist.com/node/1541253.

*The Wall Street Journal Europe*. 1998. 'The Chinese Model?'. 23 October 1998.

Woo, Wing Thye. 2003. 'The Macroeconomic Consequences of China's Partially-Reformed Economy'. *China Perspectives*, no. 50 (December). http://chinaperspectives.revues.org/686.

Wu, Jinglian. 2004. *Understanding and Interpreting Chinese Economic Reform*. Mason, OH: South-Western.

Wu, Qing. 2001. 'The Challenges Facing China's Financial Services Industry'. In *China and the Global Business Revolution*, by Peter Nolan, 813–38. New York: Palgrave Macmillan.

Xie, Ping. 1999. 'Bank Restructuring in China'. *BIS Policy Papers* 6: 124–29.

Zheng, Bijian. 2011. *China's Road to Peaceful Rise: Observations on Its Cause, Basis, Connotation and Prospect*. Abingdon, UK; New York: Routledge.

# 5 The development of a sound and sustainable banking model (2003–07)

In 2003 the first Chairman of the CBRC, Liu Mingkang, declared that the principal goal of banking reform was to fundamentally improve bank governance and risk management to order to prevent any further build-up of credit or operational risk and establish a sound and sustainable banking model. While China's officials had become aware of the risks posed by NPLs and large-scale fraud after the AFC, regulators had yet to establish the necessary governance mechanisms and systems of risk management that could address these threats effectively. Despite the sector having undergone a costly process of recapitalisation and NPL disposal, poor economic conditions had prevented further reform. According to international standards of prudential regulation, the Big Four banks had a negative capital adequacy rate and were insolvent (Liu, Mingkang 刘明康 2009a). China's officials seized upon the opportunity provided by improved domestic and international economic conditions, along with the enhanced financial strength of the state, to take an active role in the reform of the banking sector. The CBRC, in conjunction with other government agencies, would actively drive the development of a new system of corporate governance in China's large state-owned banks brought about by the programme of shareholding reform and listing announced by Jiang Zemin at the 2002 National Financial Work Meeting. Fundamental progress occurred throughout the banking sector. New city commercial banks and rural commercial banks were formed through mergers, with the initial focus of regulators on instituting systems of governance and risk management. While the state had a high level of engagement with international consulting firms and investment banks, minority investors and international financial regulators, it selectively adopted international practices. Party governance systems remained deeply embedded within the banking system, and were refined and adapted to the new corporate governance system.

The state's approach to reform was criticised by other parties. New CBRC Head Liu Mingkang felt obligated to defend the active role of the Chinese state after 2004 IMF Acting Managing Director Anne Krueger claimed that emerging market economies had failed to 'to put the past behind them' and showed only 'skin-deep' commitment to market reform, with politicians avoiding 'the pain' associated with such reform (Krueger 2004). In response, Liu emphasised the state's crucial role in 'grasping the rhythm' of reform and implementing it in an ordered and balanced fashion (Liu, Mingkang 刘明康 2004). *Red Capitalism* authors Walter and Howie claimed that China's banking system had arrived at 'the end of reform' in the year 2005 because reforms were not part of a journey towards a free market system (Walter and Howie 2012, 14).

## Improving banking supervision

There was a clear focus on improving banking supervision after the appointment of Wen Jiabao as Premier following the retirement of Zhu Rongji in 2003. Wen was a career bureaucrat and former head Head of the General Office of the Chinese Communist Party (CCP) Central Committee. His appointment as Secretary of the Central Finance Work Committee, an organisation that had centralised systems of party governance in the banking sector, had allowed him to gain a strong understanding of the problems facing the banking sector. Under Wen, the party chose to close down the Central Finance Work Committee and focus reform efforts on improving banking supervision. It was widely felt by experts, such as those in the State Council Research and Development Centre, that banking supervision under the PBoC had been inadequate, particularly given the alarming cases of bank fraud that had come to light since the late 1990s (Yang 2004). It is unclear whether the matter was discussed at the Second National Financial Work Meeting, though PBoC Governor Dai Xianglong himself acknowledged the weak state of bank supervision (Li, Junling 李峻岭 2002).

The decision to establish CBRC was reached after vigorous debate within the party that involved wide consultation with banking professionals and academics. Certain parties, such as scholars Professor Chen Gong Meng of HK Polytechnic University and Yi Xianrong of Financial Research Centre of Chinese Academy of Social Sciences (CASS), argued that the problem of weak banking supervision should be resolved through the reform of human resource mechanisms, strengthening the legal framework and improving regulators' grasp of important regulatory concepts (Ding, Nan 宁南 2003). An official interviewed argued that the principal issue had been the lack of resources allocated to banking supervision (Interview with government official, 10 October 2014). A review of the existing organisational arrangement took place. There was a feeling that the dual responsibility for banking supervision and monetary policy created a conflict of interest for the PBoC. Deputy Vice Director Wei Jianing of the State Council Research and Development Centre's Macro Department suggested that it was 'highly likely' the PBoC implemented more expansionary monetary policy 'from the perspective of bank managers to protect the interests of commercial banks' (Ding, Nan 宁南 2003). Wei's view that the regulatory and monetary policy functions should be split and a separate institution for banking supervision be established formed part of an official report to the CFWC from the State Council Research and Development Centre in 2002. The report also raised two potential alternatives, the creation of a bank supervisory bureau within the PBoC, and the establishment of a super-regulatory body covering the finance, insurance and securities sectors. Some within the party asserted that the PBoC should retain the banking supervisory function. In January 2003 an article was published in *Jinrong Shibao*, the official newspaper of China's financial industry, advocating for the current model of regulation and pointing to the evolution of the United States model as a sign of the declining relevance of sectoral regulation (*Financial Times* 金融时报 2002). Ultimately China's leaders elected to establish the CBRC in March 2003, despite some media reports suggesting that the bureau option had been chosen (see for example: Kynge 2002; *Sina Finance* 2002).

It is argued that the decision taken under Wen Jiabao to establish a separate regulatory agency in 2003, the CBRC, was likely a pragmatic decision based on which institutional form was best suited to ensure the safety of the financial system. The creation of a new agency would allow Wen, as a new leader, to have a strong influence over its organisational culture and push a new approach to regulation. The CBRC had a clear focus on banking supervision. This ring-fencing of the regulatory function allowed Wen to avoid the unnecessary bureaucratic challenges involved with creating a super-regulator and provided the new Head of the CBRC, Liu Mingkang, with a clear mandate through which to 'maintain a safe, sound and efficient financial system in China' (Liu 2003a).

The appointment of Liu Mingkang as the official to head the CBRC was based on his previous experience with restoring stability to the banking sector, his international outlook, his experience with corporate governance reforms, and his passion and commitment for the banking industry. Liu aimed to 'grasp the two ends and bring the middle forward', to drive improvement of all parts of the banking system (Liu, Mingkang 刘明康 2009a, 130). Liu had established a reputation as a 'firefighter' in the financial sector. He was appointed by the party to head up both Everbright Bank in 1999 and BoC in 2000 in the wake of the corruption scandals involving Zhu Xiaohua and Wang Xuebing respectively (Naughton 2003). Liu was a career banker, having worked in the banking sector since the beginning of Reform and Opening, who had gained rare international experience while at BoC. Liu was posted to London, where he obtained an MBA from the Cass Business School, University of London. He returned to the banking sector upon his return but also held important bureaucratic posts in China including Vice Governor of Fujian, Vice Governor of the PBoC and as a member of PBoC's monetary policy committee. Liu managed the restructuring and IPO of the Bank of China Hong Kong. He was also involved with the beginning of corporate governance reform and the transition of BoC's bloated, so-called 'honorary board of directors' towards a more streamlined and operational form (Liu, Mingkang 刘明康 2009a, 127). One CBRC staff member recently commented that CBRC was 'like a baby of Liu's'. Liu was extremely passionate about his job and would often give written notes on the reports of junior staff members. In this way, he was considered by the CBRC official concerned as 'easier to touch' than his successor Shang Fulin, a career bureaucrat (Interview with CBRC official, 19 March 2015). Wen Jiabao maintained a close relationship with Liu, who commented that 'he likes to sit down and talk with us. We pick the most important issues where we need his guidance' (Kuhn 2010, 268).

## The CBRC

> The CBRC, with strong support from the Chinese government, has actively pursued its statutory mandate for safety and soundness of the banking sector through promulgating a prudential framework benchmarked to international standards and continuously improving supervisory effectiveness. This effort is facilitated by substantial enhancement in corporate governance and risk management in the Chinese banking industry through three decades of reform and opening up.
>
> (IMF Financial System Stability Assessment Report for
> China (IMF 2011, 71))

The mandate of the CBRC as regulator of China's banking system, noted above by the IMF, was formally enshrined in the *Law of the People's Republic of China on Banking Regulation and Supervision* passed in December 2003. The CBRC was designated a ministerial-level institution, on par with the PBoC and above the vice-ministerial level of the large state-owned banks. Approximately 200 of the 400 original employees at the CBRC were transferred from the PBoC. The CFWC also contributed 120 employees (Naughton 2003, 3).

A CBRC official commented that CBRC's distinguishing feature was its high degree of exchange with the outside world, which was largely motivated by a desire to learn from the regulatory experience of other countries (Interview with CBRC official, 11 March 2015). On 10 May 2003 the CBRC International Advisory Council was established, 'indicating that the CBRC is committed to learn from international best practices and benchmark its supervisory practices against the international level' (CBRC 2007, 120). The council was made up of highly qualified senior regulators and bankers from developed countries such as former Chairman of the FSA Sir Howard Davies and CBRC Chief Advisor and former Chairman of the Hong Kong Securities and Futures Commission Andrew Sheng. The importance of the IAC function was underlined by the presence of Wen Jiabao at the first IAC meeting in November 2003. At the meetings council members would respond to briefings from CBRC senior officials, while the Presidents of the Big Four state-owned banks would also attend. From August 2003, Liu began to sign a series of MOUs which created a platform for cooperation with other financial regulators globally, with agreements reached with thirty-three countries or territories by 2008 (Liu, Mingkang 刘明康 2009a, 6). Liu was vocal about his desire for international institutions involved in banking supervision to serve the needs of developing countries such as China. In July 2003, Liu wrote a letter to Mr Jaime Caruana, Chairman of the Basel Committee on Banking Supervision, in which he stated that Basel II 'addresses the need of "internationally-active banks" in G10 countries' and could 'disadvantage banks in emerging markets'. Liu signalled that given Basel II's unsuitability, China would remain on Basel I for a few years. He called for the Basel Committee to assist with developing an internal ratings system for credit risk that was tailored to the needs of developing countries, thereby contributing 'to the safety and soundness of national and international financial systems' (Liu 2003b). The open engagement with the international financial community helped improve the perception of China's banking system internationally.

The CBRC has received criticism from the Western media and international financial institutions because, despite its open culture, its lack of independence is considered to have prevented the implementation of market reforms seen in the West. In the 'People's Republic of China: Financial System Stability Assessment', completed in 2011, the IMF identified that State Council control of 'budgeting arrangements, external headcount approval requirements and authority' threatened to 'compromise CBRC effectiveness and could affect operational independence'. The IMF felt that CBRC's place within the administrative system limited its ability to develop a 'forward-looking approach to resource planning', to evaluate staff in a transparent (presumably market-orientated) manner and remunerate staff at a level that would allow CBRC to attract the necessary human capital needed to cope with an increasingly complex and demanding regulatory environment (IMF 2011, 64). In a follow-up report released in 2017, the IMF noted that staff numbers had not increased for 10 years, despite the greater complexity and interconnectedness of China's banking system (IMF 2017). A CBRC official questioned on this issue confirmed that both the headcount, determined by the centrally controlled State Commission Office for Public Sector Reform, and the quality and retention of staff was a significant issue. As of March 2015, there had been no increase in salaries since the establishment of CBRC, including any adjustment for inflation.

While CBRC actively incorporates international standards of regulation, its function within China's bureaucratic system reflects historical patterns of political and economic organisation. As part of this system, it has a duty to implement the reform vision of party leaders. One CBRC official confirmed that the strong bureaucratic presence in the banking sector was a legacy of China's culture and history. She suggested that CBRC staff needed to 'understand its own system and its merits' and 'avoid the disadvantages' (Interview with CBRC official, 13 March 2015). When questioned on this topic, another CBRC official responded that CBRC's independence from the bureaucratic system was unimportant and that no government department could ever be truly independent of the objectives of the state. The official acknowledged that while small conflicts could occur between different arms of the state, there was no fundamental conflict with the common goal of stable economic development. He believed that it was a strength of China's bureaucracy that state organs were unified in striving for this common goal (Interview with CBRC official, 19 March 2015).

The sense of duty and responsibility of CBRC officials to the state's wider goal of stable development is a continuation of the role of scholar-officials in China within a politically united, centrally controlled bureaucracy for over 1,000 years. Many CBRC officials asked about their motivation for working at CBRC identified a strong sense of pride in guiding the direction of the banking sector and making a contribution to the country's prosperity. One CBRC official explained that she was most proud of her work relating to macroeconomic policies, principally because many of her reports went to the State Council level. She described a sense of pride knowing that her efforts would provide support to the country's leaders, influence the economy and hopefully improve the welfare of the people (Interview with CBRC official, 20 March 2015). The responsibility of officials in ensuring the well-being of citizens was a fundamental tenet of Confucianism, adopted as the state doctrine by Emperor Wu of the Han dynasty, more than 2,000 years earlier (Dawson 1964). Since that time, officials have been preoccupied with how best to fulfil this role through solving fundamental problems of food production, famine, water supply, and political stability (Will 1990; Nolan 2004). Interviews revealed that the mind-set has not fundamentally changed. When asked of the motivations of the leaders of the Big Four banks, one official quoted the Confucian saying 'a good scholar can become an official', explaining that many top banking officials had higher political aspirations and viewed their role in the bank as part of a political career within the bureaucratic system (Interview with CBRC official, 20 March 2015).

## Shareholding reform

Shareholding reform was the first step in changing the governance systems of China's banks. Liu Mingkang points out that, unlike in 1998–99 when the state 'spent money but did not buy a mechanism', this time the state had 'spent money and bought a mechanism' (Liu, Mingkang 刘明康 2009a, 126). Reforms would enable the development of a mixed ownership model within China's banks as discussed by party leaders at the 3rd Plenum of the 16th Party Congress in 2003. Jiang Zemin had confirmed at the Second National Financial Work Meeting that the state would retain control of its largest banks, which would be listed as whole entities as part of 'an important exploration of effective forms of public ownership' (Du, Hua 杜华 2007, 458). The success or failure of these reforms had enormous implications for the entire economy. There was much debate about the pros and cons of shareholding reform within the party, with officials concerned about the potential for economic instability or the loss of economic welfare from society. According to an article in the *Ming Daily* (21 April 1997), Jiang Zemin had been forced to defend the concept to party insiders prior to the 15th Party Congress, quoting Engels' view that shareholding reform was 'no longer private production' but instead 'profit-seeking joint production' (as cited in Ma 2010, 19). Through the publication *Economic Perspective* (Jingjixue Dongtai), academics voiced their support for shareholding reform as a form of 'public ownership with Chinese socialist characteristics', asserting that 'as long as the shareholding system can maintain and enhance the value of public capital, it should be regarded as a form of public ownership' (as cited in Ma 2010, 22).

Shareholding reform began a process of adapting Western principles of corporate governance within China's economic system. *China's Company Law* and *Commercial Bank Law* together formed the guiding legal framework for shareholding reform. According to these laws, the state became a shareholder of a modern shareholding company. This was a fundamental shift. Central Huijin Investments was established by the PBoC in December 2003 to exercise the state's function as an investor in major state-owned financial enterprises. The limited liability of the state as an investor was enshrined by law, replacing what previously had been an implicit guarantee of total support from the state in the case of financial distress. The articles of association, which accorded with both laws, provided the legal basis for the establishment of a modern structure of corporate governance for each bank. They called for the establishment of a shareholders' general meeting, a vehicle through which shareholders would elect members of a two-tier board structure, the board of directors and board of supervisors, and approve the annual budget and major investments. The board of the directors was responsible for guiding the bank's overall strategy and establishing a basic management structure. It was the duty of the board of supervisors to provide a check on the activities of the board and senior management and the financial operations of the bank, and ensure that the bank has met the necessary standards of risk management and regulatory compliance. The structure was supported by committees focusing on particular aspects of governance. These reported to either the board of directors or board of supervisors. Committees for risk management, audit, strategic development and personnel and remuneration typically reported into the board of directors.

As banking regulator, the CBRC drove the reform process and issued financial licences to the new shareholding companies. While Liu Mingkang acknowledged the challenge of transforming corporate governance practices, he vowed that 'my house will be responsible for making sure it will be a 'never-again story' through corporate governance and transparency' (Kynge 2003). In March 2004, the CBRC issued the *Guidelines on Corporate Governance Reforms and Supervision of Bank of China and Construction Bank of China*, a document that provided the first detailed vision of reform, namely to develop the banks 'into modern and internationally competitive joint-stock commercial banks' within 3 years. The guidelines explicitly stated that the banks' motive was one of profit maximisation and encouraged banks to streamline the personnel structure and introduce incentives for management. Within the new corporate governance structure, it was imperative for banks to 'have in place sound mechanisms for decision-making, internal controls and risk management'. Banks were encouraged to introduce foreign and domestic strategic investors in order to diversify equity structure, and learn from the 'international advanced management expertise, technology and methodology' of world-leading banks. In addition, the guidelines emphasised improved information disclosure and prudent accounting policies (CBRC 2004).

As the dominant shareholder across China's centrally controlled banks, it was the responsibility of Huijin (along with the MOF, which also held 50 per cent of ICBC and ABC shares and 28 per cent of BoCom) to act as a shareholder and not a government agency. Huijin Vice Chairman Jesse Wang summed up the change in the nature of banks' relationship with the statement:

> We're not [the banks'] mother-in-law, but they report to us as shareholders. One of our major missions is to help them restructure. … We want shareholders to get more returns on equity and on assets, so our directors trouble them every day.
>
> (Browne 2005)

The board of directors was composed of the firm's top management, acting as executive directors, along with non-executive directors. In the case of BoC and CCB, these were formally employed and remunerated by Huijin (Hu 2004a).

The incorporation of Western principles of corporate governance was by no means an acknowledgement by officials of the superiority of a Western model of corporate governance. Head of ICBC Jiang Jianqing remarked:

> What I especially wish to make clear is that the historically accumulated problems of China's state-owned banks are not caused by the fact that they didn't have a board of directors. Rather, they cannot be separated from the innumerable closely inter-related factors, including China's economic structure, the credit structure, the reform of SOEs, and the economic transition.
>
> (Ling and Zhang 2003)

Banking officials viewed shareholding reform as a means to improve bank governance and help resolve problems of asset quality and operational risk. New PBoC Head Zhou Xiaochuan pointed out that:

> if the banks rely on gradual improvement of asset quality, it will take a very long time and not meet the demand made of the financial system by the economy as a whole, and there could be conflicts between this and the need to support economic growth. Therefore, in this respect, we need new thinking and new measures.
>
> (*The Banker* 2003)

Officials hoped that the programme of shareholding reform would provide a means to 'change the method of long-term reliance on state credit and financial support' (Liu, Mingkang 刘明康 2009a, 119).

Western structures of corporate governance were established to complement party governance rather than replace it outright. An article published in the Chinese journal *Qiushi* in December 2003 promulgating Party views on reform stated 'we cannot indiscriminately copy capitalist democracy … and if we adopt their model, it is bound to lead to chaos'. Instead it was necessary to 'further raise the party's level of governance' through bringing about 'systematized, standardised and procedural decision-making' and to 'improve decision-making mechanisms' (*BBC Monitoring Asia Pacific* 2003). There was an emphasis on the development of 'scientific concepts' of restraint and supervision of personnel and also the use of law when exercising power. The party's appointment system was an integral part of this vision of governance. After the establishment of the corporate governance structure, appointment powers remained within the party. The party's COD retained the authority to appoint the top executives within the Big Five state-owned banks. A party committee, set up to deal with party-related matters such as the monitoring and discipline of officials, existed within each bank. According to the article, the vision was to 'intensify reform of the cadre personnel system' indicating that the use of this parallel structure would continue to evolve alongside newly formed corporate governance structures (*BBC Monitoring Asia Pacific* 2003). It could even be said that the party was learning from these structures to improve upon its own system. While, as one official commented, party structures were not ostensibly involved with the day-to-day running of the banks or in commercial decisions, the ultimate accountability of officials to the party defined the character of the system (Interview with government official, 10 October 2014). As such, China's bankers are compared to other officials rather than international bankers and the levels of remuneration for directors and executives in the banking sector is one representation of this.

Agencies such as the CBRC, PBoC and MOF were subject to party governance and the conceptions of reform which originated at the highest levels of the party. China's bureaucratic system ensured that officials would implement reforms according to the reform principles of the party centre and not pursue the neoliberal agenda favoured by the West. This is evident from the party's actions with respect to PBoC's ownership of Huijin. Huijin belonged to the PBoC during the recapitalisation of CCB and BoC, which utilised foreign exchange reserves administered by the PBoC-administered SAFE. The recapitalisation wiped out the MOF's shareholding and made Huijin the dominant shareholder following recapitalisation. It has been suggested the ' "market-based" approach' of the PBoC, which also impacted SOEs and the securities sector 'violated every norm of bureaucratic behaviour' (Walter and Howie 2012, 19). There was wide criticism of the PBoC's approach within China's bureaucratic system. An article on the National Development and Reform Commission (NDRC) website publicly denounced the PBoC, claiming it had wrongly assumed fiscal responsibilities of the MOF and suggested that the PBoC 'stop grabbing more power' (Browne 2005). This criticism of Zhou was linked by Western journalists to a so-called 'anti-reform agenda' (McGregor 2006). After the recapitalisation of CCB and BoC, the party chose to gradually transfer control of Huijin to the MOF. It appears likely that the PBoC lost control of Huijin because it was perceived to have exceeded its authority and attempted to implement a reform agenda that did not accord with the principles of the party centre. During ICBC's recapitalisation, MOF was allowed to retain a 50 per cent shareholding and by the time of ABC's recapitalisation Huijin had been acquired by a sovereign wealth fund, the China Investment Corporation, which was under effective MOF control.

## Financial restructuring of the large state-owned banks

Officials felt a heavy weight of responsibility to deliver improvements to bank governance given the enormous cost of recapitalisation and NPL stripping. Zhou

Xiaochuan publicly assured Chinese citizens that the decision to use China's foreign exchange reserves to recapitalise the banks followed a long period of research and debate by officials (Jin 2004). PWC Partner David Wu estimates the total cost for this round of recapitalisation of the Big Four to be approximately RMB 3.6 trillion or approximately RMB 2,800 per person in China in 2010 (David Wu 吴卫军 2010). The financial restructuring was necessary to remove the historical burden of economic transition from China's banks and give them the best opportunity to operate as sound and sustainable financial enterprises. This recapitalisation provided China's banks with an equity base that would allow them to meet the minimum requirements for capital adequacy as set out in Basel I. In addition to recapitalisation, China's banks also underwent another round of NPL stripping. In the case of CCB, 2003 financial data revealed the value of equity to be equal to – RMB 115.477 billion (Liu, Mingkang 刘明康 2009a, 123). The NPLs of CCB were auctioned to Cinda AMC at 50 per cent of face value. As this exceeded the estimate value of the bad loans concerned, it therefore provided another means to contribute equity to CCB (Liu, Mingkang 刘明康 2009a, 124). The state also recapitalised the large state-owned banks further by returning previously distributed earnings, including income tax paid (Liu, Mingkang 刘明康 2009a). Where any positive equity existed prior to the capital injection, it was generally used to bolster loan loss provisions.

## Auditing of the large state-owned banks

China's large state-owned banks were also audited for the first time by international accounting firms. Each audit required enormous resources. The audit of CCB required over 1.2 million hours of labour (Walter and Howie 2013). Executive Assistant President of BoC Zhu Min (now Deputy Managing Director of the IMF) said 'the PwC people went everywhere. They went to the branches because they have to sign off on their NPL figures, unless they want to become KPMG-PwC' (Kynge 2004). Auditors were typically appointed after trial audits of branches had produced satisfactory results. This was a highly significant first step towards greater transparency, a step that required China's leadership to allow international firms access to the minute details of its financial system. Bank employees were initially highly reluctant to divulge such details, though auditors were able to gradually overcome this resistance. The audits were vital to providing assurance to international investors about financial information such as NPL levels (Kynge 2004).

## Minority investors

### *Reasons for the introduction of minority investors*

Minority investors were introduced so that the banking sector could incorporate ideas and technology from outside to facilitate the transformation of the banking sector. As Liu Mingkang suggests, 'the main reason for bringing in investors was not to bring in capital, but rather to bring in advanced management experience and technological methods' (Liu, Mingkang 刘明康 2009a, 134). The introduction of minority investors was a requirement of the State Council group on SOCB shareholding reform. Minority investors could improve systems of internal control and risk management, assist with the training of management personnel, and encourage innovative product development and better service. Minority investors would also bring life to the new shareholding system and corporate governance structure. The rights of minority investors were exercised through the new governance structure, causing this process to become more robust than it would be under total state ownership. A further reason for the introduction of minority shareholders was to give confidence to international financial markets. The decision of international financial institutions to invest in China's banks, reached after performing due diligence, was an important step towards listing. It amounted to an acknowledgement by these institutions that China's banks were ultimately capable of entering the world of international financial markets (David Wu 吴卫军 2009).

In December 2003, CBRC published regulations that reflected the state's desire to find investors that were best suited to drive the transformation of China's large state-owned banks. Overseas financial institutions that wished to become minority investors had to possess the necessary scale, profitability and regulatory record and had to demonstrate a long-term interest in China's economic development. Shareholding for individual and total holdings by foreign financial institutions was limited to 20 per cent and 25 per cent respectively (CBRC 2003). During the second half of 2004, the CBRC further defined the key principles for foreign investment. These included the concept that cooperation with foreign investors would occur according to market principles and that the CBRC would not intervene in the selection and negotiation processes. CBRC would instead screen investors and monitor the investment to assess whether it had the impact desired by the state. Minority investors would be locked in for a minimum period of 3 years and were required to have representation at board level and participate in the corporate governance of the bank concerned. With regards to sovereignty, CBRC stated unequivocally that the state would not give up its absolute control of the Big Five banks (Liu, Mingkang 刘明康 2009a).

Officials were concerned that some ideas promoted by minority investors could be harmful to China's banking system. Western governments and their financial institutions had promoted a neoliberal model characterised by deregulation and financial liberalisation. In the eyes of China's officials, adoption of this model had created a dangerous and insufficiently regulated global financial system that was highly vulnerable to financial crises. These ideas were seen as a potential threat to the stability of China's banking sector and potentially its entire economy. Officials felt a strong weight of responsibility to protect China's banking sector against a crisis that could derail China's economic reform programme and create social instability. Officials were also concerned that if foreign banks gained a high degree of influence over China's banking sector, the sector would not be effective in implementing the country's reform goals or serving the real economy. A critique published in *Securities Market Weekly* suggested that China's corporate governance reforms could create a layer of professional managers whose interests in short-term profits will be aligned with those of foreign capitalists. The authors alleged that managers would employ 'complex technical terms' to deceive policymakers and advance their own interests to the detriment of the country. According to the article,

> under the guidance of market-orientated corporations, the financial system is now progressively separating itself from the fundamental benefits of modernisation, by itself becoming part of an international capital chain of interests which at its core benefits the United States as the financial imperial power.
>
> (*Zhengquan Shichang Zhoukan* 证券市场周刊 2005)

There was intense deliberation within the Party about how best to incorporate helpful ideas and technology while avoiding the spread of harmful ideas that could threaten stability and economic development. Much of the debate centred around restrictions on foreign ownership, which were directly linked to the influence that foreign financial institutions could exercise on the corporate governance of Chinese banks through seats on the board of directors. The restrictions of 20 per cent and 25 per cent for individual and total holdings by foreign financial institutions not only safeguarded the sovereignty of Chinese banks but also limited the influence of the ideas of Western financial institutions. The restrictions permitted officials to maintain the fundamental character of China's banking system. There was some support within the system for the softening of restrictions in order to create a dynamic that would support deeper internal reform of the banks. Vice Chairman of CBRC Tang Shuangning publicly raised the idea of relaxing ownership restrictions on small and medium-sized banks (Kong 2006). This was strongly considered in December 2005 when Citigroup, as part of a consortium of foreign and domestic investors, bid US$3 billion for 85 per cent of the troubled Guangdong Development Bank, 'widely considered one of the weakest banks in the country' (Kong 2006). It was argued that relinquishing control of financial enterprises was in the interests of the banking sector, which needed 'foreign groups' management expertise and corporate governance discipline' (Kong 2006). The bid implied a total foreign ownership stake of 49.9 per cent, of which 40 per cent would belong to Citigroup. As this exceeded the regulatory limit of 25 per cent, Citigroup attempted to pressure the Chinese government to relax this requirement, going as far as to ask former President Bush to write a letter of support (Shih 2011). French President Jacques Chirac also visited China personally to lend support for rival bidder Societe Generale (McGregor and Wighton 2006). After 7 months of deliberation, Wen Jiabao confirmed the party's decision that the restriction on total foreign ownership would remain at 25 per cent (Shih 2011).

### Sale to minority investors

Foreign financial institutions were initially very reluctant to invest in China's banks. Liu Mingkang reports that upon inviting investment in BoC and CCB, only four large-scale financial institutions showed interest. Of these four, Citigroup, Bank of America, Morgan Stanley and RBS, both Citigroup and Morgan Stanley later dropped out. There was no response at all to ICBC's initial invitation (Liu, Mingkang 刘明康 2009a). While financial restructuring had raised capital adequacy and lowered NPL levels, there was little confidence that Chinese banks could become sustainably profitable given their past performance. Foreign bankers were also wary of the influence of China's bureaucracy on lending, particularly with SOEs as the major clients. The project of the newly-created State-owned Assets Supervision and Administration Commission (SASAC) to restructure China's large SOEs was at an early stage, and there was also scepticism towards the goal of developing competitive and commercially-orientated firms that were state-owned. Former Chief Representative of Deutsche Bank Shanghai, Stephen Harner, stated at the time that foreign banks '... much prefer to be on their own', while another former banker commented the entry of foreign banks was 'a political favor to the government. That's it' (Leggett 2001). The fact that many investors had already taken a minority stake in small commercial banks decreased the likelihood of gaining regulatory approval for a stake in the large state-owned banks, thus further limiting the number of eligible investors. The lack of willing foreign investors caused negotiations to be long and arduous as the remaining investors bargained for a lower price.

### Transfer of knowledge from minority investors

Minority investors made a significant commitment to improving the practices of Chinese banks. As part of the negotiation process, the parties devised a comprehensive strategy for improvement that became part of a formal agreement for cooperation. Foreign financial institutions typically kept offices within Chinese

*Table 5.1* Minority investments in China's large state-owned banks

| Bank | Date of investment | Minority investor | Shareholding (%) |
| --- | --- | --- | --- |
| BoCom | August 2004 | HSBC | 19.9 |
| CCB | August 2005 | Bank of America | 8.515 |
| | | Asia Financial Holdings Pte Ltd. | 5.878 |
| BOC | December 2005 | The Royal Bank of Scotland | 10 |
| | | UBS | 1.61 |
| | | Asian Development Bank | 0.24 |
| | | Asia Financial Holdings Pte Ltd. | 5 |
| ICBC | March 2006 | Goldman Sachs Group | 6.05 |
| | | Allianz Group | 2.36 |
| | | American Express | 0.47 |

banks with the presence of a stable team to coordinate a wide range of projects. In its partnership with CCB, Bank of America committed the equivalent of fifty full-time Bank of America employees to work at the bank (Linebaugh 2006a). HSBC sent ninety-nine full-time staff to BoCom and the two banks cooperated on more than fifty separate projects. In the initial years of co-operation, HSBC staff executed more than one thousand training courses at BoCom (Liu, Mingkang 刘明康 2009a, 138, 139). Interaction between minority investors and Chinese banks occurred through representatives at the board level, meetings between the chairmen of the Chinese bank and the corresponding foreign financial institutions, and at an operational level.

Officials prioritised the improvement of systems of corporate governance, risk management and internal control. The cooperation between ICBC and Goldman Sachs had a clear focus on developing the capability to manage market risk. The two parties established a project committee and seven working groups for project implementation. There were working groups specifically for corporate governance, risk management, NPL management and staff training (Liu, Mingkang 刘明康 2009a). According to the ICBC 2007 Annual report,

> Goldman Sachs assisted the Bank in carrying out risk strategy studies, stress testing, loan portfolio risk management, country risk management, risk management for the Group's customers, and optimization of the credit business process, and put forward suggestions on improving the management of market and operational risks.
>
> (ICBC 2008, 92)

ICBC established the post of Chief Risk Officer in July 2006 to 'assist the President to supervise and decide on risk management of the Bank' (ICBC 2007, 100). RBS seconded four experts on risk management to BoC. These experts worked with BoC staff to design training courses on corporate and credit risk and also to provide a framework for classifying and processing operational risks. ADB provided BoC with advice regarding anti-money laundering, operational risk management and internal control (BoC 2007). BoCom incorporated a comprehensive range of risk management concepts from HSBC, including the concept of risk-orientated audits. The adaptation of these concepts fundamentally changed the approach of management to risk (Liu, Mingkang 刘明康 2009a). From 2006 to 2007, Bank of America and CCB worked together on six projects relating to the development of IT infrastructure and two projects relating to risk management (Liu, Mingkang 刘明康 2009a, 139). Goldman Sachs provided over 2,000 ICBC staff with training at its Pine Street Initiative, which included courses on risk management and leadership (Liu, Mingkang 刘明康 2009a, 141). At Shenzhen Development Bank, the introduction of minority investors helped address serious failures in corporate governance, brought to light following the arrest of its former Chairman and Party Secretary for the granting of illegal loans (Mitchell 2006). Chairman and CEO Frank Newman was appointed in June 2005 subsequent to an 18 per cent investment by

Newbridge Capital. Newman stabilised the bank after this scandal and central-ised the coordination of credit and management functions to reduce operational risk (Linebaugh 2006a; McMahon 2010).

Minority investors also enabled Chinese banks to introduce new products, improve customer service, and upgrade and streamline core business practices. As part of its investment into BoCom, HSBC worked with BoCom's Pacific Credit Card unit, which had issued over 10 million credit cards by 2008 with annual spending of roughly RMB 100 billion, surpassing some of the large state-owned banks (BoCom 2009a, 71). In October 2009 the two banks announced the intention to launch a credit card joint venture company due to 'the unexpected rapid growth of the business of the Existing Card Centre', the significant contri-bution of 'human resources, materials and financial resources' by Joint Venture (JV) partners and the 'huge potential of the PRC credit card market' (BoCom 2009b). American Express facilitated the development of a credit card customer service model and process within ICBC. Together the two companies jointly launched two credit cards. Allianz assisted ICBC with the development of its bank insurance agency service and helped introduced new insurance products (ICBC 2008). BoC worked with RBS Group on corporate banking projects relat-ing to aircraft financing, shipping financing, and supply chain financing (BoC 2007). In 2007, with the assistance of Bank of America, CCB rolled out a project that standardised service and sales functions in approximately 39 per cent of total branches. The project more than doubled sales volume and dropped waiting times by 29 per cent (CCB 2007, 16). BoC was able to upgrade its core business practices after reviewing RBS Group practices on with respect to treasury, plan-ning, budgeting, internal funds transfers and product pricing (BoC 2007).

## Listing of China's large state-owned banks

Officials gained significant knowledge during consultation with international firms during the shareholding reform of Bank of China (Hong Kong), which 'would pave the way for restructuring and IPO of Chinese banks' (Chin 2016). Bank of China (Hong Kong)'s reform brought together a total of twelve affiliates in Hong Kong which were 'loosely coordinated by a "Hong Kong management office"' (Chin 2016). Goldman Sachs and UBS were rewarded for their contri-butions to banking reform with the opportunity to act as lead underwriters for the bank's IPO. In his autobiography, then Goldman Sachs CEO Hank Paulson described his company's wide-ranging role as that of a 'policy advisor, manage-ment consultant and investment banker' (as cited in Chin 2016). Chinese offi-cials worked with international advisors to carve out NPLs, develop a new system of risk management, and institute corporate governance and organisa-tional structures that were in accord with international practices. Important dis-cussions were held regarding the sequencing of such reforms and costs and benefits of NPL stripping prior to listing. BoC Chairman Liu Mingkang ulti-mately favoured UBS's recommendation for a Hong Kong listing, based on the premise that the 'marginal benefit of a United States listing was not meaningful compared to the legal and accounting costs' (Chin 2016). Standard Chartered Bank was brought in as a strategic investor at the time of IPO, having committed to buying US$50 million dollars' worth of stock to bolster investor confidence and facilitate further cooperation post-listing (Irvine 2002). Bank of China (Hong Kong) provided an important reference point for the appetite of overseas investors for Chinese financial assets. While Bank of China (Hong Kong) was in a stronger financial position than the large state-owned banks on the mainland, it still had to overcome the recent scandals that had plagued its parent company BoC which had exposed the bank's weak corporate governance and poor control of operational risk.

Officials determined that banks with the most favourable financial circumstances would list first. This was part of a 'one bank, one strategy policy', aimed at reducing the difficulty of reform implementation (Liu, Mingkang 刘明康 2009a, p121). Wu Xiaoling, Vice Governor of the PBoC, commented that 'the situation varies from bank to bank, so we need to study the issue according to each bank' (Kynge and McGregor 2003). The levels of capital adequacy and NPLs of the banks were important in determining the listing order. The listing of China's large state-owned banks on the HKSE began in June 2005 with the IPO of BoCom and ended in August 2010 with the listing of ABC. Between October 2005 and September 2006, CCB, BoC and ICBC all listed on the HKSE. Governance reforms at ABC proceeded at a more gradual pace due to the bank's high NPL rate and weak financial circumstances.

Processes of corporate governance and financial restructuring occurred throughout the banking sector. Regulators hoped to expose financial institutions to external market discipline where possible. The domestic listings of shareholding banks such as Pudong Development Bank (1999), Minsheng Bank (2000) and Huaxia Bank (2003) preceded listings of the large state-owned banks. Minsheng Bank, along with other shareholding banks such as China Merchants Bank and CITIC Bank, successfully listed on the HKSE. The restructuring of city commercial banks and rural commercial banks involved mergers with other commercial banks and cooperatives. The listing of Bank of Ningbo, Bank of Beijing and Bank of Nanjing on the Shanghai Stock Exchange in 2007 marked a breakthrough for city commercial banks. In 2010, Chongqing Rural Commercial Bank was listed on the HKSE.

The success of the IPOs allowed the state to increase capital adequacy in China's banks significantly without compromising financial sovereignty. The IPOs were vastly oversubscribed as investor euphoria for grabbing a piece of China's economic growth story trumped any concerns about their weak financial state. One journalist commented after ICBC's 2006 IPO that 'in the past year, sentiment toward China's lenders has made a 180-degree shift' (Linebaugh 2006b). Shares allocated to institutional investors for the BoC listing were oversubscribed by up to twenty times, while ICBC's listing raised over US$300 billion after extraordinary demand from institutional investors for an estimated value of US$19.1 billion worth of stock (Lague 2006; Linebaugh 2006b). CCB's IPO was the largest ever in the global banking industry, while ICBC's 2006 IPO became the largest IPO ever until it was eclipsed by the US$22.1 billion IPO of ABC in 2010. CCB's capital adequacy ratio rose from 11.29 per cent to 13.57 per cent in 2005, with proceeds from the IPO being used 'for strengthening the Bank's capital base', while ICBC's rose over 4 per cent in 2006 to 14.05 per cent (CCB 2006, 4, 91; ICBC 2007, 5). This was achieved despite only a portion of the banks' total shares being available to external investors, allowing the state to retain control of its large, centrally controlled banks. Following ICBC's IPO, only 13 per cent of total shares were not subject to restriction on sale, while Huijin, MOF and the National Council for Social Security Fund of PRC together held approximately 75 per cent of total shares (ICBC 2007, 16, 19).

While raising capital was important, improving bank governance was the primary objective of listing (Liu, Mingkang 刘明康 2009a). After listing, China's banks were now required to conform to international best practices. The banks became part of a new institutional setting where newly introduced concepts of governance were now standard and were monitored and enforced by more robust laws and regulation. The public disclosure of detailed financial information, which began during preparation for listing as part of the due diligence process and continued in a manner and frequency which accorded with the rules of the HKSE, represented a huge change in the culture of the banks. The enhanced transparency facilitated more rigorous supervision of bank operations by regulators and investors, as well as third party organisations such as rating agencies. Reporting standards included specific guidelines by the HKSE on the corporate governance practices of listed firms. Within this structure, shareholders were able to exert influence on bank governance. Independent non-executive directors had a duty to protect the interests of minority shareholders. Shareholder rights were supported by a more comprehensive and effective legal system than that of the mainland.

## Corporate governance after listing

CBRC actively fostered good practices of corporate governance within Chinese banks. Liu Mingkang saw corporate governance as his 'biggest' challenge, saying that CBRC had 'taken bold steps, but they're not sufficient. The credit culture is still very weak in China. It must be nourished: discipline, incentives, education, cultivation – it's a huge endeavor' (Kuhn 2010, 270–71). Less than 1 year after listing, Bank of China (Hong Kong) Head Liu Jinbao was investigated for granting illegal loans while working in Shanghai, with a suspected connection to Shanghai property tycoon Zhou Zhengyi (Leahy and McGregor 2003). This episode demonstrated to officials that it was vital to strengthen the corporate governance framework to prevent fraud and allow it to play a greater role in guiding the commercial decisions of China's banks. As regulator, CBRC was able to exert influence through its right to examine the qualifications of top-level managers and board members and veto appointments. CBRC sets the tests which determine the competence of directors. CBRC also closely observes the board meetings of the large state-owned banks. CBRC typically sends two or three representatives to each board meeting to listen and observe, usually senior heads of departments. Jim Stent, who previously held the post of Non-executive Director of Everbright prior to joining its supervisory board, suggested that bank staff did not view this as interference but rather as a means for CBRC to understand their concerns, and that CBRC support for bank improvement was appreciated within the sector (Interview with Everbright Supervisory Board Member Jim Stent, 16 May 2015). It appears that directors less familiar with China's system and more familiar with Western forms of corporate governance experienced some frustration with CBRC's active role. One director and member of the audit committee of a Big Four bank reportedly became frustrated with what he perceived as CBRC interference and resigned from his post (Interview with PWC Partner David Wu, 3 April 2015).

At the beginning of 2006, CBRC issued the *Guideline on the Corporate Governance Reforms and Supervision of State-owned Commercial Banks*, developed from the initial guidelines for corporate governance reform of the pilot banks, CCB and BoC (CBRC 2007). This guideline standardised corporate governance procedures for state-owned banks. In April, it was further amended to create a more robust and functional structure. Banks were required to align meetings of shareholders, the two boards and senior management to facilitate communication between each tier of the corporate governance structure (CBRC 2007). The duties and incentives of each role were further refined. CBRC required banks to develop market-orientated HR management systems and, with CBRC support, establish performance evaluation schemes. In 2007, the CBRC focused on the establishment of 'sound procedures' for board meetings, improving the effectiveness of the supervisory board and developing 'the check and balance mechanism for senior management' (CBRC 2008, 72). Liu's aim to 'grasp the two ends and bring the middle forward' was also evident, as he sought to apply the standards of listed banks to the industry in general. Small and medium-sized banks were encouraged to establish a structure of corporate governance, while the *Guidance on Corporate Governance of Trust Companies* was issued in 2007 (CBRC 2008). In July 2007, the CBRC issued rules on information disclosure, which set rules on the disclosure of financial statements, corporate governance and risk management practices, and internal control procedures (CBRC 2008). Widely followed in 2007, this had become standard practice within city commercial banks by 2010, with listed banks subject to even stricter disclosure requirements as set out by CSRC (CBRC 2011a). The issuance of guidelines each year on detailed aspects of corporate governance represented a core element of CBRC's policy-making process. In 2010 the State Council asked the CBRC to consolidate these guidelines and a 'set of common principles and standards' was drafted regarding 'good corporate governance applicable to all types of commercial banks' (CBRC 2011a, 54). The following year *Guidelines on Corporate Governance of Commercial Banks (Consultative Document)* was released and previous guidelines were abolished, signifying a milestone in the policy-making process (CBRC 2011b). A CBRC official interviewed reported in 2015 that the Basel Committee for Banking Supervision (BCBS) was working with the CBRC on combining rules around information disclosure and transparency into one comprehensive document, with the capability of small-scale banks to comply with BCBS templates an important consideration (Interview with CBRC official, 13 March 2015).

The large state-owned banks introduced independent, non-executive directors into their corporate governance structure. Liu Mingkang had been encouraged by the work of a director representing the International Finance Corporation (IFC) on the board of Nanjing Commercial Bank. 'They invited an independent director called John Langlois (on to the bank's board),' Mr Liu said. 'He is a big mouth. Push, push, push. In six months [the bank] has changed quite a lot' (Kynge 2003). These directors typically had a high level of academic or professional experience in the banking sector and many had strong international experience. These directors were a force in pushing a more rigorous application of corporate governance processes. The contribution of Hong Kong directors in upgrading the audit functions of large state-owned banks through their roles on audit committees, for example, is an important part of this story that requires further examination. Liu Mingkang reported that independent directors were quick to question executive board members on CBRC reports, asking 'Why didn't we know this? What happened? And what's your plan to rectify or mitigate the risks noted by CBRC?' (Kuhn 2010, 270). In this way, non-executive directors helped to create a more open atmosphere within the board and its committees. Independent directors were able to create discussion and debate in meetings that had previously been highly stylised.

The Party remained deeply embedded within the corporate governance structure of China's banks. The COD retained de facto authority over the appointment of the board-level executives of the banks. The chairmen of centrally controlled banks were typically officials that had been rotated from positions in the central bank. BoC Chairman Xiao Gang (2003–13), CCB Chairman Guo Shuqing (2005–11) and ABC Chairman Xiang Junbo (2009–11) had all served as a Vice Governor of the central bank. BoCom Chairman Niu Ximing (2013–) had formerly assumed the post of Vice Chairman of ICBC. The new corporate governance system functioned alongside the party system and was gradually strengthened. The powers vested in the board of directors and supervisory board according to *China's Company Law* provided them the authority to supervise the performance and recommend the dismissal of directors or senior management where necessary. According to an official from the COD, appointments of provincial and large city branch heads of centrally controlled banks gradually became more competitive after listing. These were posts that had previously been allocated to officials (Sun 2012). For the recruitment of new chief risk officers and chief credit officers, CCB and BoC both hired head-hunters which operated internationally (Hu 2004b). In 2012 the office of the Central Committee published a set of rules on leaders of centrally controlled financial enterprises which summarised the philosophy of the state towards the dual responsibility of officials to the bureaucratic system and shareholders. The Head of the Financial Research Institute at the State Council's Research and Development Centre,

Ba Shusong, explained that according to these rules officials needed to integrate both responsibilities and in doing so 'achieve systemisation, standardisation and greater transparency' (PRC Central Government 2012). The state adapted its policy of rotation of officials to the appointment of auditors from 2010, favouring the benefits of greater auditor independence over establishing long-term partnerships (Gillis 2012). The principle of rotation also applies to non-executive directors, which have a maximum term of 6 years.

## Risk management

CBRC drove the adaption of international standards of risk management to Chinese conditions. In its 2011 Financial System Stability Assessment report, developed with the assistance of CBRC, the IMF commented that 'CBRC guidance is generally of high quality and was often developed directly from Basel documents' (IMF 2011, 61). While China delayed implementation of Basel II due to issues of suitability, the provision of international standards and best practices by the Basel Committee enabled risk management in China's banks 'to evolve at an accelerated pace' (Liu 2003b). The minimum capital requirements for China's banks were not adjusted, but CBRC encouraged banks to adopt the most useful elements of the other two tiers of Basel II, namely supervisory review and market discipline. CBRC has required foreign banks in China to complete surveys and questionnaires relating to regulatory practices of these banks in their home jurisdictions (He 2013, 294). In its 2009 annual report, CBRC acknowledged the contribution of such surveys in the development of standards for risk management (CBRC 2010).

## Credit risk

CBRC adopted international best practices to combat credit risk. According to the IMF, credit risk 'is the most important risk facing Chinese banks and will remain so for some time' (IMF 2011, 62). One of the most pressing tasks for CBRC upon its inception was to complete the roll-out of the five-tier loan classification system based on the United States system. In 2003 it issued a notice requiring all banking institutions to adopt this system by 2004. Implementation within RCCs followed and by the end of 2006 all banking and NBFIs employed the new loan classification system. Because the new system required banks to consider risk in a more forward-looking manner, CBRC actively implemented training programs to enable bank employees to grasp this new concept of risk (CBRC 2007). Similarly, international practices were also adopted within the credit approval process. The use of a credit score to assess loan applications became common practice in SOCBs from 2003. It was based on a business report and 3 years of audited statements (Yeung 2009). This method, along with the use of the 'five Cs of credit', which incorporate the more intangible qualities of a borrower, were both widely used by Western banks. While CBRC does not have specific rules for loan authorisation, bank practices have steadily evolved towards a greater centralisation of loan approvals (Interview with CBRC official, 19 March 2015). At China Everbright, the power of individual sub-branch Presidents to approve loans was gradually reduced and then replaced by centralised lending approval centres established in Eastern, Southern and Western China by 2004 (Yeung 2009). The lack of provisions and measures for dealing with problem assets, traditionally a weakness in the banking sector, had been addressed through the development of improved accounting standards (IMF 2011). This was achieved through the development of a modern legal framework for accounting followed by gradual convergence with International Financial Reporting Standards from 2005. It was supported by extensive visits of staff in the MOF accounting department to their counterparts in Western countries, particularly since 1999, to gain the necessary exposure and understanding of international practices (World Bank 2009).

The CBRC has been cautious with the development of financial derivatives, openly prioritising the development of functional supervision ahead of financial innovation (see for example CBRC 2008). Even before the 2008 financial crisis, Liu Mingkang felt that complex financial derivatives, such as collateralised debt obligations and credit default swaps, had the potential to create severe financial instability and that it was the role of CBRC to protect China from such instruments. The gradual development of CBRC's rules regarding derivatives and credit asset securitisation, beginning in 2004, reflected CBRC's desire to develop 'practical, transparent, and straight-forward innovations that serve the fundamental demands of the real economic sectors' (CBRC 2011a, 41). In 2017, the CBRC confirmed that there is no intention to ever introduce complex innovations such as correlation trading, re-securitisation and synthetic products (IMF 2017).

In 2004 and 2005 the CBRC and other agencies worked with the IFC to develop a legal framework that would permit the use of accounts receivable and other movable assets such as machinery or patents as collateral. This work was reported to the NPC's Legislative Affairs Work Commission and later became part of China's *2007 Property Law*. The project team visited Canada and United States to learn from their experiences. According to a CBRC official who worked on the project, certain aspects of the proposal were not accepted as were not perceived as compatible with China's legal tradition, which largely stemmed from Japanese and German civil law (Interview with CBRC official, 11 March 2015).

In addition to the adoption of international standards, the CBRC also needed to address aspects of credit risk that were specific to China's national conditions. 'The client risk statistics and early warning system' was developed by CBRC internally and completed in July 2004. It was designed to address the risk of enterprises borrowing excessive capital through multiple subsidiaries to prevent banks from gaining a full picture of their financial circumstances, thereby exploiting the lack of information sharing between China's banks. For example, following the 2004 collapse of the Delong group, an industrial and financial conglomerate with more than 100 subsidiary companies, investigations finally revealed that the group had been able to borrow an astonishing RMB20 billion in total loans (Interview with CBRC official, 12 March 2015). To combat this problem, the warning system required banks to report regularly to CBRC regarding large-scale lending, defined in 2006 as total loans to clients exceeding RMB 100 million (CBRC 2007, 74). The risk warning system, which was the first major statistical system that CBRC developed, was highly prioritised and has been upgraded twice subsequently. It remains hugely relevant due to the existence of hugely complex and diverse conglomerates in China such as Fosun International, which has more than 2,000 subsidiaries. The risk warning system 'has succeeded in helping banking institutions through the sharing of client risk information between banks' (CBRC 2007, 74).

According to a CBRC official, an important reason for the restructuring of CBRC departments in early 2015 was to enable regulators to identify the common features of credit risk and capture the synergy between different aspects of regulation. The PBoC and CBRC both issued many different regulations over the years in an attempt to improve regulatory coverage of credit risk, which is considered the oldest form of risk in China's banking system. After the restructuring, the Prudential Regulatory Department has the authority to approve all new regulation. This will provide it with the necessary top-down viewpoint to capture regulatory synergy (Interview with CBRC official, 19 March 2015).

## Operational risk

CBRC strongly prioritised the reduction of operational risk in response to the shocking cases of fraud and corruption that emerged in China's banking sector from the late 1990s to the early 2000s. CBRC employed a multi-pronged approach with the principal features being as follows: the upgrading and centralisation of IT systems in banks; educational campaigns on financial crime; on-site examinations of banks; and linking the approval of bank licenses and supervisory ratings with the capability of banks to manage operational risk. Between 2005 and 2006, the CBRC organised ten anti-crime conferences which it used to promote a series of measures designed to improve management of operational risk and prevent banking crime (CBRC 2007). Centralisation of IT systems for back office operations occurred in all commercial banks. BoCom completed a 4-year project in 2006 that centralised the processing of credit authorisation, audit and accounting documentation in the bank's back office function. The project enhanced the bank's control of operational risk and ensured there were no major incidents of fraud in the 2008 reporting period (BoCom 2008, 2009a, 2010). Foreign technology such as IBM's secure file transfer system was crucial to this process (IBM Corporation 2011). In 2007, the CBRC held a press conference to inform the media of ten major cases of bribery within financial institutions in an effort to increase transparency and change the culture within banks. By the end of 2007 CBRC had successfully resolved 106 cases of commercial bribery cases involving funds totalling RMB 13.82 million (CBRC 2008, 76).

The focus of CBRC gradually shifted from developing a robust coverage of fundamental areas of operational risk towards addressing particular areas of risk in greater detail.

## Human resources

One consequence of the rapid increase in the scale of China's banking sector, along with its increasing complexity, was that there was a shortage of qualified workers in the banking sector. Shortly after his appointment in 2005, then CCB Head Guo Shuqing admitted that 'more than 90% of the bank's risk managers are unqualified'. The problem was not limited to banks. Head of CBRC's International Department Han Mingzhi, lamented that 'we lack people who understand commercial banking and microeconomics. It is a headache for the CBRC' (*The Economist* 2005). While from 2007 to 2009 there was a drive by CBRC to appoint more staff with international experience, according to the 2011 IMF Financial Sector Assessment Program the bureaucratic limits placed on CBRC in terms of headcount and budget have limited its ability to 'attract and retain talent' (Interview with CBRC official, 13 March 2015, IMF 2011, 60). The development of the necessary human capital remained of vital importance to the transformation of China's banks.

Reforms led the Human Resources (HR) systems of banks to conform (at least partially) with those of modern capitalist enterprises while maintaining the transmission of party values and ideology to staff. There was increased emphasis on a management hierarchy that was based on the relative responsibilities and performances of workers in order to create a system that was less politicised. In 2006 BoCom made fundamental reforms to its HR management system. The new system was based on five key principles, which also reflected the new remuneration policy of the bank: internal fairness and market competitiveness, efficiency, individual and team performance, proactive career development and a consistent, standardised system (BoCom 2007). As recently as 2016, HR development at BoCom had a clear focus on party values. Staff 'followed the studies on the theoretical and practical issues of Party building, focused on Party Constitution, Party regulations and professional skill training' (BoCom 2017, 121). BoCom has continued to refine and perfect its human resources system, optimising performance assessment procedures and developing more focussed performance incentives for workers. As part of its 13th 5-year plan, BoCom planned to cultivate 2,000 experts over 3 years as part of its strategy to develop sufficient human capital (BoCom 2017).

## Legal development

China's officials are gradually developing a legal environment that will permit the bankruptcy of financial institutions as a means to contain financial risk within failed enterprises and diminish the risk of moral hazard. Cases of bankruptcy in China's banking sector up to this point had been extremely rare with the assets and liabilities of banks in financial difficulty typically taken over by another bank in an effort to maintain stability. New laws have resulted in improved property rights for banks. The development of laws regulating commercial activities such as the *Enterprise Bankruptcy Law* and the *Property Law*, both enacted in 2007, gave greater protection to the rights of banks as creditors. This new bankruptcy law gave secured creditors priority over worker's wages in the event of an enterprise closure. Property rights for creditors were much stronger than during the period of enterprise restructuring and layoffs in the 1990s, when the State Council issued regulation to ensure that worker pension and social welfare took precedence over bank rights to seize collateral (Lardy 1998). The IMF suggests that these laws have assisted with the enforcement of contracts generally in Chinese courts, particularly in urban centres (IMF 2011).

The CBRC has actively participated in the introduction of a deposit insurance scheme, achieved in 2016, and the drafting of a bankruptcy law specific to banking institutions. This has been a gradual and iterative process. As early as 2008, CBRC was charged with the drafting regulations for the bankruptcy of banking institutions and assisted with the formulation of a deposit insurance scheme (CBRC 2009). With respect to the bankruptcy law, state media reported the view of bank industry officials that 'given banks serve as the stabilizer of the economy, the ordinance must be able to minimize the aftermath of bankruptcy of banks and financial institutions and simultaneously provide the maximum protection to the interests of depositors, creditors and taxpayers ...' (Xinhua 2008). As a PBoC official pointed out, the implementation of these reforms would fundamentally challenge the relationship between banks and depositors (Interview with PBoC official, 2 April 2015). It was in the hands of the State Council and ultimately the Central Committee to determine the timing of implementation based on its relative priority compared to other economic reform initiatives and on China's national conditions. As of 2017, *Regulations on Resolving Bankruptcy Risk of Commercial Banks*, drafted by the CBRC, is currently under revision by legislators (IMF 2017).

## Interest rate reform and wealth management products

Under Zhou Xiaochuan, the PBoC increased the flexibility of bank interest rates to promote a more efficient allocation of resources. As Figure 5.1 shows, this was part of a greater process of interest rate liberalisation which started with the introduction of the concept of market-based allocation of resources by the CCP at the 14th Party Congress in 1992. Throughout Reform and Opening, the state has repressed interest rates to reduce borrowing costs and facilitate the transformation of its SOEs, including its banks. The PBoC's control over benchmark deposit and lending rates allowed banks to take advantage of the wide interest rate margins and discouraged the development of differentiated lending products based on risk. The reform measures gradually allowed banks to charge lower lending rates and offer greater returns on deposits. In 2004, upon enlarging the floating range of lending rates, Zhou said that now 'commercial banks must learn

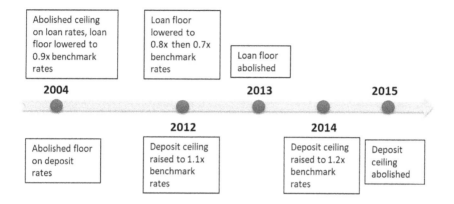

*Figure 5.1* Key milestones of interest rate liberalisation in China.
Source: data adapted from PBoC 2004; *Reuters* 2013; *The Economist* 2015.

how to price risk' and focus on capital adequacy, rather than simply on matching the relative quantities of assets and liabilities (PBoC 2004). The policy has reduced interest rate income, increased competition between banks and stimulated banks to further develop non-interest rate sources of income. It has also provided banks with an incentive to look beyond relationships with SOEs. PBoC Deputy Governor Yi Gang stated in 2015, 'it is fair to say that interest rate liberalization is the main channel to meet the increasingly diversified financial demands and promote economic development' (Yi 2015).

According to one CBRC official, the development of the wealth management sector was another means to gradually liberalise interest rates (Interview with CBRC official, 12 March 2015). Wealth management products offered a return to investors that was higher than the interest rate on deposits. The wealth management businesses of commercial banks were actively regulated by the CBRC. Policymakers wanted state-owned banks to play a central role in the wealth management industry so that they would develop greater capability to assess projects and price risk. According to CBRC Vice Chairman Wang Huaqing, commercial banks were also permitted to engage in overseas wealth management business to 'gradually get familiar with international financial markets and to build up the investment and management capability, thus to strengthen banks' overall competitiveness' (Wang 2008). The CBRC issued the Administrative Rules for Pilot Incorporation of Fund Management Companies by Commercial Banks in 2005, in conjunction with the PBoC and CSRC. The pilot project, which allowed for three of the Big Five banks to operate as the largest shareholder in fund management companies, was quickly expanded to include other commercial banks. Through the pilot project CBRC was able to expand upon its 2005 provisional regulations, issuing the *Notice on Issues Relevant to Further Regulating Commercial Banks' Wealth Management Business* in 2008, later followed by comprehensive regulations in 2011 (CBRC 2009; Li 2014). Due to their vast retail networks, banks quickly came to dominate the wealth management industry, with total assets marketed by commercial banks skyrocketing from RMB 195 billion in 2005 to RMB 3.8 trillion in 2008 (Liu, Mingkang 刘明康 2009b, 597). The practice of commercial banks of using another financial institution as an investment vehicle (usually a NBFI such as a trust company or a securities company) kept the investments off bank balance sheets.

While contributing to the banking sector's ability to price risk, the development of the wealth management sector also had the potential to reduce transparency and create scope for regulatory arbitrage. Where banks did not directly invest, the implicit guarantee of banks to investors was not well defined and products were not usually visible on the balance sheets of banks (Perry and Weltewitz 2015). The ability of investors to assess risk was limited by a lack of transparency with regard to the product and its underlying assets. The different types of financial institutions involved, along with the variable nature of their relationship with the partnering commercial bank, made it difficult to establish a uniform regulatory structure for these products.

## The lifting of restrictions on RMB business for foreign banks post-WTO entry

The state asserted its sovereignty over the banking sector and prioritised domestic policy objectives in its regulation of foreign banks and in particular through its application of WTO requirements. China had committed to allowing foreign banks to conduct local currency business with Chinese individuals by 11 December 2006, 5 years after its entry to the WTO. China's accession to the WTO and the prospect of deregulation of the financial sector attracted foreign banks in unprecedented numbers. By the end of 2005, over seventy banks from twenty countries had established operating branches in China (Dickie 2006). In November 2006, the State Council issued the *Regulations on the Administration of Foreign Invested Banks*. According to the State Council, these rules were designed to 'strengthen and improve the supervision and management of foreign banks and promote the stable operation of the banking sector' (Areddy 2006a). Policymakers elected to subject foreign banks, which operated outside the party system of governance, to the same regulatory oversight as Chinese banks, thereby 'making the industry more transparent and safer for depositors' (Areddy 2006b). The rules required foreign banks to incorporate locally in order to accept deposits and conduct other retail business including the issuance of credit cards, with banks only eligible for incorporation after 3 years of operations in China. Chinese regulators preferred local incorporation as it clearly defined CBRC as the regulator responsible for foreign banks, a policy which foreshadowed the global trend following the 2008 financial crisis. Foreign banks were given 5 years to comply with regulations on asset and liability management, which required them to reduce total loans to 75 per cent of deposits. According to Ba Shusong, Senior Official at the Development Research Centre of the State Council, the rules would create an environment of 'fair competition' between Chinese and foreign banks (Dickie 2006).

The new rules were subject to criticism externally because, while in conformance with WTO terms, they were not viewed to be in the spirit of the WTO agreement. Charlene Barshefsky, the United States Trade Representative who helped negotiate the WTO agreement, found the new rules 'troubling' and commented that 'the intent was to open the sector to the maximum extent possible' (Areddy 2006a). Local incorporation imposed significant set-up costs and inconvenience on foreign banks which perceived it as an affront to their global business model (Dickie 2006). Foreign banks would compete with Chinese banks, not for control of deposits but in high-value areas such as investment banking for Chinese multinationals, pushing improvement in customer service. The rules favoured foreign banks that had a genuine long-term interest in China's economic development. This was in keeping with the goal of policymakers for foreign competition to aid the transformation of Chinese banks.

## Conclusion

From 2003 the CBRC led reforms which, according to Liu Mingkang, made the banking sector 'much stronger and more resilient' (Liu 2010). While China's record-breaking IPOs took the headlines, between 2003 and 2009 officials were able to reduce the level of NPLs from 17.9 per cent to 1.58 per cent. Banks in compliance with capital adequacy requirements constituted 99.9 per cent of banking assets in 2009 compared with just 0.6 per cent of assets in 2003. In the same period, the loan provisioning coverage ratio grew from 19.7 per cent to 155 per cent (Liu 2010). Liu viewed this dramatic improvement as due to governance reforms, or what he termed 'the fundamental reform and opening-up of the banks' structures and mindsets', along with 'the relentless efforts of the banking supervision and regulation' (Liu, Mingkang 2010). Reforms adapted Western ideas and technology within a Chinese system. Under Liu, the CBRC implemented major reforms such as the full roll-out of the international standard five-tier loan classification system, the centralisation and upgrading of the credit approval process, and the centralisation of IT systems within China's banks. Minority investors made a significant contribution to improving the capacity of Chinese banks to manage risk, while also helping to introduce new products, improve customer service and upgrade business practices. The CBRC gradually fostered systems of corporate governance. China's bureaucratic system remained central to the governance of the banking sector. The implementation of reform by agencies such as the CBRC and PBoC reflected conceptions of reform from the party core. The sense of duty to the organisation and development of society felt by CRBC officials was a continuation of the role of scholar-officials in traditional Chinese society. According to one CBRC official, the leaders of the Big Four banks view their role as part of a political career within the bureaucratic system (Interview with CBRC official, 20 March 2015). As Premier, Wen Jiabao played a leading role in banking reform and worked closely alongside Liu Mingkang. He and other party leaders wished to avoid the 'chaos' of a Western governance model and chose to adapt the model of party governance, which appointed and monitored officials at the highest levels of China's banks. The strict limits placed on ownership of Chinese banks by minority investors, along with new regulations for foreign invested banks enacted prior to the lifting of WTO restrictions, were implemented not only to ensure sovereignty of the financial sector but also to limit the influence of dangerous ideas relating to deregulation and financial liberalisation. The greater resilience of China's banking sector would prove invaluable in confronting the 2008 GFC, which had its origins in these very same ideas.

## References

Areddy, James T. 2006a. 'Citigroup Encounters Banking Hurdles in China – New Rules May Delay Retail-Market Access; ATMs at 7-Eleven'. *The Wall Street Journal Europe*, 13 November 2006. http://global.factiva.com/redir/default.aspx?P=sa&an=WS JE000020061113e2bd0000f&cat=a&ep=ASE.

Areddy, James T. 2006b. 'China Gives Banks More Time – Global Lenders Get Lengthy Grace Periods to Meet New Rules'. *The Wall Street Journal Europe*, 29 November 2006. http://global.factiva.com/redir/default.aspx?P=sa&an=WSJE000020061129e2bt 0000v&cat=a&ep=ASE.

*BBC Monitoring Asia Pacific*. 2003. 'Journal Explains Chinese Communist Party's Views on Political Reform'. 31 December 2003. http://global.factiva.com/redir/default.aspx? P=sa&an=BBCAPP0020031231dzcv0015q&cat=a&ep=ASE.

BoC. 2007. 'Bank of China 2006 Annual Report'. Bank of China. www.boc.cn/en/ invester/ir3/200812/P020081212707644071528.pdf.

BoCom. 2007. 'Bank of Communications 2006 Annual Report'. Bank of Communications. www.bankcomm.com/BankCommSite/en/invest_relation_index.jsp?type=index.

BoCom. 2008. 'Bank of Communications 2007 Annual Report'. Bank of Communications. www.bankcomm.com/BankCommSite/en/invest_relation_index.jsp?type=index.

BoCom. 2009a. 'Bank of Communications 2008 Annual Report'. Bank of Communications. www.bankcomm.com/BankCommSite/en/invest_relation_index.jsp?type=index.

BoCom. 2009b. 'Possible Connected Transaction: Proposed Establishment of a Joint Venture Company'. Hong Kong Exchanges and Clearing Ltd. www.hkexnews.hk/ listedco/listconews/SEHK/2009/1028/LTN20091028217.pdf.

BoCom. 2010. 'Bank of Communications 2009 Annual Report'. Bank of Communications. www.bankcomm.com/BankCommSite/en/invest_relation_index.jsp?type=index.

BoCom. 2017. 'Bank of Communications 2016 Annual Report'. Bank of Communications. www.bankcomm.com/BankCommSite/shtml/zonghang/en/3182/3195/3196/82769. shtml?channelId=3182.

Browne, Andrew. 2005. 'Chinese Agency's Rising Heft Sets Stage for Battle over Banks'. *The Wall Street Journal Europe*, 22 August 2005.

CBRC. 2003. 'Jingwai Jinrong Jigou Touzi Rugu Zhongzi Jinrongjigou Banli Banfa' 境外金融机构投资入股中资金融机构管理办法 [Measures for the Administration of Overseas Financial Institutions Investment in Shares of Chinese Funded Financial Institutions]'. China Banking Regulatory Commission. www.cbrc.gov.cn/chinese/home/docDOC_ReadView/295.html.

CBRC. 2004. 'Guidelines on Corporate Governance Reforms and Supervision of Bank of China and Construction Bank of China'. China Banking Regulatory Commission. 11 March 2004. www.cbrc.gov.cn/EngdocView.do?docID=560.

CBRC. 2007. 'China Banking Regulatory Commission 2006 Annual Report'. Beijing: China Banking Regulatory Commission. www.cbrc.gov.cn/showannual.do.

CBRC. 2008. 'China Banking Regulatory Commission 2007 Annual Report'. Beijing: China Banking Regulatory Commission. www.cbrc.gov.cn/showannual.do.

CBRC. 2009. 'China Banking Regulatory Commission 2008 Annual Report'. Beijing: China Banking Regulatory Commission. www.cbrc.gov.cn/showannual.do.

CBRC. 2010. 'China Banking Regulatory Commission 2009 Annual Report'. Beijing: China Banking Regulatory Commission. www.cbrc.gov.cn/showannual.do.

CBRC. 2011a. 'China Banking Regulatory Commission 2010 Annual Report'. Beijing: China Banking Regulatory Commission. www.cbrc.gov.cn/showannual.do.

CBRC. 2011b. 'Guidelines on Corporate Governance of Commercial Banks (Consultative Document)'. 5 August 2011. www.cbrc.gov.cn/EngdocView.do?docID=20110726 E3B31F1963766665FFCB624208EAB400.

CCB. 2006. 'China Construction Bank 2005 Annual Report'. China Construction Bank. www.ccb.com/en/newinvestor/upload/1146016560100/2005e.pdf.

CCB. 2007. 'China Construction Bank 2007 Annual Report'. China Construction Bank. www.ccb.com/cn/uploads/annualreport2007.1209119082546.pdf.

Chin, David. 2016. 'BOCHK: A Breakthrough in Financial Sector Reform'. *FinanceAsia*, 28 January 2016. www.financeasia.com/News/405490,bochk-a-breakthrough-in-financial-sector-reform.aspx.

David Wu 吴卫军. 2009. *'Zouzai Kuaiji Fazhan He Yinhang Gaige de Qianyan'* 走在会计发展和银行改革的前沿 *[Walking in the Forefront of Accounting and Banking Reform]*. Beijing: Zhongguo Jinrong Chubanshe.

David Wu 吴卫军. 2010. '"Suansuan Nonghang de Gaige Dazhang" 算算农行的改革大账 [Calculating the Big Bill of ABC's Reforms]'. *Xinshiji Zhoukan* 《新世纪》周刊, 19 July 2010.

Dawson, Raymond Stanley, ed. 1964. *The Legacy of China*. Oxford, UK: Clarendon Press.

Dickie, Mure. 2006. 'China Issues Rules for Foreign Banks'. *Financial Times*, 16 November 2006, sec. ASIA-PACIFIC. http://global.factiva.com/redir/default.aspx?P=sa&an=FTFTA00020061116e2bg0001w&cat=a&ep=ASE.

Ding, Nan 宁南. 2003. '"Zhongguo Jinrong Gaoceng 'Zoumahuanjiang' de Taiqianmuhou" 中国金融高层'走马换将'的台前幕后 [Behind the Scenes of Changes of Command at the Executive Level of Chinese Finance]'. *www.people.com.cn*, 12 December 2003. www.people.com.cn/GB/jinji/34/165/20030212/921713.html.

Du, Hua 杜华, ed. 2007. *'Jinrong Gongzuo Wenxian Xuanbian (1978–2005)'* 金融工作文献选编 (一九七八——二00五). Beijing: Zhongguo Jinrong Chubanshe.

*Financial Times* 金融时报. 2002. '"Fahui Zhongyangyinhang Jianguan Youshi" 发挥中央银行的监管优势 [Bring out the Central Bank's Regulatory Advantage]'. Baidu Wenku, 28 January 2002. http://wenku.baidu.com/view/96d286d184254b35eefd34d8.html.

Gillis, Paul. 2012. 'China's Big Four Banks Rotate Auditors'. *China Accounting Blog* (blog), 16 October 2012. www.chinaaccountingblog.com/weblog/the-big-four-and-the-big.html.

He, W. P. 2013. 'Paternalistic Regulation in China's Banking Sector'. *The Chinese Journal of Comparative Law* 1 (2): 289–302. https://doi.org/10.1093/cjcl/cxt008.

Hu, Bei. 2004a. 'Reforms Give Birth to Mutant in Banking Boardrooms'. *South China Morning Post*, 18 October 2004.

Hu, Bei. 2004b. 'Party's Influence Waning at Banks'. *South China Morning Post*, 2 December 2004. http://global.factiva.com/redir/default.aspx?P=sa&an=SCMP0000200 41201e0c200007&cat=a&ep=ASE.

IBM Corporation. 2011. 'Bank of Communications: Bank of Communications Relies on IBM® for Security-Enhanced File Transfer'. Lightwell Inc. 2011. www.lightwellinc. com/wp-content/uploads/2012/04/CS-MFT-CD-BankofComm.pdf.

ICBC. 2007. 'Industrial and Commercial Bank of China 2006 Annual Report'. Industrial and Commercial Bank of China. www.icbc-ltd.com/icbc/html/download/nianbao/2007/ ICBC_H%20share%20engi-as%20printed%20Final.pdf.

ICBC. 2008. 'Industrial and Commercial Bank of China 2007 Annual Report'. Industrial and Commercial Bank of China. www.icbc-ltd.com/icbc/html/download/nianbao/2008/ E101.pdf.

IMF. 2011. 'People's Republic of China: Financial System Stability Assessment'. IMF Country Report No. 11/321. Washington, DC: International Monetary Fund.

IMF. 2017. 'People's Republic of China: Detailed Assessment Report on the Observance of Standards and Codes'. IMF Country Report No. 17/35. Washington, D.C.: International Monetary Fund.

Irvine, Steven. 2002. 'Standard Chartered to Take Stake in Bank of China HK; In a Move Set to Boost Confidence in Bank of China Hong Kong's IPO, Standard Chartered Will Take a Strategic Stake'. *FinanceAsia.com*, 9 July 2002. http://global.factiva.com/redir/ default.aspx?P=sa&an=facm000020020708dy7900004&cat=a&ep=ASE.

Jin, Hui 靳慧. 2004. '"Zhou Xiaochuan Da Zhongguojingjibao Jizhe: Waihuichubei Zhuzi Zhonghang Jianhang" 周小川答中国经济时报记者:外汇储备注资中行建行 [Zhou Xiaochuan Responds to China Economic Times Reporters: Use of Foreign Reserves for Capital Injection of BoC and CCB]'. *Dongfang Xinwang* 东方新网, 11 March 2004. http://news.eastday.com/eastday/news/node12945/node12954/userobject 1ai117408.html.

Kong, Francesco Guerrerain Hong. 2006. 'Citigroup's GDB Bid Hits Hurdle'. *Financial Times*, 21 April 2006. www.ft.com/cms/s/0/3f580f92-d0d3-11da-b160-0000779e2340. html?ft_site=falcon&desktop=true#axzz4CDxo34XT.

Krueger, Anne O. 2004. '"Meant Well, Tried Little, Failed Much: Policy Reforms in Emerging Market Economies", Remarks By Anne O. Krueger, Acting Managing Director, IMF'. International Monetary Fund, 23 March 2004. www.imf.org/external/np/ speeches/2004/032304a.htm.

Kuhn, Robert Lawrence. 2010. *How China's Leaders Think: The Inside Story of China's Reform and What This Means for the Future*. Singapore: Wiley.

Kynge, James. 2002. 'China Accord on How to Oversee Banks'. *Financial Times*, 7 February 2002. http://global.factiva.com/redir/default.aspx?P=sa&an=ftcom00020020208 dy27000ab&cat=a&ep=ASE.

Kynge, James. 2003. 'China's Banking Watchdog Plans a Revolution'. *Financial Times*, 25 November 2003.

Kynge, James. 2004. 'BoC Says PwC Willing to Certify Bad Loans'. *Financial Times (FT.com)*, 20 April 2004. http://global.factiva.com/redir/default.aspx?P=sa&an=FTCM A00020051015e04k01c4j&cat=a&ep=ASE.

Kynge, James and Richard McGregor. 2003. 'Paranoia Is Weapon of Choice against China's Banks – Beijing's Leaders Have Decided on Innovative Ways…' *Financial Times*, 24 November 2003.

Lague, David. 2006. 'Bank of China I.P.O. Raises $9.7 Billion'. *New York Times*, 24 May 2006. www.nytimes.com/2006/05/24/business/worldbusiness/24cnd-ipo.html.

Lardy, Nicholas R. 1998. *China's Unfinished Economic Revolution*. Washington, DC: Brookings Institution.

Leahy, Joe and Richard McGregor. 2003. 'BoC Woe Highlights Difficulties of Chinese Bank Reform'. *Financial Times*, 10 June 2003.

Leggett, Karby. 2001. 'Foreign Banks Mull Deals in China – HSBC's Interest in Local Bank May Be Aimed at Pleasing Officials, Regulators – WTO Won't Change Obstacles to Financial Expansion in Mainland Market Overnight'. *The Wall Street Journal Europe*, 11 December 2001.

Li, Junling 李峻岭. 2002. '"Yinhangju" Huangle Guoyouyinhang Shangshi Youle Buliangdaikuan Xuanle "银监局'黄了 国有银行上市有了 不良贷款悬了" [Bank Regulatory Body Falls through. Non-Performing Loans Cast a Shadow over the Listing of State-Owned Banks]'. *21 Shiji Jingji Baodao* 21世纪经济报道, 26 February 2002. http://business.sohu.com/90/85/article13838590.shtml.

Li, Tong. 2014. 'Shadow Banking in China: Expanding Scale, Evolving Structure'. *Journal of Financial Economic Policy* 6 (3): 198–211. https://doi.org/10.1108/JFEP-11-2013-0061.

Linebaugh, Kate. 2006a. 'How Foreign Banks Scaled the Chinese Wall – Titans Acquire Minority Stakes With Little Control of Their Own; Will the Strategy Prove Wise?'. *The Wall Street Journal*, 23 February 2006.

Linebaugh, Kate. 2006b. 'China's ICBC Sets IPO Price for a Record of at Least $19 Billion'. *The Wall Street Journal*, 20 October 2006.

Ling, Huawei and Xiaojian Zhang. 2003. '"Jiang Jianqing Xijie Gonghang" 姜建清细解工行 [Jiang Jianqing Explains ICBC in Detail]'. *Cajing Zazhi* 财经杂志, 2003.

Liu, Mingkang. 2003a. 'Turning a New Page in Banking Regulation and Supervision in China: On the Basis of Past Experiences and in Keeping Pace with Changing Times'. China Banking Regulatory Commission, 28 April 2003. www.cbrc.gov.cn/Engdoc View.do?docID=528.

Liu, Mingkang. 2003b. 'Letter from Liu Ming Kang, the Chairman of CBRC, to Mr Jaime Caruana, Chairman of the Basel Committee on Banking Supervision'. 31 July 2003. www.cbrc.gov.cn/EngdocView.do?docID=466.

Liu, Mingkang. 2010. 'Keynote Speech at Asian Financial Forum: Chinese Bankers Carry Hopes for Future Balances'. China Banking Regulatory Commission, 20 January 2010. www.cbrc.gov.cn/EngdocView.do?docID=2010012011DA7AE6925E5D48FF76107F F744C800.

Liu, Mingkang 刘明康. 2004. '"Zhongguo Guoyouyinhangde Gaige, Fazhan Yu Zhili-jiegou 中国国有银行的改革、发展与治理结构" [Reform, Development and Governance Structure of China's State-Owned Banks]'. CBRC, 19 May 2004. www.cbrc.gov. cn/chinese/home/docView/607.html.

Liu, Mingkang 刘明康, ed. 2009a. '*Zhongguo Yinhang Gaige Kaifang Sanshinian (1978–2008) Shangce*' 中国银行业改革开放30年 (1978–2008) 上册. Beijing: Beijing Jinrong Chubanshe.

Liu, Mingkang 刘明康, ed. 2009b. *'Zhongguo Yinhang Gaige Kaifang Sanshinian (1978–2008) Xiace'* 中国银行业改革开放30年 (1978–2008) 下册. Beijing: Beijing Jinrong Chubanshe.

Ma, Shu Yun. 2010. *Shareholding System Reform in China: Privatizing by Groping for Stones*. Cheltenham, UK: Edward Elgar.

McGregor, Richard. 2006. 'Ominous Undertones of an Attack on Reforms'. *Financial Times*, 28 February 2006. www.ft.com/intl/cms/s/0/47236ff8-a7fe-11da-85bc-0000779e2340.html#axzz3Sf3JaDeV.

McGregor, Richard and David Wighton. 2006. 'Citigroup Close in Bidding War for Guangdong Banking'. *Financial Times*, 19 October 2006, London edition.

McMahon, Dinny. 2010. 'End of an Era – Frank Newman Takes a Bow'. *The Wall Street Journal*, 26 May 2010. http://blogs.wsj.com/chinarealtime/2010/05/26/end-of-an-era-%E2%80%93-frank-newman-takes-a-bow/.

Mitchell, Tom. 2006. 'Shenzhen Development Bank's Ex-Chair Arrested'. *Financial Times*, 30 March 2006. www.ft.com/cms/s/0/49446304-c00f-11da-939f-0000779e2340.html.

Naughton, Barry. 2003. 'Government Reorganization: Liu Mingkang and Financial Restructuring'. *China Leadership Monitor* 7. http://media.hoover.org/sites/default/files/documents/clm7_bn.pdf.

Nolan, Peter. 2004. *China at the Crossroads*. Cambridge, UK: Polity Press.

PBoC. 2004. 'China's Monetary and Interest Rate Policy in Year 2004'. The People's Bank of China, 12 May 2004. www.pbc.gov.cn/english/130724/2830295/index.html.

Perry, Emily and Florian Weltewitz. 2015. 'Wealth Management Products in China'. *RBA Bulletin*, 59–68.

PRC Central Government. 2012. '"Fenxi: Ruhe Kandai Zhongguan Jinrong Qiye Lingdaorenyuan Guanli Guiding" 分析：如何看待中管金融企业领导人员管理规定 [Analysis: How to View Administrative Rules on Leaders of Centrally Controlled Financial Enterprises]'. The Central People's Government of the People's Republic of China, 19 March 2012. www.gov.cn/jrzg/2012-03/19/content_2094335.htm.

*Reuters*. 2013. 'Timeline-China's Interest Rate Reforms'. 20 July 2013. www.reuters.com/article/china-economy-rates/timeline-chinas-interest-rate-reforms-idUSL4N0FP33B20130719.

Shih, Victor. 2011. 'When Are Banks Sold to Foreigners? An Examination of the Politics of Selling Banks in Mexico, Korea, and China'. In *Beyond the Middle Kingdom: Comparative Perspectives on China's Capitalist Transformation*, edited by Scott Kennedy. Stanford, CA: Stanford University Press.

*Sina Finance*. 2002. '"Zhongyang Jinrong Gongzuo Huiyi Zaijing Zhaokai Yanghang Jiang Neishe 'Yinjianju" 中央金融工作会议在京召开 央行将内设'银监局' [Central Financial Work Meeting Convened: Central Bank Will Establish a 'Bank Regulatory Bureau' Internally]'. 6 February 2002. http://finance.sina.com.cn/g/20020206/171077.html.

Sun, Tao 孙弢. 2012. '"Zhongguan Jinrong Qiye 'Renshiquan' Zhizheng" 中管金融企业'人事权'之争 [The Battle for "Power over Human Resources" in Centrally Controlled Financial Enterprises]'. *Jinrong Shijie* 金融世界, 28 August 2012. http://fw.xinhua08.com/a/20120828/1011154.shtml.

*The Banker*. 2003. 'Supplement – China – All Change At Central Bank – The People's Bank Of China Has Lost Its Banking …' 1 May 2003. http://global.factiva.com/redir/default.aspx?P=sa&an=bkna000020030526dz51000cj&cat=a&ep=ASE.

*The Economist*. 2005. 'A Great Big Banking Gamble'. 27 October 2005. www.economist.com/node/5081090.

*The Economist*. 2015. 'Letting Go'. 29 October 2015. www.economist.com/news/finance-and-economics/21677238-china-liberalises-interest-rates-last-letting-go.

Walter, Carl and Fraser Howie. 2012. *Red Capitalism: The Fragile Financial Foundation of China's Extraordinary Rise*. Revised edition. Singapore: Wiley.

Walter, Carl and Fraser Howie. 2013. 'Beijing's Financial "Reform" That Wasn't'. *Wall Street Journal*, 1 July 2013, sec. Opinion. www.wsj.com/articles/SB100014241278873 234196045785756740890 45396.

Wang, Huaqing. 2008. 'Vice Chairman Wang Huaqing's Speech at the Wealth Management Seminar'. China Banking Regulatory Commission, 17 March 2008. www.cbrc.gov.cn/EngdocView.do?docID=2008032166F91A3B45D29792FF05A8AB5E9F8500.

Will, Pierre-Etienne. 1990. *Bureaucracy and Famine in Eighteenth-Century China*. Translated by Elborg Forster. Stanford, CA: Stanford University Press.

World Bank. 2009. 'Report on the Observance of Standards and Codes (ROSC) – Accounting and Auditing. People's Republic of China'. World Bank. www-wds.worldbank.org/external/default/WDSContentServer/WDSP/IB/2011/06/15/000333037_20110615021206/Rendered/PDF/625380WP0P112500Box0361486B0PUBLIC0.pdf.

Xinhua. 2008. 'China Starts Legislative Precedure on Bankruptcy of Banking Institutions'. 8 February 2008. http://english.sina.com/business/1/2008/0208/145296.html.

Yang, Dali. 2004. *Remaking the Chinese Leviathan-Market Transition and the Politics of Governance in China*. Stanford, CA: Stanford University Press.

Yeung, Godfrey. 2009. 'How Banks in China Make Lending Decisions'. *Journal of Contemporary China* 18 (59): 285–302. https://doi.org/10.1080/10670560802576034.

Yi, Gang. 2015. 'On Removal of the Deposit Interest Rate Ceiling'. The People's Bank of China, 27 October 2015. www.pbc.gov.cn/english/130724/2969444/index.html.

*Zhengquan Shichang Zhoukan* 证券市场周刊. 2005. '"Shei Caokongle Zhongguo Jingrong Tixi de Jianmai" 谁操控了中国金融系统的贱卖 [Who Is behind the Cheap Sale of China's Financial System]'. 26 December 2005. http://finance.sina.com.cn/g/20051226/09332227506.shtml.

# 6 Reacting to the global financial crisis (2008–17)

There was a heavy weight of responsibility on China's officials to ensure stable development of the banking sector after the GFC. While CBRC's prudent policies on financial innovation minimised the exposure of China's banks to the complex derivatives which helped spread the 2008 GFC, the crisis created an adverse economic environment in China through which new risks to the banking sector emerged. The GFC brought the world economy into recession, severely reduced asset values and created panic and uncertainty in financial institutions which caused credit markets to dry up globally. The total cost of the crisis was estimated at over US$22 trillion, over a third of 2008 World GDP (Melendez 2013; World Bank 2016). Due to its reliance on exports and Foreign Direct Investment (FDI), China's economy was relatively vulnerable to the effects of the crisis. The banking sector was under enormous pressure to continue to make profitable loans, maintain asset quality and control risk in this adverse economic environment. The level of debt in China's economy grew swiftly after the crisis.

The focus for China's policymakers after the crisis was to mitigate this new financial risk and maintain the stability of the financial system. The CBRC maintained a policy of close supervision and strong regulation to address areas of high credit risk. China's system of party governance played an important role in minimising risk by rooting out corruption and reducing the compensation and expenditure of officials. China's banks mitigated risk by diverting capital away from certain sectors, particularly SOEs in heavy industries where overcapacity existed, to more productive areas of the economy. The state also elected not to close down or restructure the NFBI sector, instead seeking to strengthen regulation and enable the sector to safely serve the real economy. Reform measures were implemented to improve the efficiency of capital allocation, reduce moral hazard and improve the pricing of risk by banks. The appointment of Guo Shuqing as Head of CBRC in February 2017 was indicative of the party's intention to take a more proactive approach to reducing financial risk. Guo has a deep understanding of financial risk, having previously assumed roles as Head of both CCB and CSRC, Vice Governor of PBOC and Director of SAFE.

The crisis underlined the concerns of officials for what they considered to be a dangerous and under-regulated global financial system. China's leaders had been extremely concerned about the risks posed by the global financial system long before the advent of the 2008 financial crisis, having been alarmed by the frequent occurrence of financial crises as the financial liberalisation promoted by Western countries caught on (see for example Jiang Zemin's speech in Du, Hua 杜华 2007, 455). The high degree of openness of China's economy and conse-quent exposure to the dangers of the global financial system, along with the close adoption of international standards of banking regulation, made it vital for China to advance its ideas of close supervision and strong regulation to mitigate the inherent risks of financial markets. The crisis provided an opportunity for China to raise concerns and propose solutions regarding future cooperation and govern-ance of the global financial system.

## The war of ideas over financial regulation

In the years prior to the 2008 financial crisis, China's leaders had prioritised the development of a banking system that was fundamentally sound and resilient to financial risk. The favourable economic environment, both domestically and internationally, allowed the state to deliver fundamental institutional change which lifted capital adequacy to international standards, bolstered loan loss pro-visions and reduced the NPL rate drastically. The determination of regulators to focus on financial stability during this period was likely informed by theorists such as Minsky, who warned that 'over periods of prolonged prosperity, the economy transits from financial relations that make for a stable system to finan-cial relations that make for an unstable system' (Minsky 1992, 8). Minsky sug-gested that in good times bankers would engage in excessive innovation and speculation that was ultimately unsustainable. After the crisis Liu Mingkang alluded to this pattern of behaviour, suggesting that 'people in this business (the financial sector) always have short memories', requiring banking regulators to have 'longer memories' in order to maintain a strong culture of regulation and mitigate the risk of moral hazard (Liu 2010b). From 2006 the CBRC imple-mented counter-cyclical macro-prudential policies to prevent overheating and risk contagion and increased its supervision of complex derivative-based prod-ucts (CBRC 2009).

While the crisis began with the collapse of the United States subprime housing market, its true origins lay in a free market ideology that encouraged deregulation, financial innovation and the consolidation of America's financial sector into a few very large and powerful financial institutions. Johnson and Kwak (2010) point out that the interests of regulators were 'captured' by the interests of banking insiders, whose economic and political power reinforced their free market ideology, convincing politicians and regulators alike:

> As banking became more complicated, more prestigious, and more lucra-tive, the ideology of Wall Street – that unfettered innovation and unregu-lated financial markets were good for America and the world – became the consensus position in Washington on both sides of the political aisle.
>
> (Johnson and Kwak 2010, 5)

That the crisis created such large-scale losses, forcing the bailouts and bankruptcies of flagship Western financial institutions in the United States, Europe and beyond was a strong indictment of unfettered free markets. Lehman Brothers, the world's fourth largest investment bank, went bankrupt, by some measure the biggest bankruptcy in history. Two other global investment banks, Bear Stearns and Merrill Lynch, were sold at huge discounts. In an attempt to bring stability to the financial system, the United States federal government took ownership stakes in its major banks in exchange for capital. This large-scale intervention was a clear abandonment of free market principles. In a congressional hearing after the crisis, former Federal Reserve Chairman Alan Greenspan acknowledged the flaws in his concept of self-regulation: 'I made a mistake in presuming that the self-interests of organisations, specifically banks and others, were such that they were best capable of protecting their own shareholders and their equity in the firms' (Treanor and Clark 2008).

As early as May 2008, senior Chinese banking regulators had begun arguing that,

> the western consensus on the relation between the market and the government should be reviewed. In practice, they tend to overestimate the power of the market and overlook the regulatory role of the government and this warped conception is at the root of the subprime crisis.
>
> (Anderlini 2008)

After the crisis, Liu Mingkang commented that 'the western regulatory authorities are too obsessed with innovation and market force and have neglected the role of prudential regulation' (Liu 2008b). While party insiders such as party school Vice President Zheng Bijian had already warned that financial globalisation had 'created conditions for a financial crash across the world', the fact that the most powerful and advanced country in the world allowed a global financial crisis to begin in its domestic housing market no doubt impacted upon the thought processes of China's leaders (Zheng 2011, 67). One Chinese official put it that, 'we used to see the US as our teacher but now we realise that our teacher keeps making mistakes and we've decided to quit the class' (Beattie and Dyer 2009).

## The direct impact of the crisis

To quote Liu Mingkang, the crisis caused a severe disruption to China's economy which exposed its banks to 'a more violent environment with higher credit risk, market risk and operational risk' (CBRC 2009, 11). Since 1978 a major element of China's reform strategy has been integration with the global economy through raising exports and attracting foreign direct investment. By 2007, China's exports had reached a level equivalent to approximately 35 per cent of GDP (World Bank 2018). China also received more FDI than any other country besides the United States. This high level of integration with the world economy made China highly vulnerable to external shocks caused by the crisis. The global economic slowdown reduced the demand for China's exports in important developed country markets, while overseas investors had suffered losses and become more risk adverse. Between 2008 and 2009, the total value of China's exports and FDI decreased by 16 per cent and 24 per cent respectively (World Bank 2018). China's GDP growth fell from 14.2 per cent in 2007 to 9.6 per cent in 2008 (World Bank 2018). The volatility in global markets spread to China. The Shanghai Stock Exchange Composite Index fell by almost two-thirds in 2008. Banks were exposed to greater uncertainty surrounding interest rates, prices and exchange rates. Wealth management operations were immediately thrown into turmoil. According to a report in the *China Daily*, seventeen of the forty-six Qualified Domestic Institutional Investor products offered by domestic banks fell by over 50 per cent, greatly enhancing legal and reputational risk for the banks concerned (Wang Zhenghua 2008).

China's banks also absorbed direct losses from their holdings of United States mortgage-backed securities, as well as debt and equity holdings in troubled or bankrupt financial institutions. In September 2008, BoC held a total of US$8.9 billion of mortgage-backed securities including US$3.3 billion of United States subprime mortgage-backed securities. CCB and China Merchants Bank owned US$191 million and US$70 million of Lehman brothers-related debts respectively. Some of China's banks, such as BoC and CCB, also had holdings of debt securities issued or backed by Freddie Mac and Fannie Mae. Banks also incurred losses as the value of equity investments in financial institutions declined. By October 2008 the market value of China Development Bank's £1.5 billion investment in Barclays Bank, made in 2007, had declined by more than 50 per cent (*Caijing.com.cn* 2008).

## The stimulus plan and increased bank lending

The Chinese state acted rapidly to preserve economic stability. In November 2008 Premier Wen Jiabao announced the implementation of an economic stimulus package estimated at a total of RMB 4 trillion (or US$586 billion), focused on infrastructure projects and designed to 'offset adverse global economic conditions by boosting domestic demand' (*Xinhua News Agency* 2008). According to Premier Wen, one of the key aims of the stimulus plan was to 'preserve financial stability to support economic development' (*Financial Times* 2009). Social stability was also a grave concern as approximately 20 million of China's 130 million migrant workers had lost their jobs and returned home, potentially threatening the stability of rural areas (Anderlini and Dyer 2009). While necessary, implementing the stimulus represented a major disruption to the state's programme of economic and financial reform. An article released by *Xinhua News Agency* commented that 'the macro-economic policy changes announced on Sunday are one of only a few major shifts during the 30 years since the beginning of reform and opening up in 1978' (*Xinhua News Agency* 2008). China's banking sector would play a fundamental role in the stimulus plan by providing

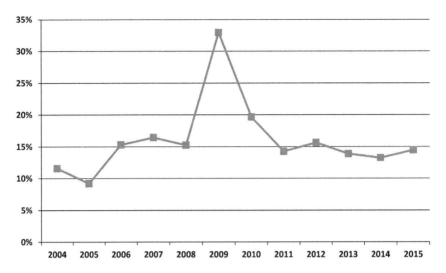

*Figure 6.1* Total loan growth (per cent) of China's banking institutions (2003–15).
Source: data adapted from CBRC 2016.

an estimated US$233 billion of funds, equivalent to 40 per cent of the total stimulus plan, to support priority infrastructure projects and other areas as designated by the plan (World Bank 2018). The expansion of credit was achieved through a removal of limits on credit growth, a relaxation of restrictions on property-related lending, and a decrease in interest rates and reserve requirements.

The banking sector played an important role in mitigating the effects of the crisis. The total credit supply of RMB 9.5 trillion represented a remarkable 32.7 per cent increase on the previous year (Liu 2010a). New loans in 2009 amounted to 31 percent of GDP (IMF 2010, 4). Almost half of the total credit for the year was distributed in the first quarter following the announcement of the stimulus plan. China's bureaucratic system made it possible for the banking sector to provide such swift support to the economy despite the uncertain economic environment. The location of banking officials within China's bureaucracy, responsive to party organs of personnel appointments and party discipline, caused them to view the implementation of government policy as a core part of their role. Everbright supervisory board member Jim Stent commented in an interview that 'in China money goes to the problem, unlike other places where it goes away from the problem' (Interview with Everbright supervisory board member Jim Stent, 16 May 2015). The reduction of the credit supply in 2010 to around RMB 8 billion further demonstrated the state's ability to control the credit supply according to circumstance (CBRC 2011, 44). The stimulus plan was highly successful in facilitating the recovery of China's economy from the crisis. In 2010 GDP growth, exports and FDI all rebounded to levels well above those recorded in 2008, restoring the confidence of consumers and financial markets. The successful execution of the stimulus plan was also vitally important for the recovery of the world economy from the crisis. The IMF praised the effective nature of China's stimulus plan, commenting that 'China has led the global recovery' (IMF 2010, 3).

The priority for the CBRC as banking regulator was to minimise the risks of the stimulus plan. The major concern was that the distribution of a large quantity of credit in a short timeframe would lower asset quality. The achievements of the CBRC prior to the crisis of developing a banking system that was more resilient to risk put the banking system in a better position to contain the risks posed by the stimulus plan. The provisioning coverage ratio had increased dramatically between 2003 and 2009 from 19.7 per cent to 155 per cent as loan loss provisioning reached over RMB 1 trillion. This gave the banking sector a much stronger buffer against potential credit risk (Liu, 2010a). CBRC measures to mitigate risk after the crisis reflected the ongoing application of a regulatory approach which Liu Mingkang characterised as 'a risk-based and consolidated supervision with strong control and great transparency', reliant on 'a set of simple, useful and effective ratios, limits and targets, modeling those used by some developed markets in the past and were later abandoned by themselves during the frenzy [of] innovation and deregulation' (Liu 2010a). To cope with the increase in credit risk, the CBRC drew upon this approach. In 2009, the CBRC raised capital adequacy standards and increased loan loss provisioning requirements in order to develop a counter-cyclical buffer. The minimum capital adequacy ratio was raised from 8 per cent to 10 per cent for small and medium-sized banks and to 11 per cent for systemically important banks. The provisioning coverage ratio was raised from 100 per cent to 130 per cent and again to 150 per cent. New guidelines were issued requiring banks to hold more liquid assets to reduce liquidity risk (CBRC 2010, 46).

The 2008 financial crisis provided an important warning to Chinese regulators about the dangers of financial contagion, excessive leverage, financial innovation and short-term behaviour by executives. The CBRC issued a number of regulations to prevent credit risk spreading to the capital markets and the real estate sector. In 2009, banks were prohibited from guaranteeing corporate bonds. Rules around the disbursement of loans were strengthened to prevent the use of funds for stock trading. The deposit requirements and interest rates for real estate loans were increased (CBRC 2010). In 2011, after some investigation, the CBRC issued the *Regulation on Leverage Management of Commercial Banks*, which 'sets forth clear-cut fundamental principles for leverage ratio supervision and measurement methodologies' (CBRC 2012, 61). Chinese regulators viewed the prevention of excessive leverage as fundamental in the prevention of speculation. The crisis also taught Chinese regulators that it was necessary to have supervisory oversight of the incentive schemes in financial institutions to avoid excessive risk-taking by banking executives. The failure of Western corporate governance in this respect reinforced the value of party governance within China's corporate governance structure. The crisis underlined the CBRC's position that China should not aspire to the excesses of financial innovation seen in the West and that derivative products must be simple, well understood by regulators and serve the needs of the real economy.

## Credit risk

The fundamental risk to China's banking sector after the crisis was credit risk due to excessive leverage. Between 2007 and 2011, when the impact of the stimulus plan was at its height, the balance sheets of Chinese financial institutions grew by 92 per cent (Xiao Geng and Sheng 2014). While China acted quickly to mitigate the impact of the GFC, it was faced with a slowing domestic and global economy with reduced trade flows. In 2014, Xi Jinping confirmed that China would have to adapt to the 'new normal' of a lower economic growth rate (*Bloomberg.com* 2014). The new economic conditions challenged China's model of export-led growth supported upstream by its large SOEs. Premier Li Keqiang stated at the NPC that 'systemic, institutional and structural problems have become 'tigers in the road' holding up development' (Branigan 2015). The stimulus plan directed credit to industries such as mining, energy and steel. The excess capacity created by this investment was compounded by weak global demand, leading to sustained low profitability in these sectors. Weak global demand had negatively impacted the manufacturing sector. The level of debt and consequent financial risk was greatest with respect to local governments and SOEs. The diminished ability of debtors to service debts not only represented a huge credit risk for China's banking sector but drove further borrowing. China's non-financial sector domestic credit to GDP ratio rose from approximately 135 per cent before the GFC to approximately 235 per cent of GDP at the end of 2016 (Chen and Joong, Shi Kang 2018). The reduction in viable commercial projects pushed lending towards areas where there was a greater dependency on collateral. Local governments relied heavily on the use of land sales to repay debt. Speculators borrowed heavily from banks to invest in China's housing market. Real estate loans rose from RMB 3.7 trillion or 15 per cent of total loans in 2006 to 17.4 trillion or 20 per cent of total loans in 2014 (Liao Min, Sun Tao and Zhang Jinfan 2016). Construction and real estate sectors reached a combined 12 per cent of GDP by 2011 (Lu Yinqiu and Tao Sun 2013, 11). Overall credit growth has continued to exceed GDP growth, with total banking assets reaching 310 per cent of GDP by 2016 (IMF 2017b, 15).

External commentators suggested that China's debt problem could cause a global financial crisis. Investor George Soros suggested that the problem 'eerily resembles what happened during the financial crisis in the U.S. in 2007–08, which was similarly fueled by credit growth' (Kishan, Cao and Ye Xie 2016). According to IMF research, international experience suggested 'China's current credit trajectory is dangerous with increasing risks of a disruptive adjustment and/or a marked growth slowdown' (Chen and Joong, Shi Kang 2018, 8). Markus Rodlauer, Deputy Director of the IMF's Asia-Pacific department, commented that 'the level of financial and corporate debt and the complexity of the financial system and rapid growth in shadow banking is on an unsustainable path' (Bulman 2016). Speculative investment through the shadow banking system contributed to increased volatility in China's stock markets, which fell 30 per cent in 3 weeks over June and July 2015 (Duggan 2015). Once again, the state faced criticism from those advocating a free market, neoliberal financial system. Shortly after the stock market fall, former Treasury Secretary and Chief Executive of Goldman Sachs Henry Paulson called for China to increase the pace of financial liberalisation and to fully open the sector to foreign financial institutions as a means to reduce market volatility. Paulson implied that the issue at hand was China's ideological opposition to markets, saying that it was 'no surprise that those ideologically opposed to markets would use recent events to make the opposite argument – that to prevent market instability, Beijing should slow the pace of financial liberalisation or perhaps even abandon market-based reforms altogether' (Paulson 2015).

The Communist Party was extremely concerned about the risk that leverage posed to financial stability. Comments from an 'authoritative person', published in the *People's Daily*, communicated the view of the party's core that 'a tree cannot grow to the heavens, high leverage inevitably brings about high risk, which if not controlled can trigger a systemic financial crisis, leading to economic recession and even eat up the savings of ordinary people, which is fatal'. The continued use of leverage to push growth was considered by the interviewee as 'having one's cake and eating it too' (Gong, Wen 龚雯, Xu, Zhifeng 许志峰 and Wu, Qiuyu 吴秋余 2016). In 2017, Central bank Governor Zhou Xiaochuan warned of the possibility of a 'Minsky moment', noting that excessive optimism in China's economy could give rise to a 'sharp correction', and urged the party to remain vigilant against financial risk (Wildau 2017b). While concerns regarding the stability of China's banking sector recalled the events surrounding the AFC, the state was undoubtedly in a stronger financial position post-GFC. The level of the central government's net assets and foreign exchange reserves, equal to 192 per cent and 21 per cent of GDP at end-2011 and end-2013 respectively, indicated there was no threat of national insolvency or a foreign exchange crisis (Xiao Geng and Sheng 2014). In response to the elevated credit risk, China's officials elected to continue to improve supervision and regulation of the banking sector rather than to liberalise the financial sector. In 2017, an IMF report noted the CBRC's 'high quality supervisory approach' reflected 'intensive investment' in improving the quality of supervisory data and its analytical systems since 2011 (IMF 2017c, 20). In 2016, the CBRC issued the *Guidelines on Comprehensive Risk Management of Banking Institutions*. The guidelines reflect learnings gained from previous provisional regulations, extensive consultation with banks and have incorporated international knowledge, most notably the requirements of *The 2012 Core Principles for Effective Banking Supervision* of the BCBS. The continued focus on regulation and supervision was part of a strategy to reduce NPL creation and lower the risk of financial instability.

The party also sought to reduce credit risk by improving the efficiency of its SOEs through reform of its mixed ownership model. In the Communiqué of the

3rd Plenum of the 18th Party Congress, the party prioritised the 'transformation of government functions' as a means to 'unwaveringly consolidate and develop the publicly owned economy' (CCP 2013). Former Communist Party Secretary and Deputy Director of the State Council Development Research Centre Chen Qingtai has proposed that the cornerstone of SOE reform going forward be the shift from 'managing SOEs' to 'managing state-owned assets' (Chen 2014b). If implemented, under this policy the state would withdraw from direct ownership of SOEs and develop its role as an investor of state-owned capital. Chen expects the liberation of SOEs from government intervention to accelerate market-orientated behaviour, foster creativity and innovation, and liberate productive forces (Chen 2012). Improvements in the efficiency of SOEs would reduce credit risk directly while the state's enhanced role as an investor would provide it with greater flexibility to prevent the misallocation of capital to sectors with over-capacity. The withdrawal of direct state ownership would also enable a full transition to a market economy in which enterprises with different ownership models would be subject to an equal and unified system of market regulation. The liberation from ownership responsibilities would enable the state to direct more resources to the supervision and regulation of markets and to the provision of public services (Chen 2014a). The state would focus on establishing invest-ment funds to maximise the profits of state-owned capital which could be held by social security and public welfare funds so that profits accrued could be used to benefit society. The state has already developed an entity which serves as the principal investment fund for centrally controlled banks, Central Huijin Invest-ments. The clear focus of Huijin in this role of investor distinguishes it from SASAC, whose role of 'managing people, business and assets' is the 'hub of many current institutional conflicts' (Chen 2014b). The reform of BoCom's mixed ownership model, which explores concepts of employee shareholding plans and stock options, has the potential to serve as a template for future owner-ship reform of China's largest banks (Wildau 2015c).

After the crisis, the state sought to mitigate credit risk in industries with over-capacity. In late 2015, Premier Li Keqiang reiterated his commitment to this policy, stating: 'We must summon our determination and set to work. For those "zombie enterprises" with absolute overcapacity, we must ruthlessly bring down the knife' (Wildau 2016a). In the short to medium term, the CBRC had a crucial role in instructing banks how to improve their credit structure, following the requirements of 'absorption, transfer, consolidation and phase-out of overcapac-ities' and the principle of 'conforming to the rules, adopting differentiated indus-trial policies, and addressing both symptoms and root causes'. Policy guidance and planning was enhanced to reduce credit risk from loans to overcapacity industries (CBRC 2014, 35, 56). The CBRC Shanghai office was praised for its efforts to reduce Shanghai banks' exposure to steel traders from RMB 220 billion in 2011 to 21.4 billion in 2016. Close supervision of the steel industry allowed regulators to detect a number of illegal practices including fake receipts, improper use of steel holdings as collateral, and the use of loans for unrelated speculative activities (Liao 2016). Chinese Premier Li Keqiang reported that iron and steel capacity was cut by over 65 million tonnes in 2016, exceeding targets, with officials aiming for a further reduction of approximately 50 million tonnes in 2017 (Li, Keqiang 2017). The IMF reported in 2017 that 20 per cent of identified centrally controlled 'zombie' SOEs had been resolved, though SOEs continued to account for around 50 per cent of outstanding 'zombie debt' (IMF 2017a, 16).

## Local government debt

Following the implementation of the stimulus plan, the increasing indebtedness of local governments rapidly became an issue which had the potential to threaten the stability of China's financial system. It is important to distinguish this phenomenon from the type of speculation that occurred in the United States housing market prior to the GFC. Local government debt in China was not built up through speculative activities which were disconnected from the real economy. The implementation of projects through local government financing vehicles (LGFVs) was a vital part of the stimulus plan which reflected the important role of local government throughout reform in the provision of a wide range of services related to infrastructure and social welfare (World Bank 2018). According to CBRC Chief Advisor Andrew Sheng, 'China's massive infrastructure investment, funded largely through LGFVs, will most likely be remembered for its critical contribution to the country's economic modernization' (Sheng n.d.). Infrastructure projects, such as those relating to roads or utilities, typically have a stable and recurring revenue stream based on the monopolistic position of local governments as the sole provider of infrastructure. Local government infrastructure investment prior to the crisis was funded through long-term loans from China Development Bank which suited the nature of returns on infrastructure investment (Sheng n.d.). After the crisis, the need for LGFVs to rollover existing infrastructure loans or take on new short- or medium-term loans reflects the maturity mismatch that occurred during the implementation of the stimulus plan rather than any fundamental misallocation of capital.

After the crisis, the banking sector as a whole took responsibility for the increase in lending to local governments. According to the IMF, while the MOF raised RMB 200 billion for local government spending, the majority of funding needs for the stimulus plan were met through bank loans supported by CBRC and PBoC guidance (Lu Yinqiu and Tao Sun 2013, 21). As by law local governments were unable to borrow directly without central government approval, LFGVs were utilised to finance infrastructure projects. According to IMF estimates, more than 80 per cent of LGFV debt at the end of 2010 was comprised of bank loans, which in turn represented 15 per cent of total corporate bank loans (Lu Yinqiu and Tao Sun 2013, 9). A national audit of local government debt undertaken by the NAO revealed the stock of local government debt to be equivalent to RMB 10.7 trillion as of the end of 2010. Of this, RMB 4.97 trillion was acquired through LGFVs (Lu Yinqiu and Tao Sun 2013, 5). A further audit by the NAO dated June 2013 revealed that local government debt had risen 67 per cent to RMB 17.9 trillion, around one-third of GDP (*The Economist* 2014). According to the audit, LGFV debt stood at RMB 7.0 trillion at end-June 2013 (Jin Hui and Rial 2016, 5). Of this, local governments had guaranteed debt worth RMB 2.7 trillion and had implicitly guaranteed a further RMB 4.3 trillion (*The Economist* 2014).

The risks posed by LGFVs and local government debt had many of the same components as the financial risks seen during the AFC. As lenders, banks were subject to the same concept of moral hazard. There was an assumption that local government would bailout LGFVs if in trouble and that local governments themselves would not be allowed to fail. As a consequence, banks put less emphasis on the commercial circumstances of the borrowing vehicle. Banks also took advantage of the stimulus plan to expand lending to LGFVs after the crisis. The non-transparent nature of local government finances, which included extra-budgetary revenue and expenditure, made it difficult for banks to assess credit risk. The complex networks of implicit and explicit guarantees from local governments or their subsidiaries to LGFVs and the provision of collateral (typically land or future government revenue) to gain funding greatly increased the challenge for banks. The dependency of local governments on land sales for revenue made them highly vulnerable to a potential collapse of the real estate market.

A collapse in the real estate market had the potential to spread to China's financial sector, whose significant exposure to medium and long-term loans in both the real estate and construction sectors was exacerbated by the increase in local government debt. If LGFVs were unable to fund the repayment of loans through land sale, a significant proportion of loans to LGFVs were likely to become non-performing. The slowdown in the housing market after 2010 outside of China's largest cities intensified concerns. An IMF working paper published in 2013 suggested that in the worst case scenario LGFP losses could lead to a bailout of banks, worsening problems of moral hazard and reducing the state's capability to deal with future financial instability (Lu Yinqiu and Tao Sun 2013).

The CBRC worked with the PBOC, MOF and the NDRC to mitigate the risk of local government debt to the financial sector. As banking regulator, CBRC's major role was to guard against the increased credit risk. CBRC had been actively developing rules and regulations to improve monitoring and risk control by banks of LGFVs since they emerged in their current form in 2005. In 2009, the CBRC developed three immediate 'bottom lines of defense' against credit risk: banning package loans to local government, prohibiting banks from making large loans to local governments for commercially unviable projects and restricting lending to local governments with poor financial circumstances or lacking the necessary levels of internal control, corporate governance and risk management (CBRC 2010). The syndication of loans was encouraged where possible to reduce loan concentration risk (CBRC 2010). In 2010, banks were required by the State Council to review every loan to LGFVs, clarify the parties responsible for the loan and re-categorise the loan based on cash flow analysis. In the eyes of the regulators, it was vital that banks were aware of the risks of their current loan portfolio, had written off bad loans promptly and established adequate loan loss provisions to prepare for any losses (CBRC 2011). In an attempt to reduce moral hazard, local governments were prohibited by the State Council from guaranteeing LGFV debt (Lu Yinqiu and Tao Sun 2013). From 2012, CBRC advised banks to reduce their total stock of LGFV loans. Credit approval was given according to the principle of 'securing credit for on-going projects, reducing credit for redundant projects and controlling credit for new projects' (CBRC 2013, 67). Processes of loan classification and disposal were further refined, while by 2014 CBRC had developed a comprehensive statistical system which monitors the different forms of LGFV debt (CBRC 2015). These measures were complemented by regulation of real estate lending designed to curb speculation and prevent a bubble in the property market.

In August 2014, China issued a revised *Budget Law* that aimed to increase the transparency of local government debt by allowing local governments to issue bonds and prohibiting further borrowing through LGFVs. State Council Directive 43 introduced specific rules including the requirement for central government approval on local government debt issuance and any land sales for financing (Sheng and Ng 2016). In 2015, bonds at a face value of RMB 3.8 trillion were issued by local governments, RMB 3.2 trillion of which represented a transfer of existing debt which lowered the debt servicing costs of local government (Lockett 2016). Successful implementation of the *Budget Law*, through the prevention of off-budget borrowing and overcoming problems of moral hazard to develop more commercially-orientated borrowing practices, is viewed by the IMF as fundamental for the state to maintain a stable debt to GDP ratio in the future and reduce the risk of contagion to the banking sector (IMF 2016a). In 2016, the State Council issued a contingency plan for local government to manage debt risk. The plan provided for the establishment of an evaluation and warning mechanism by the MOF and required local government to establish a reporting system. It also provided specific measures for local government to reduce debt based on the level of risk (State Council 2016).

## Shadow banking

Another key area of risk that had developed in China's financial sector was located in its shadow banking system, broadly defined by the Financial Stability Board (FSB) as 'the system of credit intermediation that involves entities and activities outside the regular banking system' (FSB 2011, 3). The development of credit provision outside the formal banking system was vitally important as it allowed sectors of the economy that were marginalised by the banking system to have access to credit. The traditional support of China's banks for SOEs along with the financial repression of the regular banking sector through lending quotas and interest rate regulations had limited the access of other firms to credit. The shadow banking sector grew rapidly from 2010, driven by the growth of wealth management products (WMPs). According to a CBRC official, the development of WMPs is considered as a trial for interest rate liberalisation (Interview with CBRC official, 12 March 2015). Such products, which offer a higher return, can promote the development of a more commercially-orientated allocation of credit and allow banks to develop increased capability to price risk. Despite this rapid growth, non-bank credit intermediation remains at an early stage of development in China. The FSB estimated global shadow banking at 120 per cent of GDP in 2014, while the IMF estimated shadow credit products in China to be approximately 58 per cent of GDP in 2016 (FSB 2014; IMF 2016b).

While policymakers encouraged the development non-bank credit intermediation in order to promote more commercially-orientation of credit, it also became a source of risk. Shadow banking contributed to the development of what the IMF terms 'an increasingly large, leveraged, interconnected, and opaque financial system' (IMF 2016a, 10). The strong degree of interconnectivity between the banking and shadow banking sectors greatly enhances the risk to the financial sector. According to the IMF, 'much of the nonbank credit provision in China, excluding bond financing, has consisted of commercial banks doing bank-like business away from their own balance sheets' (IMF 2014, 32). This may be achieved through the sale of trust products to wealthy clients or selling shares in WMPs. This extra layer of complexity has created a lack of transparency around the risks posed by the shadow banking sector. As Sheng and Ng point out, there is no accepted measure of the quantity of NPLs in the shadow banking system (Sheng and Ng 2016). This lack of transparency has incentivised banks to shift loans off their books which are of poor quality. In doing so, banks avoid regulations on capital adequacy and are no longer required to make loan loss provisions. While the shadow banking sector assists small and medium-sized enterprises (SMEs), many loans are also made to LGFVs and real estate developers who have found it difficult to gain funding through the regular banking sector. The IMF estimates that RMB 19 trillion or around half of total shadow credit products can be categorised as high risk as they have either poor quality loans (defined as 'nonstandard credit assets') or equities as the underlying asset (IMF 2016b, 17–18). The responsibility of banks with respect to shadow products has not been well defined. However the expected yield of WMPs, for example, appears to be roughly the same regardless of whether an explicit guarantee exists or not (IMF 2014). This likely indicates that investors in these products believe that there is an implicit guarantee from either the partnering commercial bank or issuing financial institution, a belief supported by the past restructuring of WMPs in financial difficulty. This presents a problem of moral hazard as investors are less likely to consider the risk of the investment, while the potential for a bank bailout may also push NBFIs to engage in more risky behaviour. Shareholding banks and city commercial banks have a much greater exposure to shadow credit than the Big Four banks, whose exposure is equal to approximately 1–2 per cent of assets or 10–15 per cent of 'loss-absorbing buffers' (defined as combined equity and loan-loss reserves). In contrast, the exposure of smaller banks averaged 280 per cent of total buffers (IMF 2016c, 36). These smaller banks are more reliant on the interbank market for wholesale funding, which has surged from around 10 per cent of total bank funding to over 30 per cent between 2010 and 2015 (IMF 2016c, 37). This short-term borrowing has created another source of interconnectedness between banks and other financial institutions who are net lenders on the interbank market.

The lack of transparency and regulatory coverage relative to the formal banking sector has given rise to unwelcome short-term financial innovations which have led to 'financialisation, usurious lending, Ponzi schemes, fraud and outright abuse of controls and regulations' (Sheng and Ng 2016, xxiii). The high yields offered by China's peer-to-peer (P2P) lending sector, for example, has resulted in loans growing ten-fold between 2013 and 2015, reaching a total of RMB 982 billion (*Bloomberg.com* 2016). The lack of regulatory coverage in the P2P sector has allowed lending platforms to engage in a number of criminal practices, such as illegal fundraising, misappropriation of funds and other fraudulent behaviour. As of end-September 2016, industry website Wangdaizhijia reported that while there were over 4,000 platforms currently operating, more than 2,000 platforms had closed down ('"Wangdaizhijia Shuju" 网贷之家数据 [Wangdaizhijia Data]' n.d.). The central government and police reported that in 2015 illegal fundraising cases rose by 70 per cent and involved funds totalling approximately RMB 250 billion and affected more than 1.5 million people (Wang Yuqian 2016). In the worst case, a leading P2P service provider named Ezubo defrauded 900,000 people out of over RMB 50 billion in a Ponzi scheme which diverted funds to the founder's own investment projects (Mitchell 2016; Wang Yuqian 2016). In August 2016, Fosun Chairman Guo Guangchang went as far as to characterise the entire P2P sector as 'basically a scam' (Moshinsky 2016).

Instead of choosing to close down or restructure the NFBI sector, the state chose to mitigate the risks of the shadow banking system. This policy response reflects the important role of NBFIs in allocating capital to the real economy. The range of financial institutions involved in shadow banking activities necessitated a strong degree of cooperation between the CBRC, PBoC, CSRC and other regulatory agencies to develop regulation and prevent regulatory arbitrage across financial sectors. In August 2013, the inter-ministerial joint meeting system for financial regulation and coordination was established by the State Council (State Council 国务院 n.d.). The first joint regulation issued, *Notice 127 [2014] of the PBoC*, standardised interbank lending in order to prevent banks channelling liquidity into shadow finance assets and thereby 'accelerate the normalized development of asset securitization' (CBRC n.d.b). The State Council issued another notice in late 2013, jointly drafted by the CBRC and other agencies, which clearly defined supervisory responsibilities for shadow banking (CBRC 2014). The Financial Stability and Development Committee was established in November 2017 to coordinate financial reform. It is likely to prioritise the mitigation of risks associated with a fragmented regulatory system by reducing regulatory arbitrage and improving regulatory coverage across financial sectors. The committee is headed by Vice Premier Ma Kai (*Xinhua News Agency* 2017). That same month, new rules for asset management products were jointly announced by the PBoC, CBRC and other regulatory agencies which 'aimed at unifying regulatory practices across the financial industry' (Mitchell 2017). These must be adopted by financial institutions by 30 June 2019.

The CBRC has worked to mitigate the risks of the shadow banking sector through greater transparency, enhanced regulation and supervision of shadow banking activities and the establishment of firewalls between the formal banking sector and the various parts of the shadow banking sector. The new rules for asset management will increase the transparency of asset portfolios and reduce the economic incentives for financial institutions to engage in complex and non-transparent shadow banking practices. In 2017, after new CBRC Head Guo Shuqing had assumed office, the CBRC issued new regulations on the shadow banking sector. *Circular No. 46 (Yin Jian Ban Fa [2017])* aimed to shorten the long, cross-financial sector chains of banking institutions and reduce corporate leverage (KPMG 2017). Previously, the CBRC has issued regulations designed to move assets related to wealth management activities and trust business back on to bank balance sheets and for provisions to be made accordingly (CBRC 2012, 2013). The CBRC has also enhanced supervision and monitoring of bank off-balance sheet assets, drafting new rules for managing the off-sheet activities of commercial banks, increasing on-site examinations and developing a comprehensive system for credit classification, capital calculation and provisioning that covered off-balance sheet assets as well as non-credit assets (CBRC 2014, 2015). Regulations issued have focused on the partnership between banks and NFBIs. Banks were urged to review the financial circumstances and risk management capabilities of their business partners to prevent exposure to unwanted financial risk (CBRC 2013). Other regulations have been aimed at cleaning up these partnerships by improving information disclosure and curbing illegal practices such as the use of wealth management funds for trust loans (CBRC 2012). CBRC has issued regulations which have limited the scope of trust activities to traditional trust business along with wealth management (Sheng and Ng 2016, 198). Trust companies have been banned from running non-standardised cash pool and trust bill business, absorbing interbank deposits and investing in open-ended securities and equities of non-listed companies (CBRC 2011, 2013, 2015). Banks were required to establish 'an independent organizational and management system to strictly separate wealth management funds from banks' own funds', thereby reducing the risk of contagion (CBRC 2014, 109). The CBRC has introduced regulations that restrict the level of a bank's WMP investments in 'non-standard assets' to 35 per cent of total WMP assets or 4 per cent of total bank assets. According to *China Confidential*, the *Financial Times'* emerging markets research service, WMP investments in non-standard assets across the banking sector fell from 45 per cent end-2012 to 25 per cent by mid-2014 (Xiao Qi 2014). The construction of an electronic information registry system has facilitated improved supervision of bank WMPs (Sheng and Ng 2016). The IMF reported in 2017 that 'bank claims on NBFIs and off-balance sheet WMPs have largely stopped growing on a month-to-month basis after booming in recent years' (IMF 2017b, 6).

The inherent risks in the growing P2P lending and broader internet finance sector made the development of a comprehensive regulatory framework for the sector a priority for CBRC in 2016. In April, regulators in major centres of P2P lending including Beijing, Shanghai and Shenzhen temporarily stopped approval of new financial services firms in an attempt to bring order to the sector (Wu 2016). In developing a regulatory framework for P2P lending and other forms of internet finance, the CBRC has employed the same pragmatic approach seen throughout Reform and Opening of issuing a series of exploratory regulations. The exploratory regulations were replaced by a set of comprehensive regulations on internet finance issued in August 2016, *the Guiding Opinions on Promoting the Healthy Development of Internet Finance (Guiding Opinions)*, jointly issued by the CBRC and nine other ministries or government bodies (HKMB 2015b). Regulators leveraged off international experience in developing these regulations, with particular consideration given to the United States and United Kingdom where P2P platforms were already well developed and of significant scale (Interview with CBRC official, 17 March 2015). The regulations limit the scope of activities undertaken by P2P lending platforms which are forbidden from raising money for their own projects, pooling funds from lenders and guaranteeing investors a specific rate of return (Wildau 2015d, 2016b). The rules are designed to establish a clear firewall between P2P platforms and other financial sectors. Platforms are not permitted to take deposits, sell WMPs or asset management plans, use funds for mortgage down payments, engage in crowdfunding and asset securitisation, or re-package and sell debts from trust companies or investment funds (Wang Yuqian 2016; Wu Hongyuran 2015). The new rules required P2P platforms to entrust lenders' funds with banks to prevent fraud (Wu Hongyuran 2015). To increase transparency and promote investor education, P2P platforms are required to disclose to borrowers and lenders their role as a financial intermediary, review lender and borrower qualifications and notify investors regarding the risk profile of borrowers (Wildau 2015d; Wang Yuqian 2016). 'The era of wild growth in Internet finance has ended and a new spring has finally come', said Liu Yang, Chief Executive Officer of leading platform Miniu98.com (Wong 2015).

## Party initiatives to reduce expenditure and stop corrupt practices

In response to the adverse economic conditions in the financial sector, the party utilised its control over personnel to reduce bank expenditure by lowering salaries, including those of the senior executives of China's largest banks. In 2015 the salaries of the Chairman and Presidents of China's five largest banks all fell by approximately 50 per cent. As a former Senior Researcher of Development Research Center of State Council pointed out, it was more appropriate to compare China's banking executives with senior government officials than with foreign bankers (Interview with Wang Dashu, 25 March 2015). ICBC Chairman Jiang Jianqing's salary of RMB 550,000 was equivalent to just 0.3 per cent of JP Morgan Chase & Co CEO Jamie Dimon's salary of US$27 million (*Reuters* 2016, 2). The support of banking executives for this policy was directly related to their identity as bureaucrats who, in keeping with the role of scholar-officials in China's history, had desire for higher political office. The Chairman of CCB, Wang Hongzhang, voiced his support for the pay cuts: 'Cutting salaries was an extremely correct decision by central authorities and is a good policy to solve the problem of fair pay for leadership cadres' (Wildau 2015b). CCB Head Zhang Jianguo's surprising claim that China's banks were 'a disadvantaged group', made at a meeting of the Chinese People's Political Consultative Conference, was met with great amusement by party leaders in attendance, including Premier Li Keqiang (Li, Jiaxin 李佳欣 2015). The economic slowdown also resulted in layoffs, with the 'Big Four' banks reporting a total reduction of around 25,000 workers in the first 6 months of 2016 (Dong Jing, Wu Hongyuran and Han Wei 2016).

Xi Jinping's anti-corruption campaign created shockwaves across the banking sector. Xi Jinping had warned in his first speech to the Politburo that corruption had the potential to 'doom the party and the state' by undermining their legitimacy (Bradsher 2012). The banking sector was a priority area for the campaign given the potential for financial instability and loss of public welfare as a result of corrupt practices. Wang Qishan led the investigations into banking officials through his role as Head of the Central Commission for Discipline Inspection (CCDI), the party institution responsible for the internal control of officials. The President of ABC, Zhang Yun, was demoted within the Communist Party following an investigation by the CCDI and was forced to resign from his position in December 2015 (Cendrowski 2015). Li Changjun, former President of the Beijing branch of the Export-Import Bank of China was detained after reportedly admitting to issuing letters of credit or guarantee for personal purposes (Wu, Zhang and Wu 2017). Bank of Beijing board member Lu Haijun and Mao Xiaofeng, the President of Minsheng Bank (considered China's first 'private bank'), were other high-profile casualities of the campaign (Wildau 2015a). In late 2015 the CCDI began a 2-month investigation of staff at regulators and financial institutions that included the CBRC, large state-owned banks and policy banks. CCDI investigators attributed cases of corruption to 'a loosened grip by the party'. Investigations uncovered cases of officials taking bribes, misusing public funds and taking advantage of regulatory loopholes for private gain (Ren 2016). In April 2017 Yang Jiacai, Assistant Chairman of CBRC, was 'reportedly placed under investigation in relation to a loan scandal in Hubei province' (Zhuang 2017). This followed the detention of Xiang Junbo, Head of the China Insurance Regulatory Commission, that same month on suspicion of involvement in corrupt practices (Feng 2017). The CCDI reported in November 2015 that four bank regulators were demoted for violating party procedures, including Wang Yanyou, Communist Party Scretary at the China Banking Association and former Head of the Innovative Supervision department (*South China Morning Post* 2015). Premier Li Keqiang explained the goal of the campaign: 'We want to ensure that government power will be exercised with restraint and the government will live up to its due responsibilities to boost market vitality, eliminate the space for rent-seeking behaviour and uproot corruption' (Barber *et al*. 2015).

## Reducing moral hazard and encouraging efficient allocation of capital

The state implemented further reforms with the goal of reducing moral hazard and improving the efficiency of capital allocation. The overall vision for these reforms came from the 3rd Plenum of the 18th Party Congress, which stressed that the market had a 'decisive function' in the allocation of resources (CCP 2013). In May 2016, the State Council introduced a deposit insurance scheme which covered all deposit-taking financial institutions. The scheme protects deposits up to a maximum value of RMB 500,000, enough to cover the savings of 99.63 per cent of China's depositors (HKMB 2015a). Chinese officials viewed the deposit insurance scheme as part of a 'market-based framework to prevent moral hazard' as it defines the parameters through which deposits are protected in the case of bank failure (IMF 2016a, 26). The state's intention to maintain a harder budget constraint in the financial sector was further demonstrated by the advent of defaults in the mainland corporate bond sector from 2014, notably affecting the so-called 'zombie' SOEs. Creating the necessary conditions for bank failure was important not only to reduce moral hazard but also to support other market-orientated reforms such as the liberalisation of interest rates and introduction of a bankruptcy law for banking institutions. In October 2015 the last remaining controls on interest rates, namely ceilings for term deposits, were removed. This signified the completion of China's gradual liberalisation of interest rates, a process that has stimulated banks to price risk more effectively and to pay greater importance to asset quality. According to Zeng Gang, Director of Banking Research at the Institute of Finance and Banking at CASS, the *Regulations on Resolving Bankruptcy Risk of Commercial Banks*, drafted by CBRC and currently under revision by lawmakers, is designed to 'set a sound legal foundation for a bank to withdraw from the financial market at a low costs, low risks and high efficiency' while helping to 'prevent spillover risk among banking institutions' (Jiang, Xueqing 2017).

To ensure that the banking sector was able serve the real economy, regulators continued to develop all types of banking institutions. As Figure 6.2 demonstrates, shareholding banks, city commercial banks and rural financial institutions continued to increase in scale and gain market share relative to the large state-owned banks. These banking institutions made an invaluable contribution to China's economic development. Each type of banking institution served a particular purpose. City commercial banks have had a natural focus on the provincial economy and have served the needs of SMEs. The governance and risk management reforms of these banks, as noted in the previous chapter, are ongoing and subject to constant improvement. The merger of financial institutions has been commonplace in the formation of city commercial banks and rural commercial banks. It has facilitated the pooling of financial resources that has strengthened these institutions and provided the foundations for more rapid transformation. Bank of Jilin, originally established as Changchun City Commercial Bank in 1997, was created through a merger with Jilin and Liaoyuan City Commercial Banks. Regulators approved the subsequent absorption of other

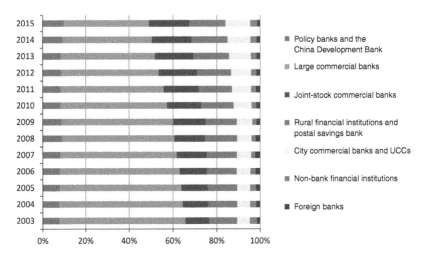

*Figure 6.2* Share of assets among China's banking institutions (2003–15).
Source: data adapted from CBRC 2016.

city commercial banks in Jilin province and the strategic partnership with South Korea's Hana Bank in an effort to allow the bank to develop the scale and knowledge to serve Jilin's economy effectively (*Reuters* n.d.). Zhongyuan Bank signed an agreement with the Grameen Trust to establish the Grameen microcredit programme 'based on the principle of social business'. The bank, which was formed in 2014 through the merger of thirteen commercial banks, will cooperate with experts from Grameen Trust to develop pilot branches in Henan province. If successful, the pilot will form the basis for the expansion of the microloan programme across its nationwide branch network (*The Daily Star* 2016). As Figure 6.2 shows, the market share of foreign banks has remained relatively stable at approximately 1.5–2 per cent of banking assets (CBRC 2016). In November 2017, the CBRC announced it would reduce limits on foreign ownership of Chinese banks (excluding private banks), broaden the scope of foreign banks activity and adjust supervisory requirements in order to allow greater participation of foreign banks in China's banking sector (CBRC n.d.a).

In March 2014 CBRC Head Shang Fulin announced that the state had approved the establishment of five private banks with a total of ten private investors (Gough 2014). According to a CBRC official, the state placed importance on the emergence of private banks to serve the needs of the real economy and particularly small enterprises. The official pointed out that this was an appropriate time for the introduction of private banks given the banking sector's relatively advanced stage of regulatory development and the continued growth of the SMEs which had created 'bottlenecks' for bank capital (Interview with CBRC official, 12 March 2015). The most important criteria for selecting private banks were the ability of banks to manage risk, the attitude of investors towards regulation, the track record of investors in business and the amount of net capital. It was also important for each bank to have a differentiated strategy and market positioning (CBRC 2015). By now a few large private corporations had emerged in China, such as Tencent and Alibaba, which became major investors in pilot banks registered in Shenzhen and Zhejiang provinces respectively. These two banks, WeBank and MYbank, were highly innovative in that they did not have brick and mortar branches, while Alibaba and Tencent hoped to utilise 'big data' from small businesses using Alibaba's Taobao online trading platform and Tencent's social networking platform to improve lending decisions. Tencent and Alibaba had already established strong footholds in internet finance through recent highly successful ventures into internet-based money market funds and payment platforms. The five banks were part of a pilot programme that would allow for the pragmatic development of a regulatory framework for private banks. CBRC announced in June 2016 its intention to consider further applications to expand the pilot on private banking (*Reuters* 2015).

## China's global engagement

After the 2008 financial crisis, China sought to promote its philosophy of close regulation of the financial sector to preserve global financial stability. To achieve this, China took on a more leading role in the governance of a global financial system which its leaders viewed as fundamentally unstable. This was of vital importance to China's own financial stability given the increasingly interconnected nature of the global financial system and the strong emphasis globally on a shared set of regulatory principles and standards. Prior to the crisis, China did not have a strong voice in institutions of global financial governance. Western developed countries had designed and controlled these institutions, beginning with establishment of the global lender of last resort in a crisis, the IMF at the Bretton Woods Conference in 1944. The Basel Committee of Banking Supervision and the Financial Stability Forum were later established by the G10 and G7 respectively. In Asia the voting rights of the Asian Development Bank have been dominated by Japan, the United States and European countries, with the President a Japanese citizen by convention. Together these countries promoted a regime of financial liberalisation and deregulation of the global financial system in an era described by financial crisis historian Kindleberger as '…the most tumultuous in international monetary history' (Kindleberger and Aliber 2005, 277). In a 2015 interview, Li Keqiang stated: 'We are ready to continue to play our role in building the current international financial system. We are also ready to work with other countries to help make the system more just, reasonable and balanced' (Barber, Pilling and Anderlini 2015).

China's voice in the governance of the global financial system grew after the GFC. Former Minsheng bank President Dong Wenbiao commented that in 2004 Chinese representatives felt like 'sitting at the back' during World Bank meetings (Dong Wenbiao, Chairman of Minsheng Bank 2014). Post-GFC, China's banks had now become some of the largest in the world in terms of capital, enhancing the legitimacy of China's regulatory philosophy. Many of the foreign financial institutions that had invested in China's banks sold much or all of their stakes after the crisis with some seeking badly needed capital from China's financial sector. In late 2007, China Investment Corporation made a US$5 billion dollar investment in Morgan Stanley (Santini and Areddy 2007). Furthermore, given severity of the crisis, its resolution demanded a solution that required institutional change and would allow the participation of all major economies in global financial governance. Martin Wolf wrote that the frequent G20 summits following the financial crisis demonstrated how 'the G20 has become the principal body driving the global response to the crisis' (Wolf 2009). The G20, originally established 'with the aim of studying, reviewing, and promoting high-level discussion of policy issues pertaining to the promotion of international financial stability', served to coordinate countries' response to the crisis and reform of the international financial system (Ramachandran 2015). In 2009, China was a member of the G20 working group 'Enhancing Sound Regulation and Strengthening Transparency'. China participated in the drafting of 'Strengthening Prudential Supervision', a policy proposal for the 2009 G20 summit in London (CBRC 2010). The decision to replace the Financial Stability Forum, established by the G7, with the FSB, with all G20 states as members, followed this same pattern. The FSB 'promotes international financial stability' by 'coordinating national financial authorities and international standard-setting bodies as they work toward developing strong regulatory, supervisory and other financial sector policies' (FSB 2017). In 2009 China became a member of both the FSB and the Basel Committee on Banking Supervision. The CBRC was delegated one of China's three seats on the FSB and has actively participated in its work, while Chairman Liu Mingkang was appointed FSB's Vice Chairman of the Standing Committee on Supervisory and Regulatory Cooperation (CBRC 2010). From this point, 'CBRC has been actively engaged in standard-setting under the BCBS in a multi-leveled, substantial manner' (CBRC 2010, 63). Liu Mingkang commented that 'we will use these positions as an opportunity to share views, draw lessons and contribute to enhancing supervision both in China and internationally. Together, we will build a more efficient and transparent international financial system' (Liu 2009). At the IMF, China's voting rights eventually increased from 3.8 per cent to 6 per cent in late 2015, though strong resistance from United States Congress delayed these reforms for 5 years. China's voting share remained substantially lower than that of the United States (16.5 per cent), who did not give up its veto power (*Asia Times* 2015). China also had greater representation in the senior ranks of these organisations. For example former PBoC Deputy Governor Zhu Min served as Deputy Director of the IMF between 2011 and 2016, and was succeeded by another Chinese national, Zhang Tao. Liu Mingkang reflected that 'cooperation and exchanges among regulators will not only promote the financial prosperity and stability, a cornerstone of our mission, but also safeguard the world civilisation in a larger sense' (Liu 2008a).

In October 2013, China's leaders announced the establishment of the Asian Infrastructure Investment Bank with the goal to 'address the daunting infrastructure needs in Asia' (AIIB n.d.). The bank is closely linked to China's One Belt, One Road initiative to develop infrastructure and commercial relationships through building 'on the history of ancient trade networks and cultural interaction between China and Central and Southeast Asia' (Nolan n.d.). Premier Li Keqiang emphasised China's desire to 'work with others to uphold the existing international financial system', further explaining that '[The AIIB] is intended to be a supplement to the current international financial system' (Barber Pilling and Anderlini 2015). China has the largest voting share with 28 per cent. The bank has fifty-seven founding members from within Asia and beyond (AIIB 2016). In its *Guiding Opinions on Enhancing the Quality and Efficiency of the Banking Industry Serving Real Economy (No. 4 [2017])*, the CBRC confirmed the banking sector's obligation to support the One Belt, One Road initiative along with other major national development policies (CBRC n.d.c).

As the CBRC strengthened its engagement with the international financial community, international standards of banking regulation issued by the BCBS became increasingly important. Chinese officials acknowledged that role of *The 2012 Core Principles for Effective Banking Supervision*, published by the BCBS, in its regulatory response to the crisis, noting the regulation 'fully embodies the post-crisis international consensus on strengthening banking supervision and places more emphasis on risk management' (IMF 2017c, 17). Compliance with both Basel II and III, which occurred over 2012 and 2013, had been achieved through a gradual incorporation of international standards within the domestic regulatory framework. The comprehensive regulations for capital requirements issued in 2010, for example, combined the knowledge of a series of rules issued post-Basel I. A CBRC official responsible for the implementation of Basel II and III stated that the priority was to ensure that implementation was achieved in a manner suitable to national conditions (Interview with CBRC official, 13 March 2015). While China had delayed full compliance with Basel II, which it considered to be unsuitable for banks in emerging markets, it largely adopted new rules and regulations issued by BCBS after the crisis. After the financial crisis, new amendments to international regulatory policies issued by BCBS, as summarised in the *Basel Core Principles*, formed the basis of regulations designed to mitigate risk including those related to capital management, leverage and liquidity risk. China adjusted the statistical rules for its off-site surveillance system to reflect the new ratios required by BCBS. A peer review administered by BCBS in September 2013 assessed China as 'compliant' with Basel II's risk-based capital standards, the highest of four possible grades. China's capital requirements were higher and applied more broadly than the minimum required Basel standards (BCBS 2016). In 2017 an assessment by the IMF confirmed that China had fully adopted the Basel III regulatory framework (IMF 2017c).

Chinese officials also utilised their representation in international organisations to advance their views on the risks posed by the global financial system. In a meeting of the IMF in 2010, Zhou Xiaochuan made a statement calling for reform of the international monetary system, stating that 'the current global financial crisis is ... primarily the result of the inappropriate financial sector in developed countries'. Zhou further emphasised that the 'primary risks to the global economy come from developed countries' and that the instability of capital flows from developed countries causes problems for emerging market economies. He also made specific suggestions for elements of financial sector reform in developed countries and asked the IMF to 'strengthen surveillance over developed countries, mature financial markets, and cross-border capital flows, in order to avoid a recurrence of the crisis' (Zhou 2010).

## Conclusion

This chapter has demonstrated how China's leaders sought to mitigate risk in the banking sector following the advent of the GFC. While the banking sector's capacity to deal with the crisis had been greatly enhanced by the dramatic improvement in capital adequacy and NPL rates recorded during the early to mid-2000s, new forms of financial risk emerged which were associated with the implementation of the stimulus plan and adverse global economic conditions. In the face of this risk, the first CBRC Chairman Liu Mingkang advocated supervisory practices that were 'invasive and interactive, keeping an eye on what banks are doing' (Liu 2010b). He also advocated the use of simple regulatory tools to address complex regulatory problems (Liu 2009). In areas of high credit risk, regulators enhanced supervision and strengthened regulation, improved transparency, developed firewalls to prevent financial contagion and ensured that banks set aside adequate provisions for losses. The problem of moral hazard was addressed by encouraging more commercial-orientated borrowing practices, while the development of a deposit insurance scheme should pave the way for a bankruptcy law specific to financial enterprises. The 'regulatory windstorm' unleashed by new CBRC Chairman Guo Shuqing has demonstrated his intent to tackle the problem of financial risk in a forceful manner. Under Guo, CBRC has pledged to 'thoroughly examine and rectify the problem of transactions with too many participants, complex structures and excessively long chains' through which funds 'take leave of the real and enter the virtual' (Wildau 2017a). China's system of party governance played an integral role in reducing risks associated with officials, ensuring that levels of executive compensation reflected the adverse economic conditions and removing corrupt officials and stamping out corrupt practices. The capability of China's leaders to restructure its economy and allocate capital more efficiently will have a large bearing on the potential for all these measures to contain the risk posed by excessive leverage in the economy. Chinese regulators' determination to guard against financial risk, almost certainly informed by Minsky's idea of an inherently unstable capitalist economy, was in stark contrast to the culture of deregulation and unbridled financial innovation advanced by America's politicians, regulators and bankers that was ultimately behind the GFC. The advent of the crisis both demonstrated the need for China to advance its own ideas on how to establish a more stable global financial system and provided it with a greater opportunity to do so through institutions such as the BCBS and the FSB.

# References

AIIB. 2016. 'Asian Infrastructure Investment Bank Subscriptions and Voting Power of Member Countries'. Asian Infrastructure Investment Bank, 22 September 2016. http://euweb.aiib.org/uploadfile/2016/0930/20160930035922477.pdf.

AIIB. n.d. 'What Is the AIIB?'. Asian Infrastructure Investment Bank. http://euweb.aiib.org/html/aboutus/introduction/aiib/?show=0.

Anderlini, Jamil. 2008. 'China Rebukes West's Lack of Regulation'. *Financial Times*, 27 May 2008. www.ft.com/cms/s/0/f404a59a-2c16-11dd-9861-000077b07658.html.

Anderlini, Jamil and Geoff Dyer. 2009. 'Downturn Causes 20m Job Losses in China'. *Financial Times*, 2 February 2009. www.ft.com/content/19c25aea-f0f5-11dd-8790-0000779fd2ac.

*Asia Times*. 2015. 'China's IMF Voting Rights Soar Nearly 60%'. 29 December 2015. http://atimes.com/2015/12/chinas-imf-voting-rights-soar-nearly-60/.

Barber, Lionel, David Pilling and Jamil Anderlini. 2015. 'Interview: Li Keqiang on China's Challenges'. *Financial Times*, 15 April 2015. www.ft.com/intl/cms/s/2/38307b3e-e28d-11e4-aa1d-00144feab7de.html?ftcamp=engage/email/content/premium/editorschoice/crm#axzz3YUFVQ6Wb.

BCBS. 2016. 'Regulatory Consistency Assessment Programme (RCAP): Assessment of Basel III G-SIB Framework and Review of D-SIB Frameworks – China'. Basel: Basel Committee on Banking Supervision.

Beattie, Alan and Geoff Dyer. 2009. 'Free-Market Ideals Survive the Crunch'. *Financial Times*, 26 November 2009. www.ft.com/content/d4744a26-dab3-11de-933d-00144feabdc0.

*Bloomberg.com*. 2014. 'Xi Says China Must Adapt to "New Normal" of Slower Growth'. 11 May 2014. www.bloomberg.com/news/articles/2014-05-11/xi-says-china-must-adapt-to-new-normal-of-slower-growth.

*Bloomberg.com*. 2016. 'China Imposes Caps on P2P Loans to Curb Shadow-Banking Risks'. 24 August 2016. www.bloomberg.com/news/articles/2016-08-24/china-imposes-caps-on-p2p-lending-to-curb-shadow-banking-risk.

Bradsher, Keith. 2012. 'China's Anticorruption Commission Investigates Senior Official'. *New York Times*, 5 December 2012. www.nytimes.com/2012/12/06/world/asia/early-target-of-chinas-anti-corruption-commission-identified.html.

Branigan, Tania. 2015. 'Chinese Premier Cuts Country's Growth Target'. *Guardian*, 5 March 2015, sec. World news. www.theguardian.com/world/2015/mar/05/chinese-premier-li-keqiang-cuts-countrys-growth-target.

Bulman, May. 2016. 'China Heading for "Financial Crisis" That Could Have "Very Serious Repercussions" for Global Economy, IMF Warns'. *The Independent*, 9 October 2016. www.independent.co.uk/news/world/asia/china-imf-financial-crisis-markus-rodlauer-economy-global-a7353236.html.

*Caijing.com.cn*. 2008. 'Financial Crisis: Impact on China'. 4 November 2008. http://english.caijing.com.cn/2008-11-04/110025848.html.

CBRC. 2009. 'China Banking Regulatory Commission 2008 Annual Report'. Beijing: China Banking Regulatory Commission. www.cbrc.gov.cn/showannual.do.

CBRC. 2010. 'China Banking Regulatory Commission 2009 Annual Report'. Beijing: China Banking Regulatory Commission. www.cbrc.gov.cn/showannual.do.

CBRC. 2011. 'China Banking Regulatory Commission 2010 Annual Report'. Beijing: China Banking Regulatory Commission. www.cbrc.gov.cn/showannual.do.

CBRC. 2012. 'China Banking Regulatory Commission 2011 Annual Report'. Beijing: China Banking Regulatory Commission. www.cbrc.gov.cn/showannual.do.

CBRC. 2013. 'China Banking Regulatory Commission 2012 Annual Report'. Beijing: China Banking Regulatory Commission. www.cbrc.gov.cn/showannual.do.

CBRC. 2014. 'China Banking Regulatory Commission 2013 Annual Report'. Beijing: China Banking Regulatory Commission. www.cbrc.gov.cn/showannual.do.

CBRC. 2015. 'China Banking Regulatory Commission 2014 Annual Report'. Beijing: China Banking Regulatory Commission. www.cbrc.gov.cn/showannual.do.

CBRC. 2016. 'China Banking Regulatory Commission 2015 Annual Report'. Beijing: China Banking Regulatory Commission. www.cbrc.gov.cn/showannual.do.

CBRC. n.d.(a) 'CBRC Sets to Further Open up the Banking Sector'. www.cbrc.gov.cn/EngdocView.do?docID=7861457BE5D64281965A84284DCB4FA2.

CBRC. n.d.(b) 'PBOC, CBRC, CSRC, CIRC and SAFE Jointly Issued the Notice on Standardizing Inter-Bank Businesses of Financial Institutions'. www.cbrc.gov.cn/EngdocView.do?docID=A9CB9480C02B4EF392748CCAD525F505.

CBRC. n.d.(c) 'The CBRC Released the Recent Focuses of Regulation and Supervision'. www.cbrc.gov.cn/EngdocView.do?docID=2921413E26A6450B8DB3A439689F666A.

CCP. 2013. 'Communiqué of the 3rd Plenum of the 18th Party Congress'. China Copyright and Media. 12 November 2013. http://chinacopyrightandmedia.wordpress.com/2013/11/12/communique-of-the-3rd-plenum-of-the-18th-party-congress/.

Cendrowski, Scott. 2015. 'China's Anti-Corruption Drive Nets Another Top Banker'. *Fortune*, 9 December 2015. http://fortune.com/2015/12/09/another-banker-caught-up-in-china-investigation/.

Chen, Qingtai. 2012. '"Guoqi Gaige Zhuanru Guozi Gaige" 国企改革转入国资改革 [SOE Reform Shifts to State-Owned Asset Reform]'. *Caijing.com.cn*, 19 May 2012. http://magazine.caijing.com.cn/2012-05-19/111852984.html.

Chen, Qingtai. 2014a. 'Managing State Capital'. *CaiXin Online*, 20 January 2014. http://english.caixin.com/2014-01-20/100631156.html.

Chen, Qingtai. 2014b. 'A Roadmap for State-Owned Assets Reform'. *Caijing Magazine*, 25 February 2014. http://english.caijing.com.cn/2014-02-25/113952281.html.

Chen, Sally and Joong, Shi Kang. 2018. 'Credit Booms – Is China Different?'. Working Paper WP/18/2. International Monetary Fund.

Dong Jing, Wu Hongyuran and Han Wei. 2016. 'China's Biggest Banks Slash Workforces'. *CaiXin Online*, 1 September 2016. http://english.caixin.com/2016-09-01/100984266.html.

Dong Wenbiao, Chairman of Minsheng Bank. 2014. 'Present and Future of China's Banking Industry'. Presentation, Cambridge, United Kingdom, 4 June .

Du, Hua 杜华, ed. 2007. *Jinrong Gongzuo Wenxian Xuanbian (1978–2005)'* 金融工作文献选编 （一九七八——二00五）. Beijing: Zhongguo Jinrong Chubanshe.

Duggan, Jennifer. 2015. 'Chinese Stock Markets Continue to Nosedive as Regulator Warns of Panic'. *Guardian*, 8 July 2015, sec. Business. www.theguardian.com/business/2015/jul/08/china-stock-markets-continue-nosedive-as-regulator-warns-of-panic.

Feng, Emily. 2017. 'Detention of China Regulator Heralds Clampdown on Insurers'. *Financial Times (FT.com)*, 15 April 2017. http://global.factiva.com/redir/default.aspx?P=sa&an=FTCMA00020170414ed4e00335&cat=a&ep=ASE.

*Financial Times*. 2009. 'Transcript: Wen Jiabao'. 2 February 2009. http://global.factiva.com/redir/default.aspx?P=sa&an=FTCOM00020090202e522001p6&cat=a&ep=ASE.

FSB. 2011. 'Shadow Banking: Strengthening Oversight and Regulation'. Basel: Financial Stability Board.

FSB. 2014. 'Global Shadow Banking Monitoring Report 2014'. Basel: Financial Stability Board.

FSB. 2017. 'About the FSB – Financial Stability Board'. www.fsb.org/about/.

Gong, Wen 龚雯, Xu, Zhifeng 许志峰 and Wu, Qiuyu 吴秋余. 2016. '"Kaiju Shouji Wen Dashi-Quanwei Renshi Tan Danqian Zhongguo Jingji" 开局首季问大势——权威人士谈当前中国经济 [Predictions at the Start of the First Quarter – an Authoritative Person Discusses China's Economy Today]'. *Renminribao* 人民日报, 9 May 2016. http://paper.people.com.cn/rmrb/html/2016-05/09/nw.D110000renmrb_2016 0509_1-02.htm.

Gough, Neil. 2014. 'China Details Plans to Liberalize Interest Rates and Encourage Private Banks'. *New York Times*, 11 March 2014. www.nytimes.com/2014/03/12/business/international/china-details-plans-to-liberalize-interest-rates-and-encourage-private-banks.html.

HKMB. 2015a. 'China Launches Deposit Insurance Scheme'. *Hong Kong Means Business*, 29 April 2015. http://hkmb.hktdc.com/en/1X0A23I9.

HKMB. 2015b. 'China Issues Guidelines on Development of Internet Finance'. *Hong Kong Means Business*, 8 June 2015. http://hkmb.hktdc.com/en/1X0A34J5.

IMF. 2010. 'People's Republic of China: 2010 Article IV Consultation – Staff Report; Staff Statement; Public Information Notice on the Executive Board Discussion'. IMF Country Report No. 10/238. Washington, DC: International Monetary Fund.

IMF. 2014. 'Global Financial Stability Report: Moving from Liquidity- to Growth-Driven Markets'. World Economic and Financial Surveys. Washington, DC: International Monetary Fund.

IMF. 2016a. 'The People's Republic of China: 2016 Article IV Consultation – Press Release; Staff Report; And Statement By The Executive Director For The People's Republic Of China'. IMF Country Report No. 16/270. Washington, DC: International Monetary Fund.

IMF. 2016b. 'The People's Republic of China: Selected Issues'. IMF Country Report No. 16/271. Washington, DC: International Monetary Fund.

IMF. 2016c. 'Global Financial Stability Report: Fostering Stability in a Low-Growth, Low-Rate Era'. World Economic and Financial Surveys. Washington, DC: International Monetary Fund.

IMF. 2017a. 'People's Republic Of China: 2017 Article IV Consultation – Press Release; Staff Report; And Statement By The Executive Director For The People's Republic of China'. IMF Country Report No. 17/247. Washington, D.C.: International Monetary Fund.

IMF. 2017b. 'People's Republic of China: Financial System Stability Assessment'. IMF Country Report No. 17/358. Washington, DC: International Monetary Fund.

IMF. 2017c. 'People's Republic of China: Detailed Assessment Report on the Observance of Standards and Codes'. IMF Country Report No. 17/35. Washington, DC: International Monetary Fund.

Jiang, Xueqing. 2017. 'China's Banking Regulator Drafting Bankruptcy Rules'. *Chinadaily.com.cn*, 10 August 2017. www.chinadaily.com.cn/business/2017-08/10/content_30 401338.htm.

Jin Hui and Isabel Rial. 2016. 'Regulating Local Government Financing Vehicles and Public-Private Partnerships in China'. Working Paper WP/16/187. Washington, DC: International Monetary Fund.

Johnson, Simon and James Kwak. 2010. *13 Bankers: The Wall Street Takeover and the next Financial Meltdown*. New York: Vintage Books.

Kindleberger, Charles P. and Robert Aliber. 2005. *Manias, Panics, and Crashes: A History of Financial Crises*. Hoboken, NJ: John Wiley & Sons.

Kishan, Saijel, Bonnie Cao and Ye Xie. 2016. 'Soros Says China's Economy Looks Like the U.S. Before the Crisis'. *Bloomberg.com*, 21 April 2016. www.bloomberg.com/news/articles/2016-04-20/soros-says-china-s-debt-fueled-economy-resembles-u-s-in-2007-08.

KPMG. 2017. '2017 Q2 China's Banking Sector: Performance of Listed Banks and Hot Topics'. https://assets.kpmg.com/content/dam/kpmg/cn/pdf/en/2017/10/china-banking-sector-performance-of-listed-banks-and-hot-topics-2017-q2.pdf.

Li, Jiaxin 李佳欣. 2015. '"Jianhang Hangzhang Shuo 'Yinhang Shi Ruoshi Qunti' Li Keqiang Weishenme Xiaole" 建行行长说'银行是弱势群体' 李克强为什么笑了 [CCB Head Says "Banks Are a Disadvantaged Group" Why Did Li Keqiang Laugh]'. *Caijing.com.cn*, 4 March 2015. http://economy.caijing.com.cn/20150304/3831682.shtml.

Li, Keqiang. 2017. 'Full Text: Report on the Work of the Government'. *Xinhua News Agency*, 16 March 2017. http://news.xinhuanet.com/english/china/2017-03/16/c_136134017.htm.

Liao, Min. 2016. 'Shanghai Shows That China Reforms Are Possible'. *Financial Times*, 29 July 2016. http://blogs.ft.com/beyond-brics/2016/07/29/shanghai-shows-that-china-reforms-are-possible/.

Liao Min, Sun Tao and Zhang Jinfan. 2016. 'China's Financial Interlinkages and Implications For Inter-Agency Coordination'. Working Paper WP/16/181. Washington, DC: International Monetary Fund.

Liu, Mingkang. 2008a. 'Chairman LIU Mingkang's Speech at British Museum: Global Financial Stability and Global Civilization'. CBRC, 5 May 2008. www.cbrc.gov.cn/EngdocView.do?docID=2008051435F5AB68C5E066C7FF85E9CAFA114B00.

Liu, Mingkang. 2008b. 'Addressing Challenges and Promoting Innovation: The Role of Regulators'. China Banking Regulatory Commission, 13 December 2008. www.cbrc.gov.cn/EngdocView.do?docID=200812231AEA0DDAE8588812FF832957DA434400.

Liu, Mingkang. 2009. 'Basic Rules Helped China Sidestep Bank Crisis What the West Could Learn from China's Firewalls'. *Financial Times*, 29 June 2009, Asia Ed1 edition, sec. COMMENT.

Liu, Mingkang. 2010a. 'Keynote Speech at Asian Financial Forum: Chinese Bankers Carry Hopes for Future Balances'. China Banking Regulatory Commission, 20 January 2010. www.cbrc.gov.cn/EngdocView.do?docID=2010012011DA7AE6925E5D48FF76107FF744C800.

Liu, Mingkang. 2010b. 'Keynote Speech at the 16th International Conference on Banking Supervision: Six Things That Make Us Concern'. China Banking Regulatory Commission, 23 September 2010. www.cbrc.gov.cn/EngdocView.do?docID=201010120E599F9AB245D490FF5BE7AD5A279B00.

Lockett, Hudson. 2016. 'China Government Bonds: No Bailouts for the Little Guys'. *Financial Times*, 15 April 2016. www.ft.com/fastft/2016/04/15/china-government-bonds-no-bailouts-for-the-little-guys/.

Lu Yinqiu and Tao Sun. 2013. 'Local Government Financing Platforms in China: A Fortune or Misfortune?'. Working Paper WP/13/243. Washington, DC: International Monetary Fund.

Melendez, Eleazar David. 2013. 'Financial Crisis Cost Tops $22 Trillion, GAO Says'. *Huffington Post*, 15 February 2013, sec. Business. www.huffingtonpost.com/2013/02/14/financial-crisis-cost-gao_n_2687553.html.

Minsky, Hyman P. 1992. 'The Financial Instability Hypothesis'. *The Jerome Levy Eco-nomics Institute Working Paper*, no. 74. http://papers.ssrn.com/sol3/papers.cfm?abstract _id=161024.

Mitchell, Tom. 2016. 'Arrests in China over $7.6bn Ponzi Scheme'. *Financial Times*, 1 February 2016. www.ft.com/cms/s/0/4ca011f4-c88f-11e5-a8ef-ea66e967dd44.html.

Mitchell, Tom. 2017. 'China Tightens Rules on Asset Management to Rein in Risky Lending'. *Financial Times*, 17 November 2017. www.ft.com/content/a8b320c2-cb89-11e7-ab18-7a9fb7d6163e.

Moshinsky, Ben. 2016. 'China's Warren Buffett Called One of Country's Fastest-Growing Industries "Basically a Scam"'. *Business Insider*, 1 September 2016. http:// uk.businessinsider.com/billionaire-guo-guangchang-called-chinese-p2p-lending-basically-a-scam-2016-9.

Nolan, Peter. n.d. 'The Silk Road by Land and Sea – A Historical Perspective'. CIRSD. www.cirsd.org/en/horizons/horizons-summer-2015-issue-no4/the-silk-road-by-land-and-sea-a-historical-perspective-.

Paulson, Henry. 2015. 'Let China's Markets Speak Truth to Power'. *Financial Times*, 22 July 2015.

Ramachandran, Jaya. 2015. 'G20 Finance Ministers Committed to Sustainable Develop-ment'. *Inter Press Service*, 9 September 2015. www.ipsnews.net/2015/09/g20-finance-ministers-committed-to-sustainable-development.

Ren, Daniel. 2016. 'Corruption Found across China's Financial Industry'. *South China Morning Post*, 5 February 2016. www.scmp.com/news/china/policies-politics/article/ 1909672/corruption-found-across-chinas-financial-industry.

*Reuters*. 2015. 'UPDATE 2-China Encourages Privately-Owned Banks, Allows More Foreign Participation'. 26 June 2015. www.reuters.com/article/china-economy-banks-idUSL3N0ZC2LA20150626.

*Reuters*. 2016. 'Update 2-China Bank Chiefs' Already Low Pay Cut in Half Even as Prob-lems Mount'. 5 April 2016. www.reuters.com/article/china-banks-pay-idUSL3N1781X0.

*Reuters*. n.d. 'S. Korea Hana to Buy $316 Mln Stake in Jilin Bank-Paper'. http://uk. reuters.com/article/hana-jilin-idUKTOE65T09520100701.

Santini, Laura and James Areddy. 2007. 'Great Wall Street of China – Morgan Deal Underlines The New Capital Flow; Who's Playing Whom?'. *The Wall Street Journal*, 20 December 2007.

Sheng, Andrew. n.d. 'Why We Shouldn't Worry about China's "Ghost Towns"'. World Economic Forum. www.weforum.org/agenda/2014/09/china-ghost-towns-lgfv-debt/.

Sheng, Andrew and Chow Soon Ng. 2016. *Shadow Banking in China: An Opportunity for Financial Reform*. Hoboken, NJ: John Wiley & Sons.

*South China Morning Post*. 2015. 'Four China Banking Regulators Demoted as Anti-Corruption Crackdown on Financial Sector Continues'. 23 November 2015. www. scmp.com/news/china/economy/article/1882019/chinas-anti-corruption-watchdog-demotes-four-banking-regulators.

State Council. 2016. 'State Council Releases Contingency Plan for Local Governments' Debt Risks'. English.gov.cn. 14 November 2016. http://english.gov.cn/policies/latest_ releases/2016/11/14/content_281475490880338.htm.

State Council 国务院. n.d. '"Guowuyuan Guanyu Tongyi Jianli Jinrong Jianguan Xietiaobu Ji Lianxihuiyi Zhidu de Pifu" 国务院关于同意建立金融监管协调部际联席会议制度的批复 [Regarding the Approval by the State Council for the Establish-ment of the Inter-Ministerial Joint Meeting System for Financial Regulation and

Coordination]'. The Central People's Government of the People's Republic of China. www.gov.cn/zwgk/2013-08/20/content_2470225.htm.

*The Daily Star*. 2016. 'China's Zhongyuan Bank to Replicate Grameen Microcredit Model'. 28 November 2016. www.thedailystar.net/business/chinas-zhongyuan-bank-replicate-grameen-microcredit-model-1321552.

*The Economist*. 2014. 'The Auditors' Footnotes'. 3 January 2014. www.economist.com/blogs/freeexchange/2014/01/chinas-debt.

Treanor, Jill and Andrew Clark. 2008. 'Greenspan – I Was Wrong about the Economy. Sort Of'. *Guardian*, 24 October 2008, sec. Business. www.theguardian.com/business/2008/oct/24/economics-creditcrunch-federal-reserve-greenspan.

Wang Yuqian. 2016. 'P2P Firms in China Get Wings Clipped by New Rules'. 25 August 2016. http://english.caixin.com/2016-08-25/100981879.html.

Wang Zhenghua. 2008. 'Banks to Recast Wealth Management Strategies'. *China Daily*, 4 December 2008. www.chinadaily.com.cn/cndy/2008-12/04/content_7269275.htm.

'"Wangdaizhijia Shuju" 网贷之家数据 [Wangdaizhijia Data]'. n.d. Wangdaizhijia 网贷之家. http://shuju.wdzj.com/industry-list.html.

Wildau, Gabriel. 2015a. 'China's Anti-Corruption Probe Broadens into Finance Sector'. *Financial Times*, 3 February 2015. www.ft.com/cms/s/0/e50b1036-ab73-11e4-8070-00144feab7de.html#axzz3qajnbVe9.

Wildau, Gabriel. 2015b. 'China Construction Bank Lauds Pay Cut as "Extremely Correct"'. *Financial Times*, March 31, 2015. www.ft.com/intl/cms/s/0/bfd6d9a2-d766-11e4-94b1-00144feab7de.html#axzz3WFizjJdR.

Wildau, Gabriel. 2015c. 'China's Bocom Sets Template for Reform at State-Owned Banks'. *Financial Times*, 17 June 2015. www.ft.com/content/ecfc3a4a-14b4-11e5-a51f-00144feabdc0.

Wildau, Gabriel. 2015d. 'China's Internet Finance Rules Tilt towards Incumbents; Financial Services: New Framework'. *Financial Times*, 28 July 2015, USA Ed1 edition, sec. COMPANIES.

Wildau, Gabriel. 2016a. 'China's State-Owned Zombie Economy'. *Financial Times*, 29 February 2016. www.ft.com/cms/s/0/253d7eb0-ca6c-11e5-84df-70594b99fc47.html.

Wildau, Gabriel. 2016b. 'China Internet Finance Crackdown Targets Fly-by-Night Operators'. *Financial Times*, 21 April 2016. www.ft.com/cms/s/0/661e7540-0786-11e6-96e5-f85cb08b0730.html.

Wildau, Gabriel. 2017a. 'China Bank Overseer Launches "Regulatory Windstorm"'. *Financial Times*, 19 April 2017. www.ft.com/content/cb0670ae-2411-11e7-8691-d5f7e0cd0a16.

Wildau, Gabriel. 2017b. 'China Central Bank Chief Warns of "Minsky Moment"'. *Financial Times*, October 19, 2017. www.ft.com/content/4bcb14c8-b4d2-11e7-a398-73d59db9e399.

Wolf, Martin. 2009. 'The West No Longer Holds All the Cards'. *Financial Times*, 24 September 2009, Surveys PIT1 edition, sec. FT REPORT – G20 IN PITTSBURGH.

Wong, Gillian. 2015. 'China Looks to Regulate Internet Finance; Central Bank Guidelines Call for Enhanced Supervision of the Sector'. *The Wall Street Journal Online*, 20 July 2015, sec. World. http://global.factiva.com/redir/default.aspx?P=sa&an=WSJO000020150718eb7i001b9&cat=a&ep=ASE.

World Bank. 2016. 'World Development Indicators: World GDP (Current US$)'. October 17, 2016. http://data.worldbank.org/indicator/NY.GDP.MKTP.CD.

World Bank. 2018. 'World Development Indicators'. 2018. http://data.worldbank.org/data-catalog/world-development-indicators.

Wu Hongyuran. 2015. 'Regulators Ready to Defog P2P Lending Sector'. 10 December 2015. http://english.caixin.com/2015-12-10/100884490.html.

Wu, Hongyuran. 2016. 'What's in a Name? If It's "P2P Lender", Gov't Says Don't Open'. 21 April 2016. http://english.caixin.com/2016-04-21/100935225.html.

Wu, Hongyuran, Yuzhe Zhang and Gang Wu. 2017. 'Former Export-Import Bank Branch President Under Investigation for Graft'. *Caixin Online*, 10 April 2017. www.caixin global.com/2017-04-10/101076484.html.

Xiao Geng and Sheng, Andrew. 2014. 'Andrew Sheng & Xiao Geng: China's Subprime Risks'. *Business Standard India*, 30 July 2014. www.business-standard.com/article/opinion/andrew-sheng-xiao-geng-china-s-subprime-risks-114073001578_1.html.

Xiao Qi. 2014. 'Guest Post: China's Shadow Finance Risks Start to Ebb'. *Financial Times*, 20 November 2014. http://blogs.ft.com/beyond-brics/2014/11/20/guest-post-chinas-shadow-finance-risks-start-to-ebb/.

*Xinhua News Agency*. 2008. 'China's 4 Trillion Yuan Stimulus to Boost Economy, Domestic Demand'. 9 November 2008. http://news.xinhuanet.com/english/2008-11/09/content_10331324.htm.

*Xinhua News Agency*. 2017. 'China Focus: China Establishes Financial Stability and Development Committee'. 8 November 2017. http://news.xinhuanet.com/english/2017-11/08/c_136737949.htm.

Zheng, Bijian. 2011. *China's Road to Peaceful Rise: Observations on Its Cause, Basis, Connotation and Prospect*. Abingdon, UK; New York: Routledge.

Zhou Xiaochuan. 2010. 'Statement by Zhou Xiaochuan Governor, People's Bank of China On Behalf of the People's Republic of China'. Twenty-First Meeting of the International Monetary and Financial Committee. Washington, DC: IMF. www.imf.org/External/spring/2010/imfc/statement/eng/chn.pdf.

Zhuang, Pinghui. 2017. 'China's Financial Sector Told to Expect New Wave of Graft Scrutiny'. *Scmp.com*, 17 April 2017. http://global.factiva.com/redir/default.aspx?P=sa &an=SCMCOM0020170417ed4h0000c&cat=a&ep=ASE.

# 7    Conclusion

This book has answered the research question: 'What factors explain the evolution of China's banking system since the establishment of the socialist market economy?'

## Part I: summary

The development of China's banking system can best be understood as an evolution of institutions which reflect historical patterns of political and economic organisation in China. China's leaders applied the concept of 'Chinese learning for the fundamental principles, Western learning for practical application' (中體西用 *zhongti xiyong*), when adopting Western ideas and technology within China's traditional political and economic system to modernise the banking sector (see Levenson 1964). China transitioned to a modern banking system with deposit-taking and lending institutions, a modern central bank and a system of financial regulation. It benefited greatly from the experience of others, incorporating technology and techniques from advanced countries and international bodies. However, modernisation of China's banking sector did not equate to Westernisation. China's highest officials, and not its financial technocrats or the international financial community, determined how reform would be implemented. The core institutional features that were particular to China, namely pragmatism, the focus on financial stability and the strong influence of party governance, defined the character of the banking sector. The incorporation of outside ideas was conditional on their suitability for Chinese conditions. Ideas that were deemed by China's leadership to be unsuitable, or even harmful, were resisted.

Deng Xiaoping's Reform and Opening policy, implemented from 1978, provided the overarching vision of reform. The goal of this policy was to modernise China's economy, thereby raising living standards and ensuring social stability for China's people. As the name of the policy suggested, Deng advocated opening China to the ideas, technology and capital of more developed countries to enable China to catch up to the West. China's leaders wanted the country, with its proud history as one of the world's oldest and most stable and prosperous civilisations, to rise again (Nolan 2017). China had suffered the humiliation of military defeats and a loss of control of its borders to foreign powers, which contributed to its economic decline. Attempts to establish a modern banking sector after the Qing dynasty ultimately failed after the advent of the Second World War, while the banking sector under the planned economy suffered due to the ideological excesses of the Cultural Revolution and other movements. To achieve this, Deng proposed a pragmatic approach to reform based on empirical evidence or 'seeking truth from facts'. China's reform path would depend on a gradual process of trial and error, as if 'groping for stones to cross the river'. Deng's ideas have remained highly influential ever since, with Xi Jinping vowing there would be 'no stop in reform, and no stop in opening up' (*Xinhua News Agency* 2012). Deng wanted China's banks to play an active role in the modernisation of China's economy by becoming 'real banks' which would be empowered to allocate capital for the purpose of promoting economic development and technological innovation (Du, Hua 杜华 2007, 9).

The below sub-sections draw out the major institutional features of the evolution of China's banking system.

### *China's bureaucratic tradition*

Policy for China's banking sector was conceived and implemented by officials through a politically united, centrally controlled bureaucracy reflective of China's bureaucratic tradition. Central to Confucian thought was the idea that officials should be virtuous and serve the interests of society as a whole in order to maintain legitimacy as rulers. The party remained deeply embedded within the banking sector during the period of research. The values and ideology of the party were transmitted through the party system to officials in the banking sector. Furthermore officials at the core of the party system, namely those within the Politburo and the Standing Committee, were responsible for the general direction of policy for China's banking sector. Regulatory agencies such as the CBRC and PBoC were subject to party governance and the conceptions of reform which originated at the highest levels of the party. The existence of party committees within each bank served as part of the bureaucratic network through which banking officials were monitored, disciplined and reminded of their responsibilities as party members. The CCDI monitored and investigated high-ranking officials. Party institutions, of which the COD was the most prominent, controlled the appointments of officials within the banking sector. Currently the COD is responsible for the appointment of the executive board members of centrally controlled financial enterprises. China's top bankers fundamentally identify themselves as officials with a political career within the bureaucratic system rather than simply as career bankers. The rotation pattern of officials to and from banking regulatory institutions and commercial banks, and to political positions beyond the sector, is indicative of this broader identity.

Party institutions of governance have adapted to the evolution of the banking sector. Before the advent of the socialist market economy, the decentralised nature of the banking sector, with its fragmented governance structure, created an environment in which local party officials were incentivised to prioritise domestic economic development ahead of national goals with respect to financial regulation, credit allocation and monetary policy. After the establishment of the socialist market economy, financial enterprises were unified and regulation became more prominent. Zhu Rongji emphasised to officials that maintaining financial order and respecting financial regulations was a core part of their duty as officials. In this way, officials remained central to governance of the banking sector even as banks became more autonomous with regards to commercial decisions. The mismanagement of financial institutions, corruption and fraud which occurred during a period of rapid economic development, culminating in the 1997 AFC, prompted reform of party governance of the financial sector. The CFWC was established to resolve these problems of financial order and refine the appointments system to enable greater central oversight of the large state-owned banks. It is from this time that Wen Jiabao, Head of the CFWC, played a central role in the development of the banking sector. Wen worked closely alongside CBRC Head Liu Mingkang to develop a system of corporate governance in banks which would complement party governance. Party officials at a high level viewed the pure imitation of a Western model of corporate governance as likely to lead to financial instability and chaos. It is widely speculated that party governance of the banking system was formalised in party documents in 2016, though it has not been possible to confirm this claim. The advantages of party governance were evident during China's rapid implementation of a large-scale economic stimulus plan, led by the banking sector, in response to the 2008 financial crisis. The system of party governance has been central to efforts to mitigate risks that have emerged in the banking sector after the crisis. Official compensation has been reduced significantly to contain bank expenditure and an anti-corruption campaign has helped identify cases of official corruption in the banking sector. Former Communist Party Secretary and Deputy Director of the State Council Development Research Centre Chen Qingtai has proposed that future SOE reform be viewed as a shift from 'managing SOEs' to 'managing state-owned assets'. If implemented, such a policy would likely require officials to govern without direct ownership of SOEs (Qingtai Chen 2014a). The party system will continue to evolve as reform progresses, just as China's bureaucratic institutions have been gradually refined over the past 2,000 years.

### *Stability*

When implementing policy for the banking sector, the first concern for China's officials was always the stability of the financial system. China's officials felt the same heavy weight of responsibility to provide a stable and prosperous society for its citizens as experienced by China's scholar-officials in traditional Chinese society. Many of these officials, particularly those serving in the first two decades of Reform and Opening, had been sent down to the countryside during the Cultural Revolution. They had first-hand experience of the devastating impact of instability brought about by the Cultural Revolution and other ideological movements. Stability had been a central focus of traditional Chinese political thought as officials attempted to find ways to solve fundamental problems of food production, famine, water supply and prevent the fall of a dynasty which inevitably brought great misfortune to the population.

The emphasis on stability fundamentally defined the approach of officials towards the regulation of a market system. The comments of China's current General Secretary Xi Jinping, made to the Politburo in 2014, that officials should '...make good use of the role of both the market, the "invisible hand", and the government, the "visible" hand' are indicative of this approach (Xi 2014, 128). As part of the gradual transition from the planned economy, China had to develop institutions of market governance and financial regulation. China's officials saw it as their duty to maintain financial order and stability in the banking sector. While the incentives created by a more market-driven economy were a valuable instrument for modernisation, officials viewed financial markets as inherently unstable and requiring close supervision and regulation. China's officials had paid close attention to the increasing number of financial crises occurring around the world as financial deregulation and liberalisation took hold from the 1970s. Institutions which would maintain financial order by monitoring and governing banks were established, refined and provided with greater resources and human capital. For bankers and regulators, the greatest challenge was to understand new concepts and adapt them effectively. The appointment of Vice Premier Zhu Rongji as Head of the central bank shortly after the establishment of the socialist market economy facilitated the political empowerment of the central bank relative to local governments and central planning ministries. This was reinforced by the 1995 *Central Bank Law*, which empowered the central bank by law to act as financial regulator and allowed for the issuance of financial rules and regulation on the basis of this power.

Banking regulators were preoccupied with the question of how to maintain financial order in the banking sector and render mechanisms of regulation effective throughout the reform period. As Head of the central bank, Zhu helped make officials aware of their duty to support the healthy operation of China's new banking regulatory framework. He also sought to maintain basic financial order through the issuance of regulations that addressed illegal financial activity and segregated banking operations from the security, trust and insurance sectors to minimise the risks of financial contagion. Regulators were concerned with how to devise and implement regulation to address fundamental issues such as the illegal establishment of financial institutions and the illegal financing that had undermined state policy efforts to direct capital to productive areas of the economy. The PBoC established and developed early systems of internal control such as its audit function. As part of reforms that transformed China's banks from specialised banks to SOCBs, China introduced concepts of risk management, including asset and liability management and capital adequacy management, from advanced countries. The adoption of the BCBS's 1988 Basel Accord for capital adequacy marked an important step in China's journey towards the progressive adoption of international standards of financial regulation. China's regulators continued to address the basic questions of how best to manage financial risk and maintain financial order by constantly updating and refining regulatory institutions.

The AFC alerted officials to the systemic risks posed by the insufficiently regulated global financial system. The sudden withdrawal of short-term capital flows brought countries affected by the crisis into recession and forced a cycle of currency devaluations in the region, leaving its banking systems with a lower net worth and higher levels of bad debt. The countries concerned had pursued an agenda of deregulation and financial liberalisation. Bail-outs by the IMF imposed conditions that undermined the economic sovereignty of governments in the region. The threat of the global financial system manifested itself in China through a payments crisis suffered by China's 'red chips' and ITICs in Guangdong that had borrowed heavily from international commercial banks. This spread to other financial institutions and threatened the entire financial sector. Wang Qishan, the official entrusted by party leaders in Beijing with the responsibility to resolve the turmoil in Guangdong, balanced the potential economic instability created by closures and bankruptcies of financial institutions with the potential threat of future systemic risk. The bankruptcy of GITIC, in particular, served to reduce moral hazard and increase the accountability of China's financial institutions.

The crisis defined a reform response that aimed to develop a more resilient banking system in the face of potential future external shocks. China's officials implemented reform measures to reduce credit risk and develop a more robust system of regulation based on international standards to manage this risk. The state recapitalised China's large banks to bring capital adequacy levels in line with the requirements of the Basel Accord. Officials studied the experience of other countries, including the Savings and Loan crisis in the United States, to establish AMCs for the large-scale purchase of NPLs from the large state-owned banks. The PBoC developed improved regulations for the recognition, investigation and reporting of NPLs. A new system of loan classification, based on international standards, was introduced and this required officials to consider the quality and risks of all loans. Credit approval processes were standardised in large state-owned banks, with loan assessment committees introduced at the branch level, providing a valuable check on the power of loan officers. Cases of large-scale fraud at banks emerged as regulators and auditors began to address issues of operational risk.

Officials made the decision to establish the CBRC in order to ensure the safety of China's banking system. The creation of a new agency allowed China's central policymakers to have a strong influence over its organisational culture. Liu Mingkang was selected to head the CBRC. Premier Wen and Liu maintained a close dialogue regarding the direction of the CBRC (Kuhn 2010). Liu had a reputation as a 'firefighter' in the banking sector, having restored stability to two major banks caught up in corruption scandals. Under Liu, the CBRC successfully strengthened regulation and reformed the governance of state-owned banks, thereby reducing credit risk dramatically and allowing banks to build up a capital buffer to absorb future shocks. This was achieved through a regulatory philosophy of close, interactive regulation and supervision of banks along with the use of simple models and ratios to detect risk (Liu 2010). CBRC successfully guided the large state-owned banks through shareholding reforms and listing. As a result, banks' capacity to manage risk was enhanced by the implementation of a new two-tier corporate governance structure with independent non-executive directors that included a risk management committee, audit by international accounting firms, and a greater focus by Huijin and minority shareholders on commercial lending and profitability. Minority investors introduced prior to listing contributed valuable ideas and techniques for managing risk to China's large state-owned banks.

From 2008, the main focus for CBRC was to mitigate the new forms of financial risk which emerged as a result of the GFC. To do so, the CBRC maintained its philosophy of close supervision and interaction with banking institutions. In areas of high credit risk, regulators enhanced supervision and strengthened regulation, improved transparency, developed firewalls to prevent financial contagion and ensured that banks set aside adequate provisions for losses. Problems of moral hazard were addressed through the establishment of a deposit insurance scheme, creating the conditions for a forthcoming bankruptcy law for financial enterprises.

### The war of ideas over financial regulation

China's officials strived to adopt knowledge from the West in a manner that was suitable to China's national conditions. China's officials were faced with ideas about reform from self-interested Western-educated bankers and government officials with a more sophisticated understanding of modern banking systems. China's officials chose to adopt Western ideas selectively. Officials felt that the neoliberal model promoted by the West had led to a dangerous and insufficiently regulated global financial system which was vulnerable to financial crises. They rejected this model in favour of a model that featured close supervision and regulation of the financial system. Liu Mingkang, for instance, was strongly opposed to Western-inspired trends of financial deregulation and innovation. The market was viewed as a 'double-edged sword' that had the potential to allocate resources more efficiently but from which financial instability and chaos could also emerge if not sufficiently regulated. In this respect, China's officials were likely informed by theorists such as Minsky, who warned of the fundamental instability of markets.

In acquiring ideas about financial regulation from the West, China's officials were also wary of the economic self-interest of Western countries and their financial institutions. General Secretary Jiang Zemin pointed out that 'developed Western countries have already made control of international finance a strategic measure for global control' (Du, Hua 杜华 2007, 454). The deregulation of the global financial services industry had given rise to the development of large financial conglomerates which had aggressively pursued cross border M&A

deals across the developing world, with China viewed as the next major prize. Self-interested foreign financial institutions wished to gain control of China's best financial assets, advocating financial deregulation, withdrawal of party governance from the sector, the break-up and privatisation of the large state-owned banks, and the introduction of foreign competition. This self-interest was advanced through an argument, supported by a neoliberal model, that Chinese officials needed to step aside and allow international financial conglomerates to take control of the financial sector in order to provide more efficient allocation of capital and market discipline. This argument persisted beyond the 2008 financial crisis as demonstrated by Hank Paulson's repeated claims that China needs to increase the pace of market reform and financial liberalisation (*The Economic Times* 2008; Paulson 2015).

The main purpose of engagement with the West was to adopt modern management practices, technology and international best practices in financial regulation to facilitate the development of a stable, well-regulated banking system that promoted economic development by serving the real economy. China's officials established close dialogue with foreign regulators, bankers and international institutions from the beginning of reform and opening. After the establishment of the socialist market economy, China progressively adopted international standards of financial regulation, beginning with the 1988 Basel Capital Accord. The implementation of an international loan classification system followed consultation with PWC and other leading foreign advisers. The CBRC, which is guided by an International Advisory Council, has utilised Basel documents as the basis for domestic regulations on risk management. China's banks and ATMs have depended on technology from Western corporations such as IBM, Hewlett Packard, Intel and Microsoft (Nolan 2013). Prior to listing, foreign firms were invited to act as minority investors in order to bring life to the new corporate governance structure and transfer knowledge of management practices and technological methods. International accounting firms regularly audit Chinese banks, a process that began as preparation for listing. After listing on the HKSE, China's banks were exposed to an 'international' institutional setting with more rigorous laws and regulations.

China's officials have played a key role in defining the character of China's banking system during this process of knowledge acquisition. Western technology and techniques were incorporated within a Chinese system. While there have undoubtedly been elements of convergence, China's banking system has not converged substantially with any Western banking model. Throughout reform, important decisions made by officials have reflected China's own reform priorities. While international firms were heavily involved in the restructuring of GDE and bankruptcy of GITIC, officials prioritised the stability of the financial system ahead of the interests of international creditors. China's officials managed integration with WTO in the banking sector by introducing foreign competition to promote reform while limiting foreign control of China's financial assets. The influence of the ideas of minority investors with respect to banking reform was restricted by strict ownership limits. Despite extensive consultation with international firms and examination of international case studies and reform proposals, Jiang Zemin rejected the Western neoliberal discourse in favour of a shareholding reform which he described as 'an important exploration of effective forms of public ownership' (Du, Hua 杜华 2007, 458). Listing was part of a process of transformation of China's financial enterprises that began at the start of Reform and Opening. China's officials were wary of the risks of the United States model of corporate governance, which were laid bare during the 2008 financial crisis. To mitigate risk, China's leaders integrated this system within the party's own governance model and continued to refine systems of appointment and discipline of top officials while maintaining compensation levels far below levels seen in the West. CBRC's first Head Liu Mingkang sought to apply principles of regulation that were abandoned by developed countries 'during the frenzy [of] innovation and deregulation' (Liu 2010).

*Pragmatism*

The pragmatic approach to reform advocated by Deng Xiaoping, for which he borrowed the Chinese idiom 'seeking truth from facts', was an important feature of institutional change in the banking sector. The overall goals of reform in the banking sector were clearly articulated, namely to liberate productive forces and modernise the economy, to aid in the transformation of SOEs and develop public infrastructure, to maintain financial stability and prevent financial chaos undermining the reform agenda. However policymakers did not have a fixed view for how to achieve these goals, or what the particular set of regulatory institutions needed to look like. The process of developing these institutions was highly exploratory and built on guiding documents such as the *Commercial Bank Law* and *Central Bank Law*. Even the most important regulations issued were provisional in nature, and comprehensive regulations were only issued after a series of trial regulations, a process that often took place over a number of years. The gradual incorporation of international standards aimed to ensure their suitability within China's domestic regulatory framework. Officials were preoccupied with how best to regulate the socialist market economy and how to adapt party systems of governance as a regulatory system was established and banks became more commercially autonomous. Reform was often a reaction to observations or particular events that brought to light issues in the banking sector. The establishment of the socialist market economy was itself a response to a lack of financial stability and the need to empower banks to take on the responsibility of distributing capital to SOEs. The AFC alerted officials to the dangers of premature integration into the global financial system and the systemic risk of NPLs. It defined a regulatory response that aimed to improve the credit culture and develop a more robust regulatory system. According to Wang Qishan, 'the 1997 Asian financial crisis helped us gain a deeper understanding of the need to establish principles for commercial credit in accordance with international practices' (Qide Chen 1999). The creation of the CBRC was aimed to address weak bank supervision. It is argued that the decision taken under Wen Jiabao to establish a separate regulatory agency in 2003, the CBRC, was likely a pragmatic decision based on which institutional form was best suited to ensure the safety of the financial system. The incorporation of Western principles of corporate governance in China's banks was a means to an end, with a view to improving asset quality by developing a new mechanism of governance. China made pragmatic efforts to mitigate the risks that emerged from the 2008 financial crisis. The rapidly implemented stimulus plan represented a major shift from long-term economic policy. Series of regulations were issued to address areas of credit risk which emerged following the crisis such as the high level of local government debt or the opaque and under-regulated shadow banking sector.

## Part II: research contribution

This book enables outsiders to better understand the reform path of China's banking system since the establishment of the socialist market economy. It relies on primary sources that shed light on the thought processes of China's officials with respect to reform of the banking system. The book's characterisation of change in China's banking sector as an institutional evolution is in contrast to the main body of literature, which evaluates its change according to the degree of implementation of free market policies. The book also makes a contribution to the research by making the argument of an institutional evolution over the particular timeframe of the research. It details the institutional change from the establishment of the socialist market economy, through the AFC, shareholding reform and the reaction to the GFC.

This book uses original sources to shed light on banking reform in China over the research period in question. The views of Chinese officials on banking reform were obtained through ten semi-structured interviews with CBRC officials in CBRC headquarters in Beijing, primarily conducted in March and April 2015. This perspective was further enhanced by interviews with a variety of past and present stakeholders in China's banking system including current and former central bank employees, a member of the supervisory board of a centrally controlled financial enterprise, a former researcher at the Development Research Centre at the State Council, a partner at an international accounting and advisory firm, an economist at a foreign commercial bank, a former President of an occupation school for the banking sector, and the former Head of Credit Planning at a local commercial bank. Many of these interviews were conducted in Chinese. These original sources were supplemented by the use of Chinese language books and articles which have been rarely cited, if at all, in previous English language publications on China's banking sector: *30 years of Reform and Opening in the Banking Industry*, edited by former Head of CBRC and BoC Liu Mingkang, and *Jinrong Gongzuo Wenxian Xuanbian (1978–2005)* 金融工作文献选编 （一九七八——二00五）, a collation of speeches made by officials for the financial sector, are important examples.

### Institutional evolution

This book contributes to the body of literature that views development in the context of an institutional evolution. Its conceptual framework relies on the work of Geoffrey Hodgson, who defines institutions as 'systems of established and embedded social rules that structure social interactions' (Hodgson 2006, 18). Hodgson asserts that institutions are embedded in the country's history, culture and politics. The implication is that historical patterns of political and economic organisation persist in institutions, making them path dependent and subject to an evolutionary process of development. This book has identified the main institutional features that explain the development of China's banking system since the establishment of the socialist market economy. These account for the fundamental character of China's banking system as it has gradually constructed institutions to regulate and govern the banking sector in the context of the market economy, while adopting technology and practices from developed countries.

This approach can be contrasted with the orthodox view of reform, which attempts to use a single theoretical framework or universal laws and principles to analyse China's banking system. The orthodox view utilises a single theoretical framework that is derived from neoliberalism and advocates for free markets and limited state intervention so as to maximise the efficiency of resource allocation through market forces. The principal work cited in this book that uses such a framework is *Red Capitalism* by Walter and Howie. In their characterisation of China's banking system, Walter and Howie reject the premise that historical patterns of political and economic organisation are of importance, stating that 'China's economy is no different from any other' (Walter and Howie 2012, xvii). The orthodox view of reform is supported by the academic literature, institutions of global financial governance and by large international financial conglomerates and their governments. Its theoretical framework rejects the idea of an active state to promote economic development and considers state intervention in the banking sector as detrimental to the efficient allocation of capital. The orthodox view of reform advocates for policies of financial deregulation and liberalisation. This book rejects the use of this theoretical framework to analyse the evolution of China's banking system on the basis that it neglects historical patterns of political and economic organisation that have been central to the gradual, experimental reform which has occurred.

### Implications of China's reform approach

China's policymakers took a different path to that of other countries and this made all the difference to the outcome of China's banking sector reforms. Officials chose to 'grope for stones' rather than the implement the 'big bang' approach to reform seen in many other developing countries. Global financial conglomerates have not succeeded in buying up China's best financial assets and have only a small market share of the banking sector. China has pursued its own model of reform that emphasises financial stability. Its regulatory philosophy allowed it to cope relatively well during the 1997 AFC and 2008 GFC. Given that the banking systems of China's South East Asian neighbours were more advanced at the time, it is likely that if China had pursued policies of deregulation and an open capital account, its banking system would not have survived the 1997 AFC. At the least, managing the crisis may have required IMF intervention and the neoliberal policies attached to a bailout would have entailed a significant loss of economic sovereignty.

The transformation of China's banking sector could not have been achieved without the active, interventionist role of the state. The state was responsible for the gradual construction of institutions designed to closely supervise and regulate the market. Protectionist policies such as control over interest rates and the capital account have provided space for the stable transformation of China's banks and facilitated regulatory development. This book has shown how the state played a fundamental role, determining the timing of reform based on national conditions and implementing reform in an ordered and balanced fashion. The state set the ultimate targets for banking reform, stressing that its banks should serve the real economy and ultimately the needs of society. In this way, the evolution of China's banking system challenges basic ideas of market efficiency and efficient allocation of resources that do not take into account institutional control.

The state's ability to drive constant improvement in the banking sector also separates it from other countries. They have turned what was an insolvent, poorly regulated banking system into one which is sustainably profitable, exceeds international standards of regulation and has a low rate of NPLs. China now has some of the largest banks in the world. As of 2015 the FT500, which provides an annual measure of the world's largest companies, included twelve banks from China, more than any other country ('FT 500 2015' n.d.). China's success can be attributed to a number of factors. China's openness to external ideas and particularly its adoption of international best practices have been integral to raising regulatory and banking standards. Officials have been very open to ideas that would improve the banking sector's ability to serve the real economy. Throughout reform, central policymakers have been willing to release control of the banking system in order to promote its development. Competition from other financial institutions such as shareholding banks, city commercial banks and foreign banks has provided a continual stimulus for the reform and development of China's large state-owned banks.

### *China and the future governance of the global financial system*

China's increasing influence on institutions such as the G20, BCBS and the FSB will allow it to promote its own ideas on reform of the global financial system. The principal aim of reform for China will be to make the global financial system more stable. Its policymakers are very concerned about global financial stability, particularly given the high number of financial crises experienced in both the developing and developed worlds since the 1970s. After the recent GFC, China has taken on a leadership role in the G20, which has become the de facto body responsible for policy discussions and initiatives for the reform of the global financial system. China also became an active member of both the FSB and BCBS after the crisis. It is likely that in the future China will continue to foster cooperation with other regulatory agencies and international institutions, and support the development of an international financial system with a shared emphasis on close regulation and supervision. China will continue to raise concerns about the risks posed by financial systems in developed countries and the instability of cross border capital flows. China will strongly encourage developed countries to comply fully with the international banking standards set out in Basel III. China will continue to advocate for greater representation of developing countries in global financial governance and seek reforms to international regulatory standards to ensure they are appropriate for the banking systems of these countries. China will seek to promote an international regulatory regime that puts safety and soundness ahead of market efficiency or the interests of international financial conglomerates. It is also argued that China will provide an opposing voice to developed countries such as the United States that have advocated for the deregulation or premature liberalisation of domestic financial systems. China will emphasise close regulation and supervision of domestic financial systems along with the pragmatic adoption of international standards according to each country's national conditions.

## Part III: the future of China's banking sector

In the less than 25 years since the establishment of the socialist market economy, the banking sector has undergone a remarkable transformation. The scale of the banking sector has increased enormously. In 1992 the volume of credit extended by state-owned banks was recorded as RMB 350 billion (Chen, Yuan 1993). The total credit supply in 2009 reached RMB 9.6 trillion, over 27 times larger than in 1992 (CBRC 2010, 44). Total assets in the banking sector have increased from RMB 27.6 trillion in 2003 to RMB 199.3 trillion in 2015, a per annum growth rate of approximately 18 per cent (CBRC 2016). China has developed a regulatory system that has gradually become more robust and resilient to risk. China's banking system was considered by external commentators to be technically insolvent in the 1990s (Liu, Mingkang 刘明康 2009). Today levels of asset quality and loan provisions exceed international standards. After the AFC, Moody's considered China's NPL rate to be 'much worse than even the most pessimistic of the official indications', and was perhaps as much as 40–50 per cent (Kynge 1998). The average NPL rate of the banking sector has decreased to just 1.9 per cent as of 2015 (CBRC 2016, 196). China's large state-owned banks have been transformed into unified, autonomous, commercial enterprises. Administrative influence over these banks has been refined so that there is less interference in commercial decisions. The introduction of modern corporate governance structures, minority investors and subjecting banks to an institutional setting with more rigorous regulations and enhanced transparency have all fundamentally improved bank governance. The landscape of China's banking sector has changed also. While the large state-owned banks still dominate China's banking sector, the share of banking assets of shareholding banks and local city commercial banks has risen substantially.

Reform of the banking sector and the transformation of its banks will continue in the future. The General Secretary Xi Jinping's vow that there would be 'no stop in reform, no stop in opening up' indicates that reform of the banking sector is set to continue according to the same philosophical principles. In the communique of the 3rd Plenum of the 18th Party Congress in 2013, the party demonstrated its intent to commitment to further develop the socialist market economy, 'to liberate and develop social productive forces', to seek truth from facts and strive for 'progress through stability'. 'Enhancing the people's welfare' remains the primary goal of economic development (CCP 2013).

The 3rd plenum points to two broad areas of focus for the banking sector. The first area is the 'perfection of modern market systems' in order to 'raise the efficiency and fairness of resource allocation' (CCP 2013). Perfecting systems of market regulation falls within the broader concept of perfecting modern market systems. CBRC and other government bodies will continue to implement new laws and regulations to mitigate areas of high risk such as local government debt or the shadow banking system. Recent reforms at CBRC have created an organisational structure that encourages a clear and consistent approach across different regulatory spaces. This trend of unification of systems and removal of regulatory arbitrage should continue, not only within CBRC but between CBRC and other regulatory agencies. The establishment of the Financial Stability and Development Committee in 2017 is evidence of this. China will also attempt to reduce moral hazard by establishing a harder budget constraint in the banking sector. The CBRC has participated in the drafting of a bankruptcy law for banking institutions that is under consideration by lawmakers. The formal establishment of such a law, in conjunction with the recently established deposit insurance scheme, will provide the basis for the closure of troubled banks while protecting the interests of depositors and maintaining financial stability. The recent removal of the last remaining controls on interest rates should promote improvement in the pricing of risk and assessment of asset quality by banks. The healthy development of the shadow banking sector, with greater transparency and improved regulatory coverage, is vital to effective liberalisation of interest rates as it enables sectors of the economy which were marginalised by the banking system to have access to credit at a higher effective cost of financing.

The second area of focus for the banking sector is the 'transformation of government functions' through structural reform (CCP 2013). While the Big Four have lost significant market share over the reform period, the banking sector remains dominated by banks which are majority owned and controlled by the central government. These are followed by banks controlled by local governments, while private banks remain at a very early stage of development. This means that reform of the large state-owned banks is integral to any future reform agenda. CBRC has taken an active approach in gradually developing mechanisms of corporate governance within the large state-owned banks and integrating them with the party governance structure. The CBRC is steadily introducing more market-orientated appointments of senior management. However a high degree of administrative control is retained through the appointment of executive board members, which diminishes the accountability of the board to shareholders. The continuation of this high degree of administrative control subsequent to the listing process has maintained the existing bias of large banks towards government-supported sectors and undermines efforts to promote more market-orientated allocation of capital.

While incremental improvements in governance have occurred, China's policymakers are currently considering adjusting the governance structure to accelerate the adoption of market-orientated behaviour. This can be compared to the way that shareholding reform and listing provided a new institutional setting through which improvements in asset quality accelerated. State policymakers are advocating SOE reform which shifts administrative control from 'managing SOEs' to 'managing state-owned assets' (Qingtai Chen 2014b). While it is unclear if such a policy will be implemented, it is a serious proposition that implies that the state would withdraw from direct ownership in the commanding heights of the economy. This policy is designed to liberate SOEs from government intervention while also liberating state-owned capital so that it can be used more effectively (Qingtai Chen 2014a). The state would focus on establishing investment funds to maximise the profits of state-owned capital, a significant proportion of which could be held by social security and public welfare funds to benefit society. It is unclear how quickly reform would proceed in the banking sector. The state's concern for economic stability has often caused reform in the banking sector to follow that of other state-owned sectors. However the banking sector already has a well-established investment fund in the form of Central Huijin Investments. In this respect Huijin compares favourably to SASAC, whose role of 'managing people, business and assets' is the 'hub of many current institutional conflicts' (Qingtai Chen 2014b). The mixed ownership reform plan recently announced for BoCom is considered to be a potential template for the first stages of governance reform in the large state-owned banks (Wildau 2015). It explores concepts of employee shareholding plans and stock options. The intention of the state is for this new governance structure to accelerate market-orientated behaviour, foster creativity and innovation, and liberate productive forces (Qingtai Chen 2012). Policymakers will hope to improve the international competitiveness of Chinese banks. Governance reform will be a highly exploratory process which will require a further evolution of the role of party governance in enterprises. China's officials will continue to grope for stones as they cross this new river.

## References

CBRC. 2010. 'China Banking Regulatory Commission 2009 Annual Report'. Beijing: China Banking Regulatory Commission. www.cbrc.gov.cn/showannual.do.
CBRC. 2016. 'China Banking Regulatory Commission 2015 Annual Report'. Beijing: China Banking Regulatory Commission. www.cbrc.gov.cn/showannual.do.

CCP. 2013. 'Communiqué of the 3rd Plenum of the 18th Party Congress'. China Copyright and Media, 12 November 2013. http://chinacopyrightandmedia.wordpress.com/2013/11/12/communique-of-the-3rd-plenum-of-the-18th-party-congress/.

Chen, Qide. 1999. 'Financial Legislation Crucial for Integration'. *China Daily*, 30 September 1999. http://global.factiva.com/redir/default.aspx?P=sa&an=chndly0020010903dv9u000de&cat=a&ep=ASE.

Chen, Qingtai. 2012. '"Guoqi Gaige Zhuanru Guozi Gaige" 国企改革转入国资改革 [SOE Reform Shifts to State-Owned Asset Reform]'. *Caijing.com.cn*, 19 May 2012. http://magazine.caijing.com.cn/2012-05-19/111852984.html.

Chen, Qingtai. 2014a. 'Managing State Capital'. *CaiXin Online*, 20 January 2014. http://english.caixin.com/2014-01-20/100631156.html.

Chen, Qingtai. 2014b. 'A Roadmap for State-Owned Assets Reform'. *Caijing Magazine*, 25 February 2014. http://english.caijing.com.cn/2014-02-25/113952281.html.

Chen, Yuan. 1993. 'Almanac of China's Finance and Banking 1993'.

Du, Hua 杜华, ed. 2007. *'Jinrong Gongzuo Wenxian Xuanbian (1978–2005)'* 金融工作文献选编 （一九七八——二*00*五）. Beijing: Zhongguo Jinrong Chubanshe.

'FT 500 2015'. n.d. *Financial Times*. www.ft.com/content/a352a706-16a0-11e5-b07f-00144feabdc0.

Hodgson, Geoffrey M. 2006. 'What Are Institutions?'. *Journal of Economic Issues* 40 (1): 1–25.

Kuhn, Robert Lawrence. 2010. *How China's Leaders Think: The Inside Story of China's Reform and What This Means for the Future*. Singapore: Wiley.

Kynge, James. 1998. 'ASIA-PACIFIC – China Considers Debt Restructuring Methods'. *Financial Times*, 16 July 1998.

Levenson, Joseph Richmond. 1964. *Confucian China and Its Modern Fate*. Vol. 1. Berkeley and Los Angeles, CA: University of California Press.

Liu, Mingkang. 2010. 'Keynote Speech at Asian Financial Forum: Chinese Bankers Carry Hopes for Future Balances'. China Banking Regulatory Commission, 20 January 2010. www.cbrc.gov.cn/EngdocView.do?docID=2010012011DA7AE6925E5D48FF76107FF744C800.

Nolan, Peter. 2013. *Is China Buying the World?* Cambridge, UK: Polity.

Nolan, Peter. 2017. Unpublished Manuscript.

Paulson, Henry. 2015. 'Let China's Markets Speak Truth to Power'. *Financial Times*, 22 July 2015.

*The Economic Times*. 2008. 'China Shuns Paulson's Free Market Push as Meltdown Burns US,' 25 September 2008. http://economictimes.indiatimes.com/news/international/china-shuns-paulsons-free-market-push-as-meltdown-burns-us/articleshow/3523794.cms.

Walter, Carl and Fraser Howie. 2012. *Red Capitalism: The Fragile Financial Foundation of China's Extraordinary Rise*. Revised edition. Singapore: Wiley.

Wildau, Gabriel. 2015. 'China's Bocom Sets Template for Reform at State-Owned Banks'. *Financial Times*, 17 June 2015. www.ft.com/content/ecfc3a4a-14b4-11e5-a51f-00144feabdc0.

Xi, Jinping. 2014. *The Governance of China*. Beijing: Foreign Languages Press.

*Xinhua News Agency*. 2012. 'Xi Jinping Vows No Stop in Reform, Opening Up'. 12 November 2012. http://news.xinhuanet.com/english/china/2012-12/11/c_132034269.htm.

# Index

Page numbers in **bold** denote tables, those in *italics* denote figures.

For Product Safety Concerns and Information please contact our EU
representative  GPSR@taylorandfrancis.com
Taylor & Francis Verlag GmbH, Kaufingerstraße 24, 80331 München, Germany

www.ingramcontent.com/pod-product-compliance
Ingram Content Group UK Ltd.
Pitfield, Milton Keynes, MK11 3LW, UK
UKHW020951180425
457613UK00019B/626